Municipal Services and Employees in the Modern City

Historical Urban Studies

Series editors: *Richard Rodger* and *Jean-Luc Pinol*

Municipal Services and Employees in the Modern City

New Historic Approaches

Edited by

MICHÈLE DAGENAIS, IRENE MAVER
and PIERRE-YVES SAUNIER

ASHGATE

Published by
Ashgate Publishing Limited
Gower House
Croft House
Aldershot
Hampshire GU11 3HR
England

Ashgate Publishing Company
Suite 420
101 Cherry Street
Burlington, VT 05401-4405
USA

Ashgate website: http//www.ashgate.com

British Library Cataloguing in Publication Data
Municipal services and employees in the modern city : new
  historic approaches. – (Historical urban studies)
  1. Sociology, Urban. 2. Municipal services – History – 19th
  century 3. Municipal services – History – 20th century
  4. Municipal employees and officials – History – 19th
  century 5.Municipal employees and officials – History –
  20th century
  I. Dagenais, Michèle II. Maver, Irene III. Saunier,
  Pierre-Yves
  307.7'6'09034

Library of Congress Cataloging-in-Publication Data
Municipal services and employees in the modern city : new historic approaches
/ edited by Michèle Dagenais, Irene Maver, and Pierre-Yves Saunier.
    p. cm. – (Historical urban studies series)
  Includes bibliographical references.
  ISBN 0-7546-0333-4
  1. Municipal services--Cross-cultural studies. 2. Municipal officials and
employees--Cross-cultural studies. 3. Municipal services--History. I.
Dagenais, Michèle, 1957- II. Maver, Irene. III. Saunier, Pierre-Yves.
IV. Historical urban studies.

HD4431. M89 2002
331.7'6135263216--dc21   2002027913

ISBN 0 7546 0333 4

Contents

Historical Urban Studies Series
General Editors Preface

Density and proximity are two of the defining characteristics of the urban dimension. It is these that identify a place as uniquely urban, though the threshold for such pressure points varies from place to place. What is considered an important cluster in one context may not be considered so elsewhere. A third defining characteristic is functionality – the commercial or strategic position of a town or city which conveys an advantage over other places. Over time, these functional advantages may diminish, or the balance of advantage may change within a hierarchy of towns. To understand how the relative importance of towns shifts over time and space is to grasp a set of relationships which is fundamental to the study of urban history.

Towns and cities are products of history, yet have themselves helped to shape history. As the proportion of urban dwellers has increased, so the urban dimension has proved a legitimate unit of analysis through which to understand the spectrum of human experience and to explore the cumulative memory of past generations. Though obscured by layers of economic, social and political change, the study of the urban milieu provides insights into the functioning of human relationships and, if urban historians themselves are not directly concerned with current policy studies, few contemporary concerns can be understood without reference to the historical development of towns and cities.

This longer historical perspective is essential to an understanding of social processes. Crime, housing conditions and property values, health and education, discrimination and deviance, and the formulation of regulations and social policies to deal with them were, and remain, amongst the perennial preoccupations within towns and cities. No historical period has a monopoly of these concerns. They recur in successive generations, albeit in varying mixtures and strengths; the details may differ.

The central forces of class, power and authority in the city remain the organisers. If this was the case for different periods, so it was for different geographical entities and cultures. Both scientific knowledge and technical information were available across Europe and showed little respect for frontiers. Yet despite common concerns and access to broadly similar knowledge, different solutions to urban problems were proposed and adopted by towns and cities in different parts of Europe. This comparative dimension informs urban historians as to which were systematic factors and which were of a purely local nature: general and particular forces can be distinguished.

These analytical frameworks, considered in a comparative context, inform the books in this series.

Université de Tours   Jean Luc Pinol
University of Leicester   Richard Rodger

Acknowledgments

Special thanks to Irene Maver, who devoted a lot of time and care to make our English fit for publication, and to Dorothy Mallon who acted as a benevolent go-between. Pierre-Yves Saunier would also like to dedicate this book to the late William B. Cohen, family friend and scholar of municipal government.

List of contributors

Emmanuel Bellanger is completing a history thesis at the Université Paris 8, France. His theme is the municipal activities and personnel of the Parisian suburbs in the nineteenth and twentieth centuries. He has recently published *Pantin. Mémoires de ville, mémoires de communaux*, (2001). He is also the author of two articles, 'L'Ecole nationale d'administration municipale. Des "sans grade" devenus secrétaires généraux' (2001) and 'Spécificité, continuité et uniformisation de l'administration communale dans les mairies communistes de la banlieue parisienne 1920–2001' (2001).

Michèle Dagenais is an associate professor in the history department at the Université de Montréal. Her main research interest is the development of the municipal domain, both in Canadian cities and in a broader comparative perspective. She has published papers on municipal administrations, urban governance, municipal policies related to leisure and culture, and a book entitled *Des pouvoirs et des hommes: l'administration municipale de Montréal, 1900–1950* (2000).

Filippo De Pieri holds a research appointment at the Department of Architectural Design, Politecnico di Torino, Turin, Italy. He has researched, lectured and written about the history of Italian cities in the nineteenth and twentieth centuries. His PhD dissertation, on institutional conflicts and urban design in early nineteenth-century Turin (1999) is currently being prepared for publication. He has recently published with Denis Bocquet 'Public works and municipal government in two Italian capital cities: comparing technical bureaucracies in Turin and Rome, 1848–88' (2002).

Roberto Ferretti is a temporary researcher for the Dipartimento di discipline storiche, Università di Bologna, Italy. He defended his PhD in 1999 under the title of 'Professions and the political systems: the engineers in France and Italy (1900–1945)'. He has recently published 'Le case per il popolo. L'edilizia popolare a Bologna tra liberalismo e fascismo' (2000). His current research is on the training and institutional function of public managers after the Second World War.

Amy S. Greenberg is associate professor of history at Pennsylvania State University. She is the author of *Cause for Alarm: The Volunteer Fire*

Department in the Nineteenth-Century City (1998) as well as articles on nineteenth-century American urban development, masculinity, violence and political culture. She is currently working on a study of nineteenth-century territorial expansionism and American culture.

Irene Maver is a lecturer in Scottish history at the University of Glasgow. Her current research interests focus on urban Scotland from the eighteenth century, although her original doctoral research concentrated on Glasgow's municipal government in the nineteenth and early twentieth centuries. She has written *Glasgow* (2000), a general history of the city, and is currently working on a history of Edinburgh. Before entering an academic career, she worked full-time for the British public sector trade union, NALGO, now incorporated into UNISON.

Cristina Mehrtens holds a PhD in history from the University of Miami and a bachelor's degree in architecture and urbanism from the University of São Paulo. She was a professor of architecture at the Catholic University in Campinas and served as an architect for the State Housing Agency (CDHU) in São Paulo. She is currently teaching at the School of Continuing Studies and is working on an oral history project about Cuba in the 1950s at the Center for Latin American Studies, University of Miami. She is the author of numerous journal articles and contributed to *The Brazil Reader* (1999).

Jean-Yves Nevers is a political sociologist at the Centre National de La Recherche Scientifique at the University of Toulouse, France. His research interests include change in municipal government, local policies and public management. He is the author of several articles appearing in *Revue française de science politique*, *International Journal of Regional and Urban Research* and *Revue française de sociologie*.

Pierre-Yves Saunier is a researcher in history at the Centre National de la Recherche Scientifique, in Lyon, France. He has published different historical studies of municipal employees and services. His current research deals with transnational circulations during the nineteenth and twentieth centuries. His latest publication in this area is 'Sketches from the urban international: voluntary societies, international organizations and US foundations at the city's bedside, 1900–1960' (2001). He has recently edited a theme issue of *Contemporary European History* dedicated to the theme of municipal connections (2002).

Bénédicte Zimmermann is *maître de conférences* at the Ecole des hautes études en sciences sociales, in Paris. Her research interests are in the history and sociology of the categories of social organization in Germany and France. With Claude Didry and Peter Wagner, she edited

Le travail et la nation. Histoire croisée de la France et de l'Allemagne (1999) and she is the author of *La constitution du chômage en Allemagne. Entre professions et territoires* (2001).

CHAPTER ONE

Tales of the periphery: an outline survey of municipal employees and services in the nineteenth and twentieth centuries

Michèle Dagenais and Pierre-Yves Saunier

Any scholarly inquiry into the history of municipal employees and services in the modern city immediately involves consideration of the roles played by local institutions and the particular processes that contributed towards shaping the urban fabric. Indeed, to study the subject entails a rediscovery, from models and maps, of the constituent dynamics of cities since the beginning of the nineteenth century, and how, over time, patterns can be traced in the way services and locations were organized. Urban transformation was underpinned by structural development, and the municipal workforce was an integral and increasingly prominent part of the agencies of change. The reference to 'the periphery' in this introductory chapter does not relate to the subject's place in the definition of modern cities, but to the relatively sparse amount of attention it has received from historical scholarship. This book aims to redress the balance by suggesting that the municipal experience should be more central to urban studies. Its focus of analysis ranges across Europe and the Americas, from high-ranking bureaucrats to firefighters, touching upon engineers, accountants, town clerks and minor public servants along the way. Most of the contributions were originally presented at the 'municipal services and employees' session of the Fourth International Conference on Urban History, held in Venice in September 1998. They were subsequently modified and other essays were added, with the aim of producing a more complete and comprehensive volume.

The contributions have their own priorities and impulses, yet they incorporate a number of shared features. They provide detailed information on how change was formulated or resisted within the administrative apparatus. They offer insight into a sector of the 'white-collar' class and the degree of commitment to public values and an ideology of service, often at times of social and political upheaval. They explore the course of relationships between local and central government, and the shifting bounds of municipal interventionism over a broad period. And they use a social history approach to interpret the day-to-day responsibilities and routine of administration. Together with these points in common, the contributions also display differences and distinctions. Inevitably, they reflect diverse traditions of municipal governance, a characteristic that makes comparative analyses of urban administration all the more rewarding. Yet individually they are also influenced by the constraints of existing historiography, whether the paucity of comparative case studies or the uneven distribution of relevant primary source material. The task of describing the specific background to each of the countries covered far exceeds our knowledge, interpretive skills and linguistic abilities, which is why each contributor was asked to incorporate basic bibliographical information to help the reader to explore further. But an outline of the broad intellectual and practical conditions to which the researches were exposed is a necessary preliminary, before we can consider some of the common questions shared by the participants.

In this introductory chapter we will first elaborate on why municipal employees and services is a relevant and revealing theme in urban history, and then go on to analyse the strengths and weaknesses of existing scholarship. With particular reference to the contributions to this book, we will consider the consolidation of civic expansionism from the mid-nineteenth century. Next, we will examine the complex relationships that emerged between the executive and administrative spheres of local government, the changing role of central government and employees' responses to the needs and directives of the often highly politicized municipal power-base. Finally, we will look to further research approaches to open out this important, yet underrated, aspect of urban history.

Researching municipal employees and services

It is tempting to plunge into the repertory of academic discourse to provide a convenient explanation for the importance of studying municipal employees and services. We could claim, for instance, that the subject has been ignored by historians and must be rescued from obscurity. But that would not be (wholly) true. We could build on trends in urban history, stressing how far the success of the 'urban governance' approach, in political science as well as history, justifies research on municipal employees and services as integral components of a wider system of government.[1] It would be relevant, in this context, to refer to the recent 'rediscovery' of the municipal dimension by scholars of sociological history, especially in France.[2] But all that would be too easy. Alternatively, we could highlight recent developments in the study of the social and cultural history of government to demonstrate how municipal administration, its organization and servants, constitute a great laboratory for exploring aspects of the theme further.[3] But that would be too trendy. Last, but not least, we could elaborate on the 'dull' aspects of municipal bureaucracy to make it look like a cursed and unglamorous subject, in need of historical rehabilitation. But that would be too inhibiting. Instead, what we intend to do in this introductory section is to offer our own reasons for being interested in municipal employees and services, and point the way forward for further developing research.

The first reason relates to municipalities as a locus for the formulation and implementation of public policy, part of the 'social domain' of communities that have been shaped by urbanization, democratization and industrialization. The evolution of a wide range of public policies was the outcome of close cooperation between national governments and local authorities, including municipalities. The need for cooperation could arise from conflict, and central–local relationships took many forms, from domination to subsidiarity through to autonomy. Between 1850 and 1950, albeit with varying degrees of intensity, municipalities, through their services and employees, were major influences on attempts to solve key social issues, such as unemployment, housing, public health, city planning, transport or the construction of utilities' networks. This was a period characterized by central state building, but even in the most 'centralized' systems, such as in France, the municipalities played a vital role (Cohen 1998).[4] The theme is familiar to historians. Jonathan Kahn (1997) for budgeting in the United States, Anne Hardy (1993) and Benoît Gaumer (1995) for public health in Britain, Canada and the United States, Gilles Pollet (1995) for the French welfare state, and Bénédicte Zimmermann (2001) for the *Kaiserreich* unemployment policies have expanded on the municipal contribution to the design and implementation of public policy. Italy also provides convincing evidence of interaction between the two spheres of government. For the inter-war period, Ugo Giusti (Gaspari 1999) has traced a professional trajectory from the municipal to the national civil service, based on his statistical expertise. Examples such as the *Segretaria alla Montagna*, where an organization born out of intermunicipal cooperation was turned into a state-run agency (Gaspari 1994),[5] and the *Societa Umanitaria* in Milan (Nejrotti 1994), all point to the importance of municipal officials and services as pioneering and innovative agencies of administration.

Other related themes rank high in our commitment to 'bring the municipal administration back in'; for example, the intense circulation of information between civic authorities (Hietala 1987) and the creation of municipal associations which sought to influence the decision-making process (Gaspari 1998, Beckstein 1991). This leads into our second area of our interest, which considers municipalities and their place in social history. A point that should be stressed from the outset is that the local government workforce was and remains important quantitatively. The chronological limits of this volume, broadly from the mid-nineteenth century up to the 1970s, do not mean to imply that there was a rise and fall of municipal relevancy. French municipal employment 'took off' during the 1950s, the figures doubling between 1975 and 1994; this represented an increase in parallel with the activities and budgets of municipalities. In terms of numbers, 236 000 people worked in French municipal services in 1946, rising to more than a million by 1995, while British local authorities employed 2.2 million in 1993. This is obviously significant in relation to total figures for employment, especially when compared with those for central government civil servants; for example, in 1993 there were 565 000 in the United Kingdom (Byrne 1994, Bellanger et al. 2000).[6] Indeed, if we consider all the countries dealt with by the contributors in this book, the collective evidence indicates the growing scope and scale of employment in the municipal sector throughout the nineteenth and twentieth centuries.

While the rise of municipal work opportunity is an important area of study in its own right, it takes on special resonance because of the interest historians have recently displayed in the 'middling sort' and the 'professions'. The work of Jürgen Kocka (1980, 1989), Geoffrey Crossick and Heinz-Gerhard Haupt (1995) and Mariuccia Salvati (1992) has addressed the experience of a range of employees in both the public and private sectors. Of course, municipal establishments did not just relate to the clerical services in city halls; most staff members were blue-collar workers, in the utilities or public works units. Nor did all authorities operate on the scale of London County Council (LCC), which employed thousands of 'blackcoated' workers at the beginning of the twentieth century. Yet municipalities inevitably had a concentration of clerical staff, and as city halls were often the largest employer within a community, they could also be the largest administrative employer, especially in towns with a limited service industry.[7]

The characteristics of municipal clerks are illuminating for a variety of reasons, among which is the niche that they occupied in the labour market. Being hired by a civic department, even as an ordinary employee, offered promotion opportunities and, from the turn of the century, the prospect of a retirement pension. A career in government administration secured a place in the hierarchy of public power, if only at the municipal level. Along with these distinctive qualities were features shared with other clerical workers in large private enterprises. White-collar status sustained a sense of corporate belonging, even if aspirations did not necessarily match the financial rewards. Clerical work generally nourished a desire for social advancement, because it implied intellectual capability and was readily associated with the business world.[8]

Municipalities also constitute a useful case-study for those with an interest in the growth and development of the professions. Whether in the public or the private sector, at local or national level, collectively or individually, professional work was imbued with the competitive impulse: the 'system of professions' depicted by Andrew Abbott (1988). Recent research by Martin Laffin (1998) has shown how the strong link between local bureaucracy and the professions has come to be challenged under the pressures exerted by changing managerial practices: for instance, value-for-money approaches and market competition. Yet the theme of change is by no means new, and was reflected in the preoccupations of municipal professionals even before the 1980s. The continuing debate illustrates that the irregular professionalization of municipal work from the nineteenth century has had long-lasting effects, one of which, with important implications for this volume, is the tension that emerged between expertise and democracy. Various studies describe how the growth of expertise in public life had an impact on the conduct of public affairs, especially when national government was involved.[9] The arguments are familiar to historians of the Progressive Era in the United States, as well as to European scholars of the municipal 'reform' movement, such as Martin Schiesl (1977), Kenneth Finegold (1995) and Christian Topalov (1999). However, research remains patchy. Better knowledge of the practical work of public services, as well as greater understanding of employment patterns, will help to provide a clearer view of the way in which expertise gained ground in municipal affairs.

The third and final factor accounting for our interest is that administrative history offers considerable scope for understanding municipal development (Dagenais 2000a, Saunier 1997, Dumons et al. 1998). At first sight, the institutional components of the administrative apparatus can appear daunting, not least the intricacies of the legal process, internal regulations and organization charts. The human resources dimension compounds the complexity; how did the institutional base relate to employees, their assigned tasks and responsibilities, especially for intermediary and higher public servants? Unravelling this question entails research into administrative techniques, the definition of values and norms, attention to the practical details of work and daily routine, and analysis of the abundant primary literature, whether textbooks or official periodicals from professional societies, associations and trade unions.[10] There is also a range of interacting factors to take into account; for instance, recruitment and promotion procedures, the relationships between services, the connection between municipal executive and legislative powers, and the operation of commissions and agencies designed to regulate and organize municipal administration. Last, but not least, even the legal characteristics of municipal activity, usually scrutinized through law enforcement and judicial decisions, can be seen from a different perspective if the evidence of legal and administrative practices is used as source material. Indeed, municipal administration often serves as the first point of contact between citizens and the institutions of government, and is therefore a useful testing ground for approaching this kind of 'grassroots' administrative history.

The legal framework provides one of the most striking differences between the cities and countries covered by the contributors to this book. In this specific context, various 'models' of local government have provided an immediate point of contrast, notably the classical opposition between the 'French' and 'English' experience. The French model, which circulated in continental Europe as a result of revolutionary and Napoleonic expansion, is characterized by the legal conception of the municipality as a basic cell of the national state and political life, with centralizing consequences (Wunder 1995). It differs radically from the English model, based on a conception of municipalities as communities of property-owning citizens, enjoying relative autonomy on the basis of incorporation or charters. English imperial expansion, notably from the seventeenth century, encouraged the spread of the latter model. Yet, inevitably, this Western-centred approach is limited, paying scant attention to possible alternative models, such as that of China. It also crumbles if taken as a basis for more detailed comparison between the two models, or if differences 'inside' the models are investigated. For instance, arguments in favour of municipalities as the domain of 'landlord-citizens' were not unfamiliar in nineteenth-century France (Bourjol 1975), while the dialectic of central–local relations in England was often complex (Bellamy 1988). There were also practical differences of size and scale.

Thus, although they came under the aegis of a shared legal system, there were obvious organizational differences between small French cities and large ones, headed by a mayor and a member of parliament. The same can be said for the metropolitan LCC and smaller urban district councils in England. Moreover, an approach that takes account only of 'national models' fails to appreciate the diversity of municipal laws. There could be wide disparities within national borders; for instance, the variety of *Städteordnungen* or *Gemeindeordnungen* in Prussia before 1870 and then in unified Germany until 1919, the piecemeal approach to urban legislation that prevailed for a long time in Italy, or the conditions under which municipal charters were given by state legislatures in the USA. In the British context, Scotland has a different tradition of local government and a separate legal system from England and Wales. But for our purposes the most important aspects of the municipal laws do not necessarily lie in what they said or enforced, but in the way the protagonists, both individually and through municipal associations, tried to cope with them, seek accommodation and manage changes appropriate to their aims.[11]

As far as municipal employees were concerned, general or particular municipal laws or charters outlined, rather than defined, their precise role and conditions of service. The power to appoint or dismiss employees might be given to the executive or legislative branch of municipal government. The functions and appointment conditions of higher officials were sometimes written into generic municipal laws or city charters, as was the case with the German Bürgermeister or American and Irish city managers.[12] But the general conditions of municipal employees were not incorporated into these generic municipal laws. With the notable exception of Ireland, where an Act of 1926 established a central body of 'local appointment commissioners', this was the task of specific laws. For example, the 1902 *loi sur la protection de la santé publique* in France created municipal health offices and defined their responsibilities and the appointment of their directors. Statutory laws could also elaborate on the rights and duties of municipal employees. The French law of 1919, the civil service regulations introduced in several American cities from the 1890s, the Italian law of 1902 on *segretari communali* (town clerks), the Spanish law of 1924,[13] and the Local Government Acts that recurred in England and Wales (for instance, in 1875, 1888, 1894, 1929, 1931 and 1933) shared many features regarding the guarantees given to municipal employees, especially over tenure and freedom of opinion.

However, they were all subject to local constraints and controls, often inspired by particular interest groups, such as the anti-machine reform movement in the USA (Schiesl 1977) or the national government of Italy in its quest for municipal control (Romanelli 1989). The activities of different classes of municipal employees should be read in the light of these regulatory influences, as they had to move between rules, between the controlling ambitions and powers of local and central government, and of the executive and legislative branches of the latter. Conversely, one should not forget that the preparation of these laws was in most cases a joint venture, where the municipal employees and their trade unions and associations played a participatory role. The laws also often emerged from existing municipal regulations that had previously set up rules for the recruitment, promotion, management and behaviour of municipal employees (Dumons et al. 1998, for France; Adorno 1998 and Mozzarelli 1992, for Italy).

Regarding the organization of municipal services, with the exception of those under central (or state) government supervision, like capital cities, the municipalities were in total control. The history of this structural aspect of civic government is relatively unknown, as few researchers have plunged into the grim and complex world of service organization charts and regulations. Yet those intrepid or heedless enough to do so have come back with a rich picture that provides greater understanding of the constraints and limits on the way municipal policies were defined and implemented (for France, Dumons et al. 1998; Saunier 1997). They have also found evidence that organizational changes could reconcile the 'rationalizing' aspirations of the government machine and employees' conflicting claims (Dagenais 2000a, Mozzarelli 1992). In her work on Montreal, Michèle Dagenais has illustrated the value of examining structural administrative reforms, showing how the work of a private consulting firm, Griffenhagen & Co., from Chicago, can be read as much more than a play with charts and positions; it had wide implications for municipal relationships, whether employees with their work, employees with their superiors or top officials with elected representatives. These studies point to the importance of investigating the construction and reconstruction of the municipal administrative apparatus. We need greater understanding of how national laws influenced the creation of positions and services – which seems to have been crucial in the UK, for instance – in order to have a better grasp of approaches to municipal organization work, whether incrementally or more radically creative.

Reform movements both directed and reflected trends in the evolution of municipal government, and the institutions that supported such impulses are worthy of attention. Municipal associations like the *Deutsche Städtetag* in Germany, societies such as the National Association of Local Government Officers (NALGO) in the UK,[14] and information and consulting services such as the Chicago Public Administration Clearing House and the Public Administration Service were among the diverse components of the 'municipal movement' that worked in such directions at a time of intense international circulation of information and news (Saunier 2001). Nevertheless, as demonstrated by the contributions gathered here, the organizational patterns were of such dazzling variety inside each country that, in response to international inquiries about the 'usual office organization of a local authority', many national or local associations of municipalities could not answer the question, or obliquely answered by stating the absence of a 'usual way'. Such was the case of the general report on the 'Practical working of local authorities' presented by George Montagu Harris at the 1932 London Congress of the International Union of Local Authorities, where the question of administrative organization was bypassed.[15] This variety is still a challenge for historians.

Historiography: international comparisons

Potential researchers anxious to explore existing scholarship have found that there are not many accessible works on municipal employees and services. Some countries are better served than others, and the examples of the UK, France, Germany, Italy and the USA illustrate the varying degrees of development. In terms of accessibility, the state of British and French scholarship is about the same, although the perspectives taken by historians can be very different. An exploration of municipal policy has not been absent from British research; on the contrary, from housing to public health, the theme provides a continuous thread in the fabric of British urban history.[16] But the mass of employees who implemented this policy have not been the subject of sustained or serious interest. Irene Maver (2000: 69) mentions the 'often shadowy presence' of municipal officials in historical analyses of local government, while Gloria Clifton (1992: 4) has shown how the intensive studies of Victorian-era municipal policies concentrated overwhelmingly on elected representatives. The consolidated bibliography on urban history and the survey of doctoral and master's theses compiled by Richard Rodger (1994) confirms the accuracy of these statements, for both published and unpublished research.

Nevertheless, a recent, if territorially scattered, interest has emerged. Maver has written several pieces on Glasgow (Maver 2000, Fraser and Maver 1996), focusing on the role of municipal managers and town clerks in implementing public policy and shaping (and exploiting) the image of civic virtue. Another area of writing relates to London's municipal employees and services. Gloria Clifton (1989, 1992) and Susan Pennybacker (1995) have made outstanding contributions to research on the London County Council (1889–1965) and its predecessor, the Metropolitan Board of Works (1856–89). Pennybacker's incursions in the world of LCC staffing and organization are major landmarks for students of municipal employees and services because of her range of coverage, from the social and cultural life of clerical staff to her analysis of the 'direct labour' experiment in the works department. Clifton extensively covers the administrative machinery, management practices, recruitment and conditions, workforce origins and the 'out of work life' of the various grades of staff of the Metropolitan Board of Works. The fact that, at the time of writing, neither historian has pursued these research interests, and indeed Clifton is working for a navy museum somewhere in the UK, might well be a sign of the relative academic lack of interest in the two books and their specific contribution to knowledge about municipal employees and services.

The French landscape is at first sight different. National civil servants have left a distinctive mark on literature. From Balzac's *Les employés* (1844) to Flaubert's *Bouvard et Pécuchet* (1881), the bureaucrat has been a cherished object of derision. While municipal servants were never accorded such literary honours, they nevertheless acquired an ambiguous reputation. In France, '*un travail à la Ville*' (a job for the municipality) is still taken as synonymous with a position combining a second-rate wage with a pressureless job. Indeed, until recently, the whole field of municipal administration seems to have been a second-rate subject for historians. On the academic front, Claude Pennetier (Bellanger et al. 2000: 5), has stressed the complexity of the subject. He argues that factors such as weak professional identity, the mix of white- and blue-collar workers, and employer–employee relationships that fluctuated between authoritarianism and accommodation may be responsible for restricting the appeal of the municipal workforce, especially for social historians. On the other hand, during the 1980s there was renewed interest in the local dimension to political history, expressed, for instance, in research on French mayors (Agulhon et al. 1986, Georges 1989). Working-class history has also inspired research into left-wing control of municipalities, notably in the Parisian Red Belt (Fourcaut 1980, 1992, Brunet 1981), although the employees in charge of implementing policy were not identified as important actors in the political process. In furtherance of their interests in bureaucracy, it was jurists, political scientists and sociologists who paid the closest attention to municipal employees and services. Work by Catherine Lecomte (1987, 1989), Jean-Claude Thoenig (1982), Dominique Lorrain (1991) and Jean-Yves Nevers (1983) illustrate a trend that developed in the 1980s. From the beginning of the 1990s, French historians used these works as a basis for developing their own research. This bore fruit in a crop of student master theses developed in Paris under the direction of Claude Pennetier from 1994 onwards, and in the work of Bruno Dumons, Gilles Pollet and Pierre-Yves Saunier in Lyons. They focused particularly on the role of different ranking civic officials, the range of services and the organization of the municipal machinery (Bellanger et al. 2000, Dumons et al. 1998).

These scattered landscapes contrast with the vigorous field of study on municipal personnel and services in Germany and Italy. They can be considered as strongholds of the subject, having pioneered research into issues that are only beginning to be investigated elsewhere. The German experience is probably the most widely known. Work on professional urban administrators evolved in the context of change within the bureaucratic structure of German cities, represented by the shift from domination by social elites acting as honorary municipal executive officials (especially in the Western Prussian *Magistrat*) to the professionalization of civic positions and careers. Honorary administrators did not disappear: in 1910 there were still 2845 in Dresden, of whom 2011 worked unpaid for the municipality. In Berlin, the number of non-paid staff was 10 087.[17] However, *Hunbesoldete Beamte* (honorary officials) gradually gave way to *Berufsbeamte* (professional officials). Historians have analysed both groups. The honorary administrators, who worked in the *Magistrat* or in the numerous specialized commissions of the municipal apparatus, form the theme of several books emanating from the *Bürgertum* studies in Bielefeld, in particular Ludovica Scarpa's investigation of Berlin (1995). Particular interest has been taken in the role of professional administrators from the mid-nineteenth century to the fall of the Weimar Republic in 1933 (Blotevogel 1990, Fischer 1995, Grottrup 1973, Krabbe 1985). Case studies have been written about the technicians of planning, architecture and utilities (Fisch 1988, Scarpa 1983, Schott 1999) and the *Oberbürgermeister* (Croon et al. 1971, Hofmann 1974), while Fabio Rugge (1989b) has provided Italian readers with an insightful analysis of the *Gemeindebeamte* (municipal employees) in Prussia up to 1914.

Two features of this rich German body of research are worth underlining. Firstly, it has been stimulated by the welcome existence of research institutions and publishing outlets. Centres like the *Institut für vergleichende Städtegeschichte* in Münster (Institute for Comparative Urban History) or series like the *Schriften des Deutschen Instituts für Urbanistik*, from the Stuttgart publisher Kohlhammer, have promoted the history of municipal employees and services. This is not surprising, if we consider that the *Deutsches Institut für Urbanistik* (Berlin) is the heir of the *Kommunalwissenschaftliche Institut*, one of many institutions created by the German municipal movement during the early twentieth century to encourage research and training in municipal administration (Rugge 1989a). A second point worth noting is that the research output of German historians comes to an abrupt halt with the demise of the Weimar Republic. What subsequently happened to municipal officials and the German municipal movement, especially after the *Deutsche Gemeindeordnung* (municipal law) of 1935, is an intriguing question that remains unanswered.

Italian historiography of municipal employees and services is more chronologically complete, and recent work by Luca Baldissara illustrates the depth of analysis that characterizes this particular area of scholarship. His study of Bologna's municipal government after the Second World War (1994) was followed by an exploration of the trajectories of ideas, institutions and individuals in Italian municipalities from the 1920s to the 1950s, which incorporates the fascist era instead of treating it as a rupture (Baldissara 1998). Baldissara's work represents only one example of the innovative Italian approach to municipal studies, and a full historiographical essay would be necessary to do justice to the wealth and breadth of research output.[18] Scholarly interest in municipal services and employees was first manifested during the 1980s, when themes in public administration, social history and urban history coalesced as part of the study of Italian nation and state formation after the *Risorgimento* years. The pioneering and prolific output of this period provided strong foundations for further research, as is indicated by the Italian contributions to this volume. In particular, conferences became a major forum for interweaving the different strands of the municipal experience, and the published proceedings show how ideas were able to develop (Aimo and Bigaran 1986, Adorno and Sorba 1991, Salvati 1993). Together with the city profiles included in the monster volumes from the *Istituto Superiore d'Amministrazione Pubblica*, dedicated to the reforms instituted by Crispi at the end of the nineteenth century (ISAP 1990), and Raffaele Romanelli's key-work on municipal secretaries (1989), these first shots were soon followed by a flurry of monographs about the municipal administration of specific towns (Alaimo 1990a, Sorba 1993, Balzani 1992).

Interest in municipal employees and services assumed a very specialized dimension with the publication of *Il governo della città nell'Italia giolittiana*, whose contributions probably form the most detailed batch of data available on the organization of municipal administration (Mozzarelli 1992). Since then, the flow has not stopped, although some Italian colleagues feel that the historiography in the field is in need of a revitalizing 'second wind'. If the evidence of a recent set of conference proceedings is anything to go by (Soresina 1998), this might come from integrating the experience of municipal employees in the wider picture of white-collar workers, or from considering municipal employees in the national context, through the existence of regional or national professional markets, for example. There is also a need for further geographic diversity, with greater focus on cities in the south and east, rather than the usual centre–north cities that have attracted the lion's share of attention. Despite the limitations, two characteristics help to explain the relative vitality of Italian research. Firstly, there is fruitful collaboration between historians and scholars of public administration. The role of the Milan-based ISAP, the intensive participation of Fabio Rugge in many collective efforts previously mentioned, and the attention paid to municipal administration by leading scholars like Sabino Cassese, Guido Melis and Ettore Rotelli demonstrate the commitment of administration specialists to understanding the municipal experience. The second salient feature is the sheer versatility of Italian research. Indeed, Italy may be the only place to have developed an integrated knowledge of municipal services and employees.[19] Not only is foreign scholarship read, used and commented upon, but Italian scholars have also conducted first-hand research beyond their home base, as with Rugge and Scarpa on Germany. The price of this versatility might nevertheless be quite high. The Italian landscape is characterized by an overabundance of monographs and conference proceedings, while the big synthesis of more than 20 years of stimulating scholarship is yet to come.

To conclude this historiographical overview, the case of the USA represents a reverse image of the Italian experience, showing the relative absence of municipal employees and services from urban studies. Of course, it could be said that the diversity of legal forms of government in the USA, from commission/council to manager/council patterns through the wide range of autonomy and power allocated to mayors by city charters, makes analysis difficult as it multiplies the organizational possibilities. This is not helped by the bewildering variety of employment systems. These include a large number of popularly elected administrative positions, as well as independent commissions and boards, covering areas such as schools and parks. Coexisting alongside the extended possibilities in hiring and firing offered by the spoils system has been the development of the merit system and civil service regulations in the municipalities from the end of the 1890s. But the complexities do not explain why American historians have paid insufficient attention to the structural aspects of municipal government. Significantly, the general work of Sam Bass Warner (1968) and Eric Monkkonen (1988) on the development of the service city stresses the role of civic private organizations rather than city officials. Elsewhere the officials are often alluded to in the context of the reform movement, but they tend not to be treated as protagonists in their own right. Their exclusion is exemplified by Schiesl's account (1977) of the drive towards 'municipal efficiency', especially the chapter dedicated to 'the politics of bureaucratization'.[20] The focus on political machines and on the municipal reform movements that developed to counteract them seems to have absorbed the energy of American historians, leaving little space to consider municipal structures and employees as an integral part of the reform process.

Indeed, it is a strange irony that the efforts of American reformers to change the structures of municipal government, and their emphasis on civil service regulations, as showcased in the Municipal Program circulated by the National Municipal League in 1900, were not followed by the efforts of American historians to study these same structures. The contrast between the work of Monkkonen (1981) and Jay Berman (1987) on the police force is revealing. Both claim to analyse behaviour, growth and change in police bureaucracies. However, they take very different approaches to the subject. The historian Monkkonen deals with structural developments in a general survey chapter and an account of the development of uniformed police forces in the USA, but then goes on to concentrate on areas of policing efficiency, such as trends of arrests. Conversely, the criminologist Berman focuses on reform of the New York Police Board, emphasizing the professionalizing impact of entrance examinations and the strengthening of centralized police executive control.

This compartmentalized American approach is quite distinct from the Italian integration of the field. Jon Teaford's *Unheralded Triumph* (1984) further demonstrates the reluctance of American historians to expand on the profile of municipal officials. The chapters dedicated to executives such as the city comptrollers, corporation counsels and city chamberlains, as well as municipal technicians, fail to draw out their importance as groups or individuals. They also fall short of examining their contribution to municipal government, sticking to famous 'stars' in engineering or park supervision. A glance at Teaford's footnotes is revealing. Most of the information on employees and services comes from the professional and daily press or official reports. Conspicuous by their absence are archival records documenting the operation of the services and the careers of the officials, an approach that reflects the tenor of other American books dealing with the history of municipal government.

Of course, the availability of municipal records is very uneven in American cities, and not all communities have civic archives.[21] Moreover, the fact that autonomous boards and commissions often performed municipal functions accounts for the dearth of 'inside' material that would enable researchers to document and analyse the course of administrative change and to reconstitute individuals' careers. But the well-known wealth of private papers in American libraries and archive depositories has not been used comprehensively for these purposes. For instance, the George McAneny papers (Princeton

University and Columbia University collections) and the Leonard White papers (University of Chicago collections) are among several collections to include Civil Service Commission documents and related material.[22] The daily journal kept by White during the late 1920s, when he was one of the civil service commissioners for Chicago, is a fascinating account of his responsibilities, bringing much more light to the Commission's activities than any of its printed reports. Civil Service Commission records, such as the Philadelphia ones, also hold a considerable amount of material on organizational change, personnel classification and positions lists. The relevant holdings of municipal repositories and historical societies are far from exhaustively explored. It is clear that historical research still has a long way to go.

The expansion of municipal employees and services

The modern city referred to in the title of the present volume is one which took shape towards the middle of the nineteenth century in a period marked by the dual processes of urbanization and industrialization, characteristic of great European and American cities. The way in which particular communities and individuals interpreted these changes helped to create or redefine the role of local institutions, and contributed to the formulation of a municipal political domain, at least on the normative level. The mid-nineteenth century also corresponded to the advent of the 'governmental revolution', the setting up of a new framework of political action that followed closely upon the development of nation states (Corrigan and Sayer 1985). Along with the centralization of power and authority, management of the multiple aspects of social existence, hitherto assumed by civil society, was gradually taken over by political institutions.[23] Municipal administrations, then in formation, participated in this general reorganization of political and social relationships.[24] By law, charter and through granting specific prerogatives, they were assigned a whole range of powers and responsibilities for the governance of local concerns, at least in regard to what pertained to their jurisdiction.

The impact of urbanization and industrialization fell heavily upon municipal authorities. This occurred because, in addition to particular exigencies, higher governments, freely interpreting their role, refused to recognize the social problems provoked by these developments, which the municipalities felt to be urgent (Fecteau 1995). Within this context of frequent turmoil, a range of questions was posed at the urban level relating to community organization, town planning, public health and the management of social relations. But towns and their institutions did not respond only to this context, as compelling and troubling as it might have been. Were they not also undergoing transformation in their institutional, political and social structures?[25] The nature of such transformation becomes more transparent if municipal employees are given a central role in the formulation and implementation of public policy. Much can be learned from scrutinizing their practical responsibilities, their analytical tools, the way their actions and interventions took shape, and the context in which they operated. Analysing the work of local institutions and of those who influenced urban life requires an examination of the processes relating to initiatives and public policy, not merely on the ground, in the political and electoral arena where results are evident, but also in the background. Even if they promoted them vocally, it was rarely elected representatives who devised specific courses of municipal action. An entire preliminary effort preceded these policies and measures, which is made evident from this book.

In more than one respect, municipalities can be likened to 'laboratories' where public policy was developed from around the mid-nineteenth century.[26] The term 'public policy' is not a direct synonym for policy on behalf of the public, but instead relates to measures and interventions issuing from political, and therefore public, institutions. Indeed, an important interpretive distinction between the American and the European experience is apparent in the very origins of towns, and strongly coloured the development of what cities actually did.[27] In the case of North America, cities created their hinterland and provided a large part of the impetus for economic development in the nineteenth century. The situation was virtually reversed in the case of European cities, which were more the product of their hinterland and the result of the development of these areas. The implications of these two contrasting histories are fundamental. In the Americas, where virtually everything had to be built and developed, the municipalities competed with one another to attract the capital necessary for growth. In consequence, they found themselves in a vulnerable position when dealing with private enterprise. Wielding the borrowing power conferred on them through municipal charter, local administrations sought to attract business through the means of low-cost loans, tax breaks and relaxed regulations.[28] At the same time as municipalities had to provide a whole range of basic services to stimulate economic development in their area, they concluded agreements with companies providing public utilities that benefited the providers more than they did the population they were supposed to serve (Armstrong and Nelles 1983). These considerations go a long way towards explaining why local authorities were primarily viewed from the perspective of management, as bodies in the service of economic development and private property.[29]

European cities were in a rather different position. They represented localities indispensable to the expansion of capital and were therefore less vulnerable to the demands of private entrepreneurs, although competition among cities was not unknown. On the other hand, their leaders had to confront the problems and tensions prompted by economic and industrial development, especially the need to maintain public order and social cohesion (Maver 1995, Morris 1997). The process of redefining the role of governance also took place in a different context from that characterizing the new communities, as it appeared within a framework in which old political structures already existed. Municipalities, especially in continental Europe, tended to be seen as extensions of the central state,[30] based in part on the French model stemming from the Revolution and subsequent Napoleonic conquest. In these cases, the notion of a public service generally appeared earlier (Rodger 1993). It was a component of the municipal sphere, sometimes as early as the middle of the nineteenth century, and issues relating to local management took on a more overtly political colour.

In view of these different contexts, how did definitions of the municipal sphere of action on each continent present themselves and how did they develop? In the Americas, public water services, for example, were established to meet the needs of private enterprise, rather than in response to questions of public health (Fougères 1995, Poitras 1999). As the contribution by Amy Greenberg in this collection demonstrates, private sector initiative also was responsible for the professionalization of firefighting services. Around the mid-nineteenth century, insurance companies, anxious about the runaway costs associated with volunteer fire departments, most of which they had to bear, became the chief proponents of professionalizing and ultimately municipalizing firefighting services. Prompted by economic imperatives, the municipalities followed in their wake and became party to a process of experimentation in techniques to fight fires. By embracing new technology, in this case the steam engine, the cities became sites for the dissemination of certain kinds of innovation. Through this process, as well as through a number of others in which the municipal authorities were prodded to develop urban services, the entrepreneurial conception of local institutions lost ground to a more communal vision of their role and activities.

There was a marked divergence in the way the public services debate was conducted in large European cities, particularly those in Italy. As shown by Filippo De Pieri in the next chapter, the Turin town council adopted an altogether different attitude when it obtained important powers to control urban development. Concerned with asserting authority and establishing their expertise in running the city, especially when faced with other local bodies and with the state, the city authorities placed *l'Ufficio d'Arte*, Turin's Department of Public Works, at the forefront. Furthermore, the municipal presence became apparent through the technical and prescriptive control it came to exercise in the course of the city's transformation. Relying on powers recognized by the state, local administrators took over responsibilities of a technical nature previously assumed by other authorities, such as drawing up building codes, urban development plans and public works projects. In consequence, questions once viewed as political, as the focus of power struggles between different local bodies, were posed increasingly in technical terms, to be managed by municipal services and specialized personnel.

By the 1900s a further wave of municipal expansion had followed on from this first pioneering period of activity. This second phase is often improperly termed 'municipal socialism', because the movement was characterized by increasing interventionism on the part of public bodies.[31] Such was the case especially for cities in the UK, Germany, Italy and France, which took over a whole range of urban functions. In the course of this process, which had roots in the middle of the nineteenth century, services as diverse as gas and electricity supply, sewers, slaughterhouses, public transport and street lighting were municipalized. Similarly, in North America, this period, termed 'reformist', was characterized by an expansion in services taken over by municipal authorities and by more energetic regulation of companies supplying public utilities. This more active interventionism was legitimized by borrowing, if only rhetorically, the principles of 'businesslike management' and the scientific management of labour, then very fashionable in business circles.[32]

On both sides of the Atlantic, interventionism was stimulated by urban development and population growth as well as by a consciously political dynamic. This last factor had been consolidated by the intensification of political debate arising from electoral extension, and the consequent growth of popular participation at the local level.[33] The expansion of public administrations and their activities during the course of the nineteenth century made them more visible in the city and conferred on them increasing legitimacy. Should we not also link this interventionism to the work accomplished by the growing number of white- and blue-collar municipal employees, who were working in the various departments of these administrations and to whom the authors in this volume direct their attention? In fact, the more systematic interventions upon and within the urban domain were fed by the expertise that local managers were developing and their knowledge of the city and its inhabitants. For projects and initiatives to be effective, they had to be supported by personnel familiar with the urban environment, structures and inhabitants. Municipal initiatives evolved at the same time as new social sciences, some of which would ultimately be systematized as 'municipal science', were developing. Political institutions, national and local, would come to rely on these not only to maintain control but also to achieve a better understanding of the populations they were managing.[34] At the local level, the tensions and instability that accompanied the rise of large cities engendered a mounting preoccupation with social questions. This was the dynamic that drove German city statisticians, studied by Bénédicte Zimmermann (the author of Chapter 5 of the present volume), to perfect the instruments they needed to measure, literally, the consequences of these developments. Before intervention could take place, it was important to be familiar with, evaluate and measure social phenomena, such as problems of poverty and unemployment. Techniques of collecting and processing a mass of empirical data on living conditions lay at the heart of constructing new analytical categories and ultimately contributed to public intervention. Thus certain new areas of public initiative expanded because they had been identified, described and were empirically based.

The contribution by Christina Mertens (Chapter 8) analyses how the city administration of São Paulo in the 1930s carried out the task of constructing the urban area and at the same time a perspective from which to comprehend it. During this period various social categories, previously invisible because the municipal authorities neither identified nor named them, acquired a certain degree of materiality thanks to the work carried out by a whole stratum of social scientists in the service of the city. In seeking to capture a sense of the city and its inhabitants, to construct a range of knowledge based on urban society, they contributed to the definition of the city itself, both physically and in relation to the mood of the populace. The contributions of these technical and social engineers, both in action and in representation, took on a complexion that was all the more pronounced because it was part of a movement designed to produce a liberal and modern mode of city administration, even if the national political scene was dominated by an authoritarian and conservative regime. Thus, with reference also to Greenberg's contribution on firefighters (Chapter 3) and De Pieri's work on Turin (Chapter 2), it can be shown that the remit of local city administrations was not just a reaction to prior necessity. The organization of structures and services represented more than a simple, functional response to the growing complexity of city administration. How 'problems' were formulated, needs defined and management styles developed was the result of the intellectual, political and practical work carried out by municipal administrations and other participants on the urban scene, in a movement made familiar by studies on the 'reformist moment' (Topalov 1999).

Politics, administration and the nature of governance

Who were the people who set these municipal policies in motion? What sort of relations developed among the various groups that were evolving within local institutions? A concern with city employees directly involves the relationship between the political and the administrative spheres. A complicated question, the connections between these two spheres would merit extensive treatment by themselves. A genealogy will ultimately have to be made to draw out the discourse and practices that contributed to defining them, and creating the borders between them, so manifold were the ramifications of these processes. Clearly, this poses important questions regarding the development and history of political institutions. For our purposes, we wish to direct attention to the interplay between these two specific spheres. Nevertheless, scrutinizing the distinction between the political and the administrative, led by reformers, administrative experts and the aristocrats of political science, whose intentions were as much practical as professional and strategic, deserves far greater attention than can be afforded here. Echoing Dagenais (Chapter 7), we wish simply to draw attention to the multiplicity of the processes manifest in the functioning of municipal administration.[35]

Because marking the boundary between the political and the administrative is never clear-cut, any more than is the definition of the prerogatives and powers attached to each sphere, sources of tension between office holder and office worker were numerous. Of course, local elected representatives needed employees to direct the fortunes of their cities, and this was why they supported a certain growth in the administrative apparatus, all the while attempting to keep it within bounds. Moreover, at a time when local government was increasingly intervening in city life, those in elected office tended to rely on the expertise of their employees to reinforce their own legitimacy and shed a favourable light on their capacity to govern. This was what happened in Montreal during the 1930s when those in office, grappling with the disastrous effects of the Depression on the city, opted to team up with senior administrators. Those who had up to then sought to retain the greatest possible control over the management of civic affairs now decided to support an important reform of budgetary procedures.

Although they risked limiting the room for manoeuvre from which they had previously benefited, the elected representatives realized that the project permitted them to take the financial situation at City Hall in hand. With this information, they could more easily project an image of authority and competence, particularly useful in those difficult times.

At the same time, the collaboration between incumbents and administrators ran into its own constraints because the first group often viewed the knowledge and expertise of the second group as a threat. Some administrators owed their expertise to their technical training, some to their familiarity with city management acquired through experience, and some, indeed, to both components. If this expertise served the interests of those in office, who could take credit for it, it was also a source of tension that would advance in step with the increasing stability, scope and legitimacy of the administrative sphere. At the height of their competencies, merits and achievements, why might municipal employees not tend to stress the idea that they constituted, when all was said and done, the best guarantee for the stability and continuity of local institutions, in a kind of echo of the principles of 'businesslike management' and the separation of politics and administration?

Roberto Ferretti's contribution concerning Italian city engineers (Chapter 4) illuminates the ambiguous character of relationships between elected officials and city employees and the contradictions that ensued from the growth of a bureaucratic municipal apparatus. Here, employees' interests collided with those in elective office, although both sides comprehended the necessity of collaborating with each other so as to consolidate the municipal apparatus. But while doing their work for the city, the employees developed recognition of their own interests and specific professional identity. Thus, in the case of the city engineers, their increasing specialization and professionalism contributed to the formation of a particular group nurtured by its own expertise and endowed with a strong collective consciousness. The elected representatives showed determination when faced with the engineers' pursuit of status and their desire to maintain autonomy, and sought to label this group as mere subordinate technicians rather than professional decision makers. Numerous tensions followed from their efforts, insofar as the image projected was altogether at odds with the engineers' quest to construct a professional identity and gain public recognition for their work.

What sorts of strategies did public servants develop to counter the limitations that elected representatives wished to impose on them? In order to promote their collective identity and obtain whatever recognition for their expertise they could, many municipal employees organized their own professional associations. Just like Bellanger's twentieth-century town clerks in France, Ferretti's Italian city engineers turned in this direction. By relying on the collective strength that came with organized numbers, both groups aimed to obtain recognition at the national level that they would then use locally, as the need arose, to press for their rights and points of view. Working towards the circulation of information about available jobs and the definition of salary standards and working conditions, these associations also favoured the establishment of job banks at the regional and even national level. This allowed for greater autonomy of their members in relation to the elected representatives. Moreover, the employees did not hesitate to call upon the state to recognize their legitimacy and authority when necessary, even if the effect was to produce a certain weakening of local autonomy and thus create new sources of tension between employees and those elected to run municipal government.

If it was relatively easy for engineers to stress the technical character of their profession in order to obtain this sort of recognition, those in other categories, whose fields of competence rested on different criteria, were not prevented from relying on the same sort of strategy. This was the case for the town clerks studied by Bellanger. They successfully defined themselves as a distinctive professional group on the basis of their detailed familiarity with the local scene, acquired on the ground, and on their indispensable role as intermediaries between municipal powers and superior authorities, and the community workforce and the mayor. By stressing their ability to transcend partisan political battles and inter-union strife, the town clerks from the Parisian suburbs grew in prestige and even achieved the local and national political support that was necessary to establish their area of competence and their authority when faced with the elected administration. It is interesting to note that this class of professionals dualistically defined itself as apart from politics, but also relied on the political power-base to consolidate its position.

Employee associations seem, moreover, to have played an important role in the process of strengthening the skills of city employees. To those initiatives discussed by Bellanger in this volume (Chapter 6) may be added the activities of the British local government officers' association, NALGO, during the first decades of the twentieth century through the summer schools and qualification examinations that it developed as a means of gaining access to municipal service, or the correspondence courses and intensive courses set up in the USA in the 1930s by the International City Managers Association. The promulgation of rules for recruitment by employees' or by communes' associations (for instance, *Nederlandsche Vereiniging voor Gemeentenbelangen* in The Netherlands, *Deutsche Städtetag* in Germany, as well as the associations of Swedish communes) is another element that shows how far this area was a point of contact between the municipalities and their employees, even if relationships could veer between conflict and cooperation.[36]

The city of Toulouse illustrates yet another form of relationship between the political and administrative spheres, in which this time the trade unions were participants. Here, the local authorities openly and consciously depended upon city employees to increase their hold on the municipal apparatus, which at this point was nearly complete. As Jean-Yves Nevers explains in Chapter 9, close association between the politicians, the unions and the city employees came to be established. The cohesion of this 'iron triangle', as Nevers calls it, was based on the interests of the dominant union, on those of the political party in power and those of the higher levels of the bureaucracy, all of which were in a situation of interdependence. This particular form of co-management developed progressively during the opening decades of the twentieth century,[37] beginning when a joint committee charged with establishing the working conditions of municipal employees was set up. This was the way found by the ruling socialist party to purchase peace and obtain the adherence of city employees to its programme of municipal services development. The arrangement also permitted the party to count on the votes of employees and to benefit from a reservoir of important activists on its behalf. The uninterrupted re-election of socialists to Toulouse City Hall between 1925 and 1940 attests to the success of such collaboration, while at the same time it provided the grounds for its perpetuation.

The collaboration established between elected representatives and the municipal service administrators in Montreal during the 1930s resembles the Toulouse model, in that it also allowed for the establishment of standards of performance that would encourage the bureaucratization of municipal structures. Taking advantage of the winds of reform blowing through City Hall during the Depression, certain highly placed bureaucrats achieved the adoption of new procedures relating to critical aspects of the careers of city employees. Thus the practices governing pensions and salary scales were reviewed according to pre-established criteria that no longer took the particular circumstances of each individual employee into account. The introduction of regulations defining various aspects of public service jobs helped to limit the degree to which politicians might encroach on administrative territories. As a result, the transfer of areas of responsibility accentuated the administrative sphere to the detriment of the political area and, at the same time, increased the power of the bureaucrats. If ordinary city workers were less than enthusiastic about these reforms, because they prohibited them from presenting a personal case to secure certain privileges, they soon realized the advantages they might enjoy, particularly considering the insecurities of the Depression years. Whether through professional associations for certain groups, or unions for the rest, it could be said that the bureaucratization of labour relations was part of the process by which the position of city workers was consolidated within the municipal apparatus and their status recognized.

Several of the contributions to this volume analyse the processes that were involved in the definition of public policy and in the elaboration of the modalities surrounding the intervention of municipal administrations in the city.

An examination of the history of municipal employees and services inescapably raises the question of the degree to which city administrations had the power and capability to shape cities at both the physical and the social level. The reconstruction of various practices relating to installing water mains, building roads and public areas, establishing codes for improving the local environment, and the elaboration of new fiscal measures, allows for some response to this question. Indeed, all of these projects constitute tangible signs of the impact of municipal services and employees on the city. It is possible to reconstruct these effects from their surviving traces in lists of rental values and property owners, in geographical maps, urban development plans, organizational charts of municipal services and structures, schedules of job classifications and public service salary scales. To paraphrase Philippe Minard (2000), these relics ultimately permit us to understand how municipal administrators helped to create the urban physical and social landscape by projecting their expertise and interests onto the town.[38]

Conclusion

To attempt an outline survey of city employees and services in Europe and the Americas is like negotiating an obstacle course that requires taking short-cuts and detours, all of which may give rise to bias and misunderstandings. The undertaking also involves its share of successes as well as problems, happy discoveries and disappointments. Yet viewing, however summarily, the history of municipal administrations and their employees in São Paulo, Turin or Toulouse at once permits the main themes to emerge and brings to light the importance of certain phenomena. Without losing sight of all the essential subtle differences, it is necessary to begin by sketching certain simultaneous developments that were taking place municipally in Western cities. From the mid-nineteenth century, and for about a hundred years thereafter, a large number of cities experienced the development of their municipal governments along paths that often converged. The dynamics of political life, though strongly influenced by distinctive types of economic, social and cultural developments as well as differences of region, country and continent, were also similar on a number of levels. Questions of defining and establishing boundaries between the political and the administrative, the development of specialized municipal endeavours, the bureaucratization of labour relations, the professionalization of particular categories of employees, and the development of associations and unions show that there are as many common tendencies as there are different cities studied in the various chapters in this volume.

A certain tension between the need to use broad strokes to describe phenomena in order to bring out overall trends and the desire not to obscure their specific qualities always accompanies attempts at comparison. Much as a certain form of generalization allows for broad vistas that give the reader the impression of covering vast areas, these can also detract from the diversity of situations and the richness they entail. This uniformity, which lurks in every attempt to generalize, also depends on the current state of research. Although this introductory chapter hopes to provide a relatively exhaustive picture regarding Europe and the Americas, it must be cautioned that a number of obscure areas remain that can be attributed as much to our own limitations as to the existing scholarship. No comparison is possible between the breadth of work on the Italian municipalities and the paucity of studies on Brazilian cities. This relative meagreness of scholarly work is also apparent in the case of towns that are otherwise quite well studied, such as North American cities. Furthermore, the differences in the level of scholarly investigation into the questions that concern us cannot be attributed solely to their national orientation. Within the same country, students of urban history have exhibited considerably less interest in certain classes of cities (medium-sized cities in Great Britain) or certain regions (south-eastern USA, for example).

The act of comparison also exposes a number of snares that can render it a perilous undertaking. It is extremely difficult to stand on the cutting edge of comparison where diverse experiences meet. Despite efforts to extricate ourselves, we remain more often than not prisoners of the encompassing nation state, so resonant and pervasive in the study of the nineteenth and twentieth centuries. Therefore, whether we like it or not, comparisons are based on a given national situation, and other situations are judged in relationship to it.[39] This confinement makes sense up to a point in the case of municipalities, as their institutional history was closely linked to the formation of nation states. But at the same time, their histories cannot be understood in isolation, since the developments they underwent present similarities that are often unrelated to the national frameworks in which they were situated. There are at this point sufficiently numerous studies that demonstrate the autonomy enjoyed by municipalities in relation to the larger state, and these ought to encourage historians to undertake direct comparisons more boldly, not satisfying themselves with mere juxtaposition of municipal cases that would be meant to 'represent' national contexts. We also intend by this trying to draw comparisons according to a method that would not solely aim at labelling 'laggard' and 'pioneer' nation states, or at being concerned only with differences. Working with cities is also an introduction to the complexity of the mechanisms of initiation, borrowing, diffusion, innovation and their variations inside national borders, and it suggests slightly different ways to operate on a comparative scale.

Irene Maver, in her concluding chapter for this volume, outlines one of these possibilities. On the one hand, she assesses Glasgow's possible distinctiveness in relation to other European cities, paying attention to the operation of its civic bureaucracy. On the other hand, she considers Glasgow as a complex place that absorbed and diffused national and international innovations in the field of municipal administration and policies. The fact that Glasgow was one of the Meccas for reformers of local government and administration at the turn of the twentieth century is very encouraging for us: it shows that even one of the most praised municipalities was in search of information about municipal policy across the seas.

One way of escaping from the straitjacket of the nation state is precisely to ask the kind of questions that are situated immediately at the intersection of a number of national contexts. Should we not go beyond the statement of similarities among the various municipalities to interrogate the structural and historic circumstances that brought them into being? We must therefore study very closely how municipal administrations came to adopt similar policies, practices and measures, despite their diverse characteristics and geographical locations. The scholarly work that already exists concerning the ideas involved with city management does not preclude further detailed research into the processes that were responsible for circulating these ideas, how they became established in various municipalities and the modalities surrounding their adoption. The comparatist perspective, therefore, becomes 'trans', 'supra', 'super' or 'inter' national; the choice of term is not important.[40] What is important is that this approach becomes more than a simple instrument in the historian's hands. Comparativism can perhaps transcend some of its limits by becoming, at least in part, the very object of scholarly research. This seems particularly appropriate, since the officials and employees being studied used it so intensively. Indeed, it was comparativism in practice that various protagonists in the 'municipal movement' employed at the turn of the twentieth century, not just through their investigations, fact-finding trips, conferences and publications, but also through the rhetorical and practical transfers they derived from foreign connections.[41] The theme of city workforces and the organization of municipal services, which, as has been noted, was the focus of numerous inquiries, conventions and investigative trips reflecting local and national experiences, is promising ground for further study. We hope that this volume will contribute to encouraging further steps in this direction.

Notes

1. See, for instance, the recent edited collection of Morris and Trainor (2000).
2. As exemplified by the work of Dubois (1996, 1998, 1999).
3. See Becker and Clark (2001), *Genèses* (1999), *Actes de la Recherche en Sciences Sociales* (2000).
4. William Cohen (1998) has presented a convincing argument about the wide margin of autonomy that French municipalities had in the nineteenth century, despite control by the Prefects, the *Ministère de l'Intérieur* and the *Conseil d'Etat*. These controls need to be investigated in more depth to reach a better understanding of their limits.
5. The *Segretaria*, created in 1919 by the *Associazione Nazionale Comuni Italiani* (National Association of Italian Municipalities), was converted into a national agency by the fascist state in 1926.
6. The British figures come from Byrne (1994), 249; the French figures are quoted in Bellanger et al. (2000: 26), from the data of the *Institut National de la Statistique et des Etudes Economiques*.
7. That was the experience of London County Council in 1909, with 35 316 employees. (See Clifton, 1989: 10.) E.D. Simon, the ex-lord mayor of Manchester, wrote that his city's Corporation employed 25 000 people in 1926, and that one-tenth of the city's population was living on a municipal stipend. (Quoted by Bellamy in Rugge 1992: 51). Glasgow employed 34 000 permanent staff in 1934 (Maver, 2000: 83).
8. On public administration employees, see notably Aron (1987), Siwek-Pouydesseau (1989) and Dagenais (2000a), chapter 5. On clerical employees in general, see Kocka (1980), Lowe (1987), Dagenais (1989) and Gardey (1999).
9. For example, Furner and Supple (1990), Furner and Lacey (1993), Dubois and Dulong (1999) and McLeod (1988).
10. For a useful introduction to the world of the press and periodicals aimed at clerks, or published by clerks' organizations, see Romanelli (1989), chapter 1, as well as Lucarini (1999).
11. For approaches that involve synthesis of municipal government in Europe, see for example Rugge (1992) and Naunin (1984).
12. Though this touches upon the limits of this volume, it is worth mentioning

that the Country Management Act of 1940 established city and county managers in Eire.

13. Gregorio Nuñez, of the University of Granada, is working on the underresearched area of Spanish municipal government, employees and services. See, for instance, his 'Notes sur les stratégies et la structure du personnel dans l'administration locale en Espagne au début du XXe siècle', from the colloquium, 'Gouverner la ville en Europe, 19–20eme siècles', held at Lyons, France, June 2000.

14. The British trade union NALGO, now incorporated into UNISON, was originally the National Association of Local Government Officers, but from the late 1940s extended its sphere of recruitment to workers in the nationalized industries, notably the state-run gas and electricity monopolies. It was known subsequently as the National and Local Government Officers' Association.

15. International Union of Local Authorities, 1932, *Fifth International Congress of Local Authorities*, Brussels: International Union of Local Authorities, 28.

16. For a summarized account of urban history in Great Britain, see Anthony Sutcliffe, 'Great Britain', in Engeli and Matzerath (1989).

17. Wolfgang Hoffmann, 'Aspetti politici e sociali', in Rugge (1992), 125.

18. Carlotta Sorba (1987) has taken preliminary steps in this direction in a wider essay on the historiography of 'local administration' in Europe. We are indebted to her for our description of Italian research in the field.

19. In fact, it is amazing how, in other countries, works on municipal employees and services generally ignore the rich foreign contribution in the field, or do not integrate their questions and findings in their own framework, beginning with Dumons et al. (1998).

20. The same observation can be made about Schiesl's contribution to Ebner and Tobin (1977). His account of the housing inspectors of Los Angeles does not consider this group or their administrative support as important actors in control policy.

21. The recent episode of Mayor Rudolph Giuliani, leaving office with his papers to be managed separately from New York City records, is another sign of the uncertainty that rules the sphere of municipal archives in the USA.

22. Georges McAneny, a local leader of the municipal reform movement, was elected to different positions in New York City government during the first four decades of the twentieth century. Leonard D. White was Professor of Public Administration in the Political Science Department of the University of Chicago. He became a US civil service commissioner later in the 1930s.

23. There is a whole collection of studies into the formation of the state in the nineteenth century, which provides an excellent account of this transfer. Chief among them are Greer and Radforth (1992) and Curtis (2001). See Morris (2000), for an analysis of the processes bearing more directly on the local level, and Dumons and Pollet (2001), for two complementary perspectives.

24. For an analysis of the whole, see Isin (1992).

25. This is also the question raised in the article by Joana (1998) on the development of municipal public action in France.

26. The term appears notably in the title of the recent work edited by Topalov (1999).

27. This discussion of the towns and the development of municipal activity is strongly indebted to an essay by R.J. Morris (1989) in which he analyses the process of urbanization in Great Britain and in Canada during the nineteenth century and highlights the weak position of Canadian municipal authorities faced with private businesses.

28. The frontier towns of western Canada clearly illustrate the strategy adopted by local administrators in order to encourage local development: Artibise (1975), McDonald (1996). For other localities, see Lord (1984) and Rudin (1984). Some authors associate this expansionist strategy with 'boosterism'; see Monkkonen (1988), 141–54, and Davis (1985).

29. For the situation in American cities, see particularly Heinhorn (1991) and Monkkonen (1988). For Canadian cities, see Dagenais (2000b).

30. This definition of the municipality as an extension of the state (or of individual states, in the case of federal structures) was and is the subject of debate in a number of countries. The German argument is perhaps the most familiar, especially in its juridical dimension, with the interpretation of local government as an organ and source of sovereignty and authority (*obrigkeitliche Selbstverwaltung*) dividing jurists such as Laband, Gellinek and Preuss did at the beginning of the twentieth century. But if the strictly legal dimension is less marked (or in every case less recognized), the debate was just as lively in many other countries from the point where it concerns attempts to settle practical questions such as municipal mergers or annexations, police duties, fiscal measures or possible revamping of the municipal legislation; for an example on France, see Payre (2001). In these situations and in a number of others (the establishment of associations of municipalities, for example) we may observe how far the discussion is animated by the historic and modern nature of municipalities as social, political and economic structures. For some suggestions regarding the 'identity' element in these questions, see Saunier (1998).

31. For this term and the wealth of significations and configurations that it may reveal or mask, see especially Dogliani (1992), chapter 2, Rodger (1993), Fraser (1993), Joana (2001) and Kühl (2001).

32. In addition to the classic urban studies by Schiesl (1977), Teaford (1984) and Weaver (1979), see also Samuel Haber's excellent treatment of the existing connections between Taylorism and municipal public works services, particularly in Philadelphia (1964), and the more recent work of Hindy L. Schachter (1989).

33. On the right to vote in European cities and the consequences of its extension into the realm of municipal politics in various countries and areas, see Stieber (1998), chapter 1 for The Netherlands, Dogliani (1992) for Belgium, and Ladd (1990), chapter 1 for Germany. For North America, see Magnusson (1983).

34. Curtis (2001). On the idea of 'municipal science', see Rugge (1989a) and Payre (2001, 2002).

35. The work of Stivers (2000) and Roberts (1994) clarifies this task of drawing analytical distinctions for historical research and of analysing historical distinctions, one of the most famous examples being the dichotomy between politics and administration developed by Woodrow Wilson and Frank Goodnow in the USA at the end of the nineteenth century.

36. For an initial panorama of these initiatives, one may refer to the report published by the Fifth Congress of the International Union of Local

Authorities, where the training and improvement of employees was on the agenda (International Union of Local Authorities, 1932; see note 15, above).

37. It would be interesting to compare the way in which joint systems developed in different countries. The case of Toulouse calls for a comparison with the Whitley Councils that emerged in Great Britain after the First World War, despite their varied fortunes. For a contemporary assessment, see Hill (1935), but note that Hill was then General Secretary of the National Association of Local Government Officers (NALGO). The Whitley Councils became the focus of considerable attention from American civil service reformers, stimulated by the likes of Leonard D. White, professor of public administration at the University of Chicago. Jean-Yves Nevers quotes the words of F. Bourdon, who anachronistically found the Whitley Councils an 'inspiration' for the system developed in Toulouse. In the context of 'sites of importation', Nevers thus demonstrates the complex way in which foreign references were used ambiguously to legitimize or subvert power (Rodgers 1998).

38. Pierre Rosanvallon (1990) refers to 'l'institution du social' (the establishment of the social sphere) by the French state. Municipalities also participated in the process, we would argue.

39. For a consideration of comparativism and its limitations, especially on the question of 'exceptionalism', see the introductory chapter in Daniel T. Rodgers (1998) and Espagne (1999).

40. For an introduction to various considerations of this point, see Tyrrell (1991).

41. Beyond the references at the beginning of this introduction, we may add the article by Viviane Claude (1999) for its development of the theme of the 'autochthonous practice of comparativism'. See also the theme issue of Contemporary European History (2002) 'Municipal connections: Co-operation, links and transfers among European Cities in the Twentieth Century'.

CHAPTER TWO

Nineteenth-century municipal engineers in Turin: technical bureaucracies in the networks of local power

Filippo De Pieri

The growth of municipal technical offices in nineteenth-century Turin was closely linked with the emergence of new functions and powers of the city's local administration.[1] Its history crosses the history of modern Italy's unification, raising many questions about the way national political changes affected local processes of bureaucratization, especially in those cities that had previously been capitals of the early nineteenth-century Italian states. Such was the case of Turin which, having been for centuries the capital city of Piedmont, became the first capital of Italy in 1860, after the country's unification, only to lose this role to Florence in 1865.[2]

Important as these two key dates were for the city's history, the development of Turin's local bureaucracy followed a different chronology, less influenced by national political events than might be assumed. This was partly due to the role played by Piedmont in the process of political and legislative unification of Italy (Romeo 1963, Coppini 1994, Riall 1994, 1998). Piedmontese and Italian legislation on local administrations were closely connected; the first Italian communal and provincial law, approved in 1865, by and large reflected the Piedmontese provisional law of 1859, which had been inspired by previous laws of 1847–48 (Romanelli 1995). As a consequence, Turin's local bureaucracies were less touched than others by the administrative reforms that followed the making of Italy (De Nicolò 1996).

A better starting point for the history of the city's local administration is provided by two previous reforms, the aforementioned 1847 and 1848 municipal laws, and Piedmont's first liberal constitution, the *Statuto* of 1848. It was only after their promulgation that Turin's city council could gradually free itself from a somewhat secondary role in the government of urban affairs. From then on, the city council began to be recognized as a sort of strategic centre for urban decision making, the focus for any discussion and negotiation involving local policies and the use of local resources. The development of the city's technical bureaucracy was part of such a process.

An important element of the new functions assumed by the city council after 1848 had to do with control over urban space, and technical and normative control over the city's transformation became a key feature of the municipality's new identity. These functions also proved to be a powerful resource for local elites, one that helped them to reshape their political networks during a period when more traditional forms of urban patronage were weakening. Given the continuing importance of building and land investments for the definition of political rights and social status in nineteenth-century urban societies, the control over spatial issues was an important factor of political influence. This explained the importance of technical bureaucracies in the local power structure, and their crucial mediating role. Their story has something to say about the way local elites dealt with urban modernization issues, while providing an opportunity to test the elements of continuity and change between post-Napoleonic Piedmont and liberal Italy.

The creation of *Ufficio d'arte*

For most of the first half of the nineteenth century, Turin's municipality did not have any specific office devoted to engineering or architectural works. No architect, engineer or surveyor is registered in the lists of the city's employees for the post-Napoleonic years, and whenever specific technical works were needed, the municipality entrusted them to professionals from outside. These could sometimes accumulate several mandates, thus acting as de facto municipal officers even without filling a corresponding bureaucratic position. Such was the case of the architect Gaetano Lombardi who, from 1817 until *circa* 1825, was charged by the city with all the projects for the development of the land previously occupied within city walls. His were also the designs for the city's new cemetery and a new municipal slaughterhouse. The position partly changed after 1828, when the city hired a municipal engineer, Giovanni Barone. However, his subsequent role essentially was limited to ordinary affairs of no great importance, such as writing technical reports, surveying and assessing the city's properties, and supervising the maintenance of the city's buildings, mills and canals. The narrow scope of these activities reflected not only Barone's unexceptional technical skills but, more importantly, the limited power of the institution he worked for.

During the Restoration years, in Turin as in other modern European capital cities, control over urban space and public works was the object of a continuing conflict between different powers, at both central and local levels (Hall 1997: 276) and following. The interference of state institutions with local urban affairs was frequent, and reflected the idea that the capital city of the kingdom should enjoy a special status; control over spatial transformation could not be left to municipal authority alone. Since the *ancien régime*, such a concern was embodied in the very structure of municipal powers, with a proliferation of institutions which, although acting at the local level, had only partial links with Turin's city council. Such was the case of the *Vicariato*, a bureaucracy whose intricate province included control over Turin's rents, part of the procedures connected with the approval of designs for private buildings, and occasionally the implementation of specific public works projects.[3]

When the city's *Ufficio d'arte* (Engineering Works Office) was created in 1843 as a municipal technical office in charge of the layout and maintenance of the city's streets, sewers, canals and buildings, this state of affairs had not really changed. The birth of the office, in itself the outcome of a new set of building and street regulations, did not result in an immediate shift in the balance of local power, and the first few years of its activity did not show any consistent departure from previous practices. However, just a few years later, King Charles Albert's reforms brought major institutional transformations to Turin, paving the way for a new role for municipal government and its technical bureaucracy. The approval of the 1847 communal and provincial law and the concession of the *Statuto* in 1848 both had a long-lasting impact on the city's history. The reforms turned the city council into an elective assembly, endowed with greater moral and political legitimacy than in the recent past (Petracchi 1962). Additionally, they abolished most of the local authorities whose proliferation had previously counterbalanced the council's powers. Finally, they were followed by financial measures, notably the transfer to the city of revenues accruing from taxation, which gave the municipality the means to implement its policies without any aid or conditioning on the part of the state.[4]

As a result, Turin's administrative structure lost many of the exceptional traits that the city's status as capital had entailed in previous years.[5] In particular, the city's administration absorbed and centralized many 'technical' tasks which had previously been the province of other institutions: the drawing up of building regulations, control over private architecture, and the implementation of public works programmes and urban expansion schemes. All of these were soon recognized as important features of municipal activity. It must be stressed that such devolution of powers from central to local administration was not entirely written in the reform texts of 1848. On the contrary, it partly resulted from the political battles subsequently fought by the city council for the redefinition of its province.

Urban design schemes provide a good example of this process. The delegation to the municipality of the decisions concerning the layout of new plans for urban extension was, in fact, the partial consequence of a conflict that pitched the local authority in opposition to the central government after 1848. The proposals for a general plan for Turin had begun in 1843, against the wishes of the old municipality. After King Charles Albert's reforms, the new city council took over and successfully implemented the project, defending it from the attacks of landowners and the ministry of public works. A plan that in previous years had often been perceived as antimunicipal consequently became a symbol of the city's new decision-making role in urban issues. The conflict ended when a 1851 law officially recognized the validity of the city's arguments, stating that urban extension plans had not to be submitted to parliamentary vote, as state ministers had often argued (Levi and Olmo 1984: 11–26, De Pieri 1999). From then on, municipal autonomy in the field of urban planning remained virtually uncontested (Olmo 1989). The political dispute with central government had been won thanks to the expertise of municipal councillors such as the architect and university professor Carlo Promis, and the lawyers Giovanni Battista Cassinis and Lorenzo Ceppi. The result was that, after the 1851 law, urban design schemes were treated increasingly as matters of purely technical concern, and therefore entrusted to the city's *Ufficio d'arte*.

In fact, in the institutional context created by the reforms, the existence of municipal technical bureaucracies had important implications for the city; it was proof of their growing technical skills, and a guarantee against any future external interference in local matters. As the above example shows, the redefinition of the professional identity of the office in the early 1850s depended on the bureaucratic inheritance left by other institutions. Only selective oblivion regarding the recent past and a comprehensive idea of 'technique' helped reshape these partly heterogeneous materials into a coherent whole. The final result was the creation of a strong bureaucracy, which during the following decades was responsible for most of the urban projects promoted by the city. The autonomy and power it enjoyed were remarkable. The public works controlled by the *Ufficio d'arte*, often with minimal political control, mobilized an important proportion of the city's financial resources.

Such a result was achieved by a simple bureaucratic structure, individually led by one of the best paid among the city's officers. Only the city's treasurer and secretary were paid more than the chief engineer.[6] From the early 1850s until the early 1880s, Turin's technical bureaucracy was in fact organized around the personal skills and power of one man; chief engineer Edoardo Pecco, who replaced the previous municipal engineer in 1852.[7] As will be explained, the structure of the office under Pecco's direction displays some interesting characteristics.

The characteristics of the technical bureaucracy

Turin's municipal bureaucracy experienced sustained if not uniform growth during the decades following King Charles Albert's institutional reforms. Growth was particularly evident in the peak years of 1848–50 and 1865–67, which alternated with periods of continuous but slower expansion. The first peak was the more spectacular: from a total of 33 employees in 1848, the municipal bureaucracy more than doubled in two years, rising in 1850 to a total of 69.[8] In the second peak, between 1865 and 1867, the numbers rose from 80 to 100 employees, thus gaining 25 per cent in a three-year interval. The intermediate period between 1850 and 1865 registered an overall increase of about 16 per cent, distributed over a 15-year time span; something very similar happened after 1867.[9] However, the growth of the city's *Ufficio d'arte* did not follow the same pattern. The office did not increase at all in the first few years after 1848, and only after Edoardo Pecco's nomination as chief engineer in 1852 did a reorganization of the office allow for an expansion of staff from seven to 12 employees. This situation remained static during the two following decades. From 1855 to 1877, the personnel of the *Ufficio d'arte* kept oscillating between a total of 11 and 14 employees, and only after 1878 did this period of stagnation come to a sudden close; the regular staff rose to 18 employees in 1878, 22 in 1883, 27 in 1884, and 29 in 1889.

This remarkable phase of stability was also characterized by lack of change in the office's staff. Only four new accessions can be registered during the whole period, a figure that was reduced to a mere two for the slightly shorter time span between 1862 and 1877. Thus, for more than two decades after Pecco's nomination, the *Ufficio d'arte* remained identified with a well-defined group of employees. The majority of them were *geometri* (surveyors).[10] From its foundation in 1843 until 1861, the structure included no more than two engineers, namely the head of the office and his deputy, the *ingegnere in seconda*. Two more engineers were added to the structure in 1862–63. Throughout the period, the engineers' weight thus oscillated between approximately one-third and one-sixth of the office's overall workforce. Here again, the situation changed abruptly after 1878; six out of the seven new employees who joined the office in that year were engineers. Their entry gave engineers a new prominence in the structure (10 out of 18 employees for that year) and from that time onwards a ratio of roughly 1:1 between engineers and *geometri* became more or less the rule in the office's composition.

As these data show, the technical bureaucracy put in place by Turin's administration after 1848 was characterized by a high degree of stability and impermeability to external exchange. Very few people entered the office, and very few people left it. The engineer Pietro Borella, who chose in 1860 to resign from his post of *ingegnere in seconda* to become chief engineer of the city of Piacenza, was indeed an exception. For most of the technical employees, work for the office was perceived to be a choice of life-long service for the municipal institution. Such values were embodied by the municipal regulations of the officers' duties, which, for example, stated that the *Ufficio d'arte*'s engineers were not allowed to act as professionals or to accept any job whatsoever in addition to their normal administrative tasks. Turin's engineers also seemed to retain a strongly local profile during the period; even on the few occasions in which available positions in the technical structure were assigned through public competitions, successful candidates always proved to be local ones.[11]

In a period of evident municipal efforts at building a coherent and homogeneous bureaucratic structure, modelled on state and province administration, the technical character of the *Ufficio d'arte* never failed to pose some problems of integration with the rest of the city's bureaucracy.[12] For example, the range of salaries of municipal employees (a hierarchical classification which also served for ceremonial purposes) was never completely matched by the one used for the salaries of the technical staff. 'Technical' salaries were also periodically increased according to a particular set of regulations. Following a rule of 1843, which remained in force until 1883, all the proceeds of the copies of drawings made by the *Ufficio d'arte* for private use were divided each year between the non-engineer clerks. Figures for these proceeds are difficult to find, but it is known that in 1857 the rule resulted in an increase of annual staff salary by approximately 10 per cent. Another distinction can be found in the application of the *indennità caro-viveri*, the system which entitled municipal employees to an automatic 20 per cent salary increase every 10 years. From 1863 the rule was applied differently to the staff of the *Ufficio d'arte*; their salary increased more frequently, by 10 per cent every five years.[13] Municipal documents repeatedly explain this exceptional status as a form of compensation for the distinctive position of the technical staff in the municipal administration as a whole. Because of their specialization, technical staff had almost no possibility of internal mobility and promotion to other sectors of the local bureaucracy.

Indeed, career possibilities could be quite limited. Once they had reached the position of *aiutante ingegnere di prima classe* (first-class assistant), the *geometri* of the office could not aspire to any further advancement, the upper positions being reserved for qualified engineers. For example, the two first-class assistants in the 1840s, Luigi Delfino and Ferdinando Broggi, had very limited careers. Both had served in the office since 1843, were promoted to first class in 1848, and kept this position for the rest of their working lives; Delfino retired in 1874, Broggi in 1877. As compensation, their salary was periodically increased (1800 lire in 1856, 2000 in 1860, 2300 in 1861, 2500 in 1863). When Broggi retired, he was granted an annual pension of 3425 lire, an amount that coincided with his last effective salary.[14] Other members of the technical staff, who had started their careers from a lower post, could on the contrary benefit widely from the absence of competition (both from the outside world and from the city's other employees) and from a regular succession of internal promotions. The case of Eusebio Campagna, in the *Ufficio d'arte* since 1855, was quite spectacular. Starting with a salary of 900 lire, in the following years he climbed every step of the bureaucratic ladder, with promotions to second class in 1872 and to first class in 1877. His salary progressively increased up to a maximum of 3300 lire in 1889, a figure that still did not include either the increases of the *indennità caro-viveri* or the periodical *ad personam* allocations, which were not infrequent.

These personal advantages and disadvantages were the result of the special position of the office within the municipal bureaucracy: a small, reputable and highly centralized *enclave*, which guaranteed to most of its employees opportunities for promotion or regular increases in salary, even though their careers were from the very beginning restricted within the structure's limits. At the beginning of the 1880s, it was evident that such a situation had led to paradoxical consequences; the salaries of the *geometri* had grown so much that the younger engineers recruited in 1878 were paid considerably less. The salary range of new engineers went from 1500 to 2400 lire in 1878. In the same year, the surveyors' salaries ranged between 1800 and 2500 lire. Yet it was clear that future prospects for surveyors were becoming less bright than in the past. This was because of the growing role of qualified engineers and the narrowing opportunities for comparatively unskilled technical staff to progress, even inside the office.

The impact of temporary technical staff

As historians of nineteenth-century bureaucracy know, the way organizations could perceive and represent themselves often differed considerably from the way they actually worked. The data previously presented have traced an account of the evolution of the city's technical office as it emerged from serial official publications, such as the annual proceedings of Turin's city council. But this information cannot be relied upon without closer scrutiny. Official information often imperceptibly mixes description and prescription, blending factual analysis with reforming discourse about how things are supposed to be. In the specific case of the technical bureaucracies analysed above, the city's official sources are flawed by one striking omission: they systematically fail to recognize the role played by the office's temporary staff.

The resort to a temporary workforce was not uncommon in nineteenth-century public administrations, both inside and outside Italy.[15] It was even more common among technical bureaucracies.[16] Temporary employment of professionals could be a viable solution for carrying out definite, short-term tasks; in other cases, a period of temporary work as an apprentice could be considered the first step in a career towards permanent or semi-permanent recruitment (Melis and Varni 2000). Practices of both kinds can occasionally be found in Turin's administration, as in many other Italian ones. Yet it must be stressed that in the years following Italy's political unification the role of temporary staff working for the *Ufficio d'arte* went much further beyond these limits, to the extent of creating a sort of secondary technical office, 'temporary' (*straordinario*) only in its name, barely spoken of by official sources and never without perceptible embarrassment.

Only sparse documentary clues allow us to catch glimpses of such a structure. Its origins are, however, clear; they can be found in the wave of public works projects promoted by the city both in 1860–61 (when Turin became the capital of Italy) and after the crisis of 1864–65, when capital city status was lost (Castronovo 1987, Bracco 2000b). Two of these projects, in particular, had a long-term impact on the organization of the *Ufficio d'arte*: first, the decision to promote a detailed survey of the city, at both ground and underground levels; second, the project for the excavation of a new water canal from the Dora river (the Ceronda canal), a project meant to increase the hydraulic motive power available in the city and encourage its future industrial development. For both works, temporary technical staff were added to the office; documents of 1860–61 speak indeed of an *Ufficio d'arte provvisorio* (temporary engineering office).[17] The structure was not financed through the ordinary city budget, but from special funds accumulated for the projects. Such funds were relevant; the works and studies for the Ceronda canal, for instance, completely absorbed the annual sum of 300 000 lire given to the city by the Italian state as compensation for the capital city transfer.

Although attempts were made by the municipal council to stop the phenomenon, the presence of temporary technical staff endured well beyond the phase of the special projects of the 1860s, and became over the years one of the *Ufficio d'arte*'s most distinctive traits.[18] From this perspective, new accessions to the office are quite revealing. All of the 12 people who entered the office in 1878 and 1883 had already worked for the office, albeit in a 'temporary' capacity, for a remarkable amount of time. Engineer Giuseppe Porro, for example, had 17 years of previous service recognized by the city at the moment of his recruitment in 1878. For the surveyor Giovanni Fusello, admitted in 1883, temporary service had lasted even longer (21 years). On average, 'new' staff recruited in the period had already worked for the city for approximately 11 years. It is unclear whether this work had been constant and uninterrupted, or involved a succession of smaller, temporary tasks distributed over a longer span of time. It would seem, however, that a long, semi-permanent service had been the rule for many of the so-called temporary employees. As the mayor, Felice Rignon, put it in 1877, temporary staff had progressively become 'a group of people who spent many years studying and directing a number of long and important works, and had their salaries increased according to their "career" advancement, even though they had only been appointed on a temporary basis'.[19]

From 1878 onwards, no fewer than 17 members of this group, and possibly more, were officially recognized as permanent members of the city's technical bureaucracy. The decision, which marked the beginning of the visible growth of the office after a long period of gestation, put an end to a situation in which temporary staff, mostly made up of engineers, had begun regularly to outgrow the less skilful workforce of the *Ufficio d'arte*, at least 14, compared to 11 in 1877. With the nominations of the late 1870s, the city was finally forced implicitly to recognize the long-term impact of the special projects of the 1860s. Firstly, they had multiplied the power of the office's chief engineer, giving him more control over local professional networks and the city's financial resources than was usually admitted. Secondly, they had conditioned the recruitment policies of the city, creating a wide reservoir of skilful officers, recruited without any public statute or competition and who virtually monopolized access to the *Ufficio d'arte* for a generation.

The impact of organizational change

It is no surprise, then, that the first regularization of the office's temporary staff in 1878 provided the starting point for a wider debate, focused on the organization and control of the technical bureaucracy. Attacks on the *Ufficio d'arte* grew stronger at the end of the 1870s, prompted not only by the issue of temporary employees but also by the unsatisfying results of some of the office's recent works, such as the new parts of the embankment of the Po river (the 'Murazzi'). Symptomatic of the changed climate was the decision, taken by the city council in 1879, to appoint a special technical committee, the *Commissione consultiva d'arte*.[20] Its task was to examine the office's projects and report to the city council or the *giunta*, so as to inform the politicians about technical matters.[21]

The committee remained in charge for only three years, and the reason behind its dissolution lay in the fact that a reform of the office then came into effect that seemed to guarantee stronger political control over the office's activities. Studied in 1880 by a sub-committee of the *Commissione consultiva d'arte* whose reporter was the architect Carlo Ceppi, the reform divided the office into three sections: engineering works (*ingegneria*), control over private buildings (*edilizia*) and public architectural projects (*architettura*). Its professed purpose was to enlarge and clarify the office's task (the creation of an architectural section is particularly noteworthy), while creating a hierarchical structure of responsibility that had previously been lacking. Thanks to the 1877 and 1883 regularization of temporary staff, the new office was bigger than in the past, and was organized according to new criteria of functional articulation.[22] This did not mean that the institution would have become stronger. In fact, it could be argued, a more subtle purpose of the reform was to dismantle the small, simple, but highly centralized bureaucratic structure that had proved so effective in recent years.

The implementation of the 1880 reform was slightly delayed to make it coincide with the more general reform of the city's bureaucracy. In 1883, the 20 city offices were reorganized into nine larger ones, each under the direct control of one *assessore* of the *giunta*. Unique among them, the *Ufficio d'Arte* was, however, put under the control of both an *assessore* and the mayor. Significantly, 1883 was also the retirement year for Edoardo Pecco. Reorganization consequently affected the technical office during a period of turnover, when some of the people who had been identified with the structure in previous years appeared very close to retirement. The same applied to the case of the city's chief architect Carlo Gabetti, who retired in 1882 and whose office merged with the *Ufficio d'arte* as a result of the reform. In previous years, Gabetti's building office (*Ufficio edilizio*) had been an interesting case of strong identification between a bureaucratic position and a single employee. A relic of the old *Vicariato*'s bureaucracy, the office was made up of two people, Gabetti and his assistant, who retired in 1879. Repeated attempts to incorporate it into the *Ufficio d'arte* apparently failed for 'personal reasons', as municipal councillor Di Pollone stated in 1860. He was commenting on a situation that contrasted with the impersonal definition of roles and status that the bureaucratic organization seemed to imply.[23] For all its concerns about general principles of functional articulation and bureaucratic control, the reorganization of technical offices was thus also made possible by a generational change that weakened a consolidated system of networks of patronage and personal rivalries.

A leading role in the reform of the *Ufficio d'arte* of the late 1870s was played by a group of architects and engineers who were not part of the city's technical bureaucracy and had a direct interest in limiting the office's role. Almost all of the authors of the project of reorganization, as well as the members of the 1879 *Commissione consultiva d'arte*, came from the same *milieu*. They were recent members of the *Commissione d'ornato*, established in 1860 after the abolition of the *Consiglio degli edili*, and which had inherited the latter's tasks pertaining to the approval of private building projects. Headed by the mayor and originally composed of three architects or engineers, a doctor and three city councillors, the committee was changing in both its composition and its role by the end of the 1870s. Again, a shift can be found in 1877, when a minor reform of the institution (the election of four deputy members in addition to the eight ordinary ones) served to accelerate the process of change.

From then on, the committee was more open to external accession, and became an important point of reference for any engineer, architect or city councillor who aspired to play a major role in conditioning municipal urban projects.[24] Such was the case of Count Ernesto Balbo Bertone di Sambuy, 'perhaps the leading patron of the arts in Turin at the turn of the century', mayor of the city between 1883 and 1886 and among the promoters of Turin's foremost 'Haussmannian' project, the opening of Via Pietro Micca in 1885.[25] Both Sambuy and Ceppi were long-time members of the *Commissione d'ornato*, and tried to strengthen its role and legitimacy as the institution where major urban transformations should be discussed and designed.[26] Hence their emphasis on the need to support the activity of the *giunta* with a committee of artists and experts, while strengthening political control over the city's bureaucracy. It was the growing weight of these pressure groups, sometimes organized in professional and non-professional associations, which finally called into question the autonomy enjoyed by the *Ufficio d'arte*.[27]

Conclusion

As historians of modern Italy have shown in recent years, the study of the structure and organization of local bureaucracies provides an interesting case-study for evaluating the political and administrative cultures of Italian local elites during the decades following the country's unification (ISAP 1990). In spite of its centralizing character, the 1865 Italian communal and provincial law allowed local authorities a wide margin of autonomy in the organization of their offices (Romanelli 1988). As far as technical bureaucracies were concerned, available research seems indeed to suggest that deep-rooted differences existed, and no single administrative model was at work in nineteenth-century Italy.[28] In such a context, Turin's *Ufficio d'arte*, during the period of Pecco's direction, was clearly recognizable by a few distinctive traits. The office embodied strong bureaucratic features. Its autonomy from political influence at the municipal level was remarkable.[29] Work for the technical office was not considered compatible with the pursuit of a private professional career.[30] The staff was committed to life-long service for the municipal institution, benefiting from automatic systems of promotions and salary increases. Thanks to the systematic recourse to 'temporary' employees, chief engineer Pecco had the dual advantage of guiding a structure that was both growing in size and apparently untouched by change.

Some of these distinctions may partly be explained as a result of institutional conflict and transformation. The office's reorganization, in the early 1850s, had an important role in the delimitation of an undisputed area of municipal government. Its autonomy and prestige helped to reinforce the image of the city as an institution capable of implementing policies of great technical complexity. Years later, after the loss of capital city status, the partial devolution of power and resources from the municipal council to its technical bureaucracy certainly appeared less justified. More generally, however, the structure of the *Ufficio d'arte* appears to have been conditioned by several factors: conflicts between institutional actors for the control of political and financial resources; persistence and incorporation of *ancien régime* cultures and bureaucracies; long-term effects of short-term policies; competition between different technical representations of the city; and formation and disruption of local networks of power, linking municipal officers to local elites, and both to urban society as a whole. In short, in Turin as in other Italian cities, the growth of technical bureaucracies was not just a 'functional' response to the increased complexity of urban government, or to a change in the tasks it was called to perform. Nor may it simply be considered the effect of diffusion of technical cultures and administrative models. Both statements are certainly true. But the ways these general processes actually affected nineteenth-century urban societies were less uniform (and less 'modern' in their implications) than we often tend to think.

Notes

1. Most of the information in this chapter comes from an elaboration of data on municipal offices published in the annual proceedings of the sessions of Turin's city council, *Atti del Municipio di Torino*, Turin: Tipografia Eredi Botta; henceforth referred to as AM. These have been examined for the period between 1848 and 1890. Information on the composition of the technical offices has also been systematically compared with those provided by two annual guides to Turin's public administration, the officially published *Calendario generale pe' Regii Stati* for the period 1824–59 and the similar *Il Palmaverde* for the period 1860–80. When necessary, reference will also be made to other documents from Turin's municipal archives (*Archivio Storico del Comune di Torino*; henceforth ASCT).

2. The capital was moved again to Rome after the seizure of the pontifical city in 1870. See Caracciolo (1985).

3. The office was headed by the *Vicario* (Vicar), an officer of royal nomination, chosen among the city councillors, who acted as the king's representative before the city. Worth mentioning also is the *Consiglio degli edili* (Aediles' Council), a committee appointed by the king which gave its opinion on matters concerning architectural projects and urban extension schemes. The council included architects, engineers and a few municipal councillors. The institution was an *ancien régime* and Napoleonic heritage (Rosso 1994). For an assessment of its actual role and powers, see De Pieri (2003).

4. The base of the city's budget during the Napoleonic years, Turin's *octrois* town duties had been collected by the state after 1815, with serious consequences for local finance, which remained constantly dependent on government subsidies. Pleas for the restitution of the *octrois* were as frequent as they were unsuccessful in the Restoration years. As a result of the changed political situation, the post-1848 municipal council obtained them almost immediately. See Repaci (1927) and Bracco (2000a).

5. Thus already distancing itself, well before 1865, from a condition of Parisian-like capital city exceptionalism, and becoming closer to the typology of the municipally-led French cities studied by Cohen (1998).

6. Figures for 1863 give, respectively, 8700, 6000 and 5600 lire.

7. This was after a public competition in which nine applicants took part. According to the notification, only candidates with the dual title of architect and engineer could be admitted. The city council later decided to accept applications from engineers not having the title of architect. Such was the case of Pecco. His appointment was in fact an internal promotion, Pecco having worked with the office since 1847 (AM, 1851–52: 11, 16, 109, 202, 209, 211, 237, 394).

8. Figures refer to the so-called 'internal' offices of the city (that is, those physically located in Turin's town hall), with the exclusion of both the

technical offices and 'external' parts of the municipal administration such as the *Ufficio del Dazio*, charged after 1853 with the collection of the town duties.

9. Data available for 1883 indicate for that year a total of 117 municipal employees, which makes for a mere 17 per cent increase since 1867, over a 16-year interval. In total, the city's 'internal' offices increased by more than 250 per cent during the period 1848–83.

10. Piedmontese engineers were trained at the Faculty of Science of Turin's university until 1860, when, as an effect of Casati's 1859 reform of state education, a *Scuola di applicazione* was opened (Gabetti and Marconi 1971, Marchis 1984, Ferraresi 2000). For Italian and international comparisons, see Minesso (1995, 1996), Pfammatter (2000). For comparatively unskilled technicians such as the *misuratori* and *geometri* (surveyors), an 1845 regulation prescribed a long period of training (from three to five years) in the office of an architect, engineer or surveyor, followed by an examination at the university. In 1852, a public school for *geometri*, the *Regio Istituto Tecnico*, was opened in Turin (see Gabetti and Griseri 1973: 125–33).

11. These results contrast with those presented (admittedly for a slightly later period) by Sorba (1998), 136–42. The article, based on professional *curricula* kept in the municipal archives of Parma, shows that in other parts of Italy geographical mobility was often the rule among engineers working for local administrations. See also Ferretti in this volume.

12. An important model was Cavour's 1853 reform of the central administration (Melis 1995, 1996).

13. See articles 248, 249, 310 of the 1863 regulation for the city's offices.

14. Like many other Italian municipalities of the period, Turin did not have any general pension scheme for its employees. Pensions for each employee were fixed by the *giunta* (the city executive) at the moment of retirement. The first general regulations were approved by the city in 1882. In the state administration the position was different; pensions were calculated according to a law of 1864 (Bigaran 1990).

15. For a British example, see Clifton (1992).

16. For examples concerning the technical bureaucracies of the Italian state, see Giannetto (1999: 18–19, 46–7) and Maggi (1999: 64–5). The phenomenon was so widespread that, in the early 1890s, a special parliamentary commission was set up (Melis 1995, 1996). Information about temporary staff working for the city of Bologna can be found in Alaimo (1990a).

17. Documents on the staff of the *Ufficio d'arte provvisorio* for the years 1860–61 in ASCT, *Affari Lavori Pubblici*, cart. 7, fasc. 22 and 23.

18. Notably in 1868, when the council ordered the dismissal of all temporary staff over three months. A petition against the decision was filed, apparently without success, by six temporary employees (two engineers, two *geometri*, two draughtsmen). Pecco supported it with a memorial. (Documents in AM, 1868, I: 206–7, 214–15, and ASCT, *Affari Lavori Pubblici*, cart. 28, fasc. 10.)

19. 'Un nucleo di persone le quali nello studio e nella direzione di alcune opere importanti e lunghe passarono una serie d'anni, ed ottennero aumenti di stipendio in misura della carriera che in certo qual modo percorrevano, benché con sola nomina straordinaria.' (Report of the mayor Felice Rignon to the city's *giunta*, 21 March 1877, approved by the city council on 30 April, AM, 1877, I, 408–9.)

20. Documents about the commission for the years 1879–82 in ASCT, *Affari Lavori Pubblici*, cart. 88, fasc. 16; cart. 98, fasc. 3; cart. 107, fasc. 6; cart. 119, fasc. 2.

21. According to the 1859 government decree on municipal and provincial administration, the *giunta* was made up of the mayor and eight *assessori* (deputies). The latter were elected each year by the city council, and were usually invested with specific responsibilities. An expression of the political majority of the city council, the *giunta* handled ordinary affairs, while preparing projects and proposals to put to the council's vote.

22. Which could already be found in the structure of many technical bureaucracies of the time. The model of Paris (Châtelet 1991) was certainly an important point of reference.

23. AM, 1861, I: 62–3 (22 November 1860).

24. While 15 people had been part of the committee between 1864 and 1876, the number was increased to 27 for the period between 1877 and 1889. The phenomenon was a consequence of the addition of four deputy places, but not only for arithmetical reasons. The 1877 reform favoured the identification of the committee with a wide group of city councillors and professionals, much wider than the number of places actually available. After 1877, it became quite common for the same person to alternate periodically between the role of deputy member and the role of effective member. If a mere eight people had monopolized the nominations to the places of effective member of the *Commissione d'Ornato* during the period 1864–76 (about 88 per cent of the available places), in 1877–89 the group doubled to 16 people, again about 88 per cent of the available nominations throughout the period. Less stable in its composition, the committee seemed now to provide support for a wider pressure group.

25. Regis (1994). For information on Sambuy's role in the 1880 national Beaux-Arts exhibition and his interest in public gardens, see Visconti Cherasco (1996). Quotation from Cardoza (1997: 73).

26. A good example of such an attitude is revealed by an episode of 1881, when both Ceppi and Balbo Bertone di Sambuy resigned from the committee (and, in Ceppi's case, also from the mandate of *assessore*) in protest at the decisions of the *giunta*, which had changed the committee's project for the development of the Crocetta zone. The committee's plan had been refused on formal grounds, because of the presence of diagonally traced streets. (AM, 1881: 331–5, 15 April 1881.)

27. For a wider approach to the question, see Zucconi (1989) and Musella (1995).

28. Some useful figures for an attempt at a general overview, based on the results of an 1897 inquiry on municipal employees, can be found in Bigaran (1990).

29. Salvatore Adorno's studies (1996, 1998) on the southern Italian city of Syracuse provide a good illustration of the extent to which, during the same years but in a different context, neither the security of a long-term job nor the independence of the bureaucratic structure from the short-term results of local political conflicts could be taken for granted.

30. Examples of non-incompatibility between a private engineering profession and a public position can be found in Aurelio Alaimo's works on Bologna (1990a, 1990b). In Milan, where technical bureaucracies appear to have been weaker than in Turin, the recourse to external professionals was

common practice in the same years, and Turin's office could be evoked (in 1885) as an example of a strong local bureaucracy (Galbani 1992). For the case of Rome, see Caracciolo (1956) and Bocquet and De Pieri (2002).

CHAPTER THREE

The origins of the American municipal fire department: nineteenth-century change from an international perspective

Amy S. Greenberg

Until the mid-nineteenth century, in America and much of Europe, the crucial work of combating fire was the business of volunteers. In urban areas, especially, this was serious business. Fire was the biggest threat to the growth and prosperity of nineteenth-century cities. Open hearths, mixed zoning and haphazard building techniques led to frequent urban conflagrations, and high population density and insufficient urban water supplies ensured that fires would cause extensive damage. Urban fires were a frequent occurrence in most cities, and regularly resulted in both massive property loss and death.[1]

Responsibility for fire protection in both America and Europe lay with the municipality. Even in highly centralized countries like France, individual city governments independently provided urban city services, and the trend in both Europe and America was towards municipalization in the late nineteenth century. There have been two main schools of thought on the professionalization of services in the United States. Most historians have adopted a functionalist point of view, regarding municipalization as an example of the city's largely passive approach to urban problems. This functionalist perspective identifies innovation as the natural and necessary response to urban crises. Another group of historians has considered the professionalization of urban services from a social control perspective. According to their analysis, innovation was the offspring of elite fears about the increasing growth and disorder of urban centres. Reform was deliberately promoted to increase control over urban masses and prevent social upheaval.

Recently some historians, including the present author, have argued against both the functionalist and social control approaches. While reformers undoubtedly had mixed motives, the social control thesis remains unconvincing primarily because all societies enforce desired behaviour, and desire does not alone result in policy implementation. Likewise, the crisis model of the functionalists is problematic because it fails to explain why, in response to age-old problems, cities and their governments introduced innovations like paid fire and police departments at the specific moments they did. Furthermore, cities did not simply respond to needs. Starting in the mid-nineteenth century, they actively and aggressively intervened in order to foster economic growth and the increasing wealth of property owners. A better approach to investigating municipal employees and services is to assume that there was nothing inevitable about the introduction of services that were later taken for granted, and to base historical inquiry on a close examination of both the social forces and the political battles present at key moments of change. This is the approach to the municipalization of firefighting adopted here.[2]

In the USA, businessmen and philanthropic individuals privately organized the earliest volunteer fire companies. As companies proliferated, city governments and the firemen themselves created various overseeing committees, although the volunteer departments retained a large degree of autonomy from any governmental control until formally municipalized at mid-century. Municipalities funded volunteer company purchases of fire engines, fire hose and often fire houses as well, usually through the proceeds of chimney fines, bonds and taxes created specifically for this purpose. Well into the nineteenth century, fire companies were among the few municipally supported public institutions, and fire department allocations proved an anomaly amidst urban privatization in cities across the USA. Firemen could, and did, petition city councils for extra funds as well. Yet regardless of the financial outlay provided for these companies, urban governments found it impossible to dictate policy to the unpaid volunteers. Department officials also faced problems when trying to adjudicate difficulties within or between companies. To a large degree, volunteer companies remained almost totally autonomous. This autonomy was intensely defended by firemen as their right to choose, voluntarily, to relinquish their time and endanger their lives in the service of urban fire protection.

Volunteer firemen might not receive salaries, but they did earn both respect and honour as a result of their firefighting duties. Volunteer firemen were icons of masculinity and self-sacrifice during the first decades of the nineteenth century, publicly celebrated in parades, honoured with frequent stanzas in urban newspapers, and made the subject of heroizing prints by the popular American printmakers Currier and Ives. Participation in volunteer firefighting was one of the surest ways of proving civic virtue in urban America. Indeed, a majority of politicians in some cities served as volunteer firemen, following in the footsteps of an earlier generation of national firefighting politicians, including George Washington and Benjamin Franklin. But while early nineteenth-century urban citizens publicly celebrated their exclusively volunteer fire departments, by the 1850s and 1860s the reputations of volunteer firefighters everywhere were on the wane. Amidst accusations of rioting, disorder and inefficiency, the majority of volunteer firefighting forces in large cities in Europe, and almost every city in America, were being replaced by costly paid fire departments. At the same time, many European cities that had previously employed paid firemen significantly reorganized their brigades to increase firefighter discipline and order.

This chapter will place the municipalization of American firefighting in a comparative context, in order to illustrate and explain the almost simultaneous international fall of the urban volunteer fire company. Why did so many city governments, in so many different places, eventually decide that it was necessary to pay men to fight fires? In the process of answering this question, three regionally distinctive American cities will be compared to assess the legitimacy of accusations of violence and disorder levelled at volunteer firemen. The municipalization of firefighting will also be placed in the context of ideological, technological and organizational transformations in mid-nineteenth-century America, which helped to facilitate and justify the shift to paid fire departments. While historians have claimed that fire services in the USA were municipalized because the volunteers were becoming more uncontrollable and disorderly, this chapter will argue that professionalization was largely the result of a potent combination of three forces: steam engines that could be operated by small numbers of highly trained individuals; increasingly powerful fire insurance companies that demanded the municipalization of firefighting and offered protection from loss through private policies; and an ideology of professionalism that suggested that payment of wages would naturally result in improved service. After outlining the forces leading to the fall of the American volunteer fire department, our analysis will cross the Atlantic and consider what relevance American examples might have for explaining simultaneous transformations in Europe.

The decline of volunteer fire services

The mid-nineteenth century was a period of intense innovation by urban governments. As Eric Monkkonen and other historians have argued, the 'service city' evolved during this period as civic leaders actively worked to create a positive climate for the economic growth of the municipality (Monkkonen 1988). Paid fire departments, along with other municipal services, helped to produce this positive economic climate, and the investment in their creation was a successful gamble. The scope of this change, and the success of paid firefighting, meant that municipalization of firefighting helped to set the terms for the evolving relationship between city services and the municipality.

Yet the creation of this paid service was highly contested. One argument traditionally advanced by historians to explain why America's urban governments were willing to spend large sums of money to pay firemen, when ample numbers of men were willing to volunteer, was that the volunteers, over time, became inefficient and disorderly. America's urban volunteer fire companies were set up firstly by concerned citizens during the eighteenth century in older eastern seaboard cities like Baltimore, then during the first decades of the nineteenth century in younger mid-western cities like St Louis, and just after the 1840s Gold Rush in the meteoric Pacific coast metropolis of San Francisco. A volunteer company was generally made up of 40 to 60 men, while a volunteer department generally contained 10 or more companies by the mid-nineteenth century, loosely controlled and coordinated by a department overseeing committee. Regardless of when these departments were organized, they shared a similar developmental trajectory. All fell in the public estimation during the 1850s, after being accused of violence and disorder, and all were dismantled and replaced by paid fire departments between 1853 and 1866. Despite regional and local variations in the political, social and cultural contexts of municipalization, and despite radically distinctive patterns of immigration, class, political development and industrialization, the charges made against these and other fire departments were eerily similar. A national increase in violence among urban firemen was noted, discussed and condemned by more law-abiding American reformers in the 1840s and 1850s.

As urban citizens first began to consider paying firemen to fight fires, rather than employing volunteers, the image of the rowdy, violent volunteer was used to justify the expense of municipal forces. That certain individuals had infiltrated and 'soon changed the aspect and personnel of the department from a band of friends and brothers, to that of rioters, scalawags and thieves' was reported in cities across America. These included the three used here to illustrate the American experience, San Francisco, Baltimore and St Louis. By the mid-1850s, reformers came to the consensus that urban volunteer firefighters posed a serious threat to public order, and that firemen stood outside the law, answerable to no power greater than their own (Lynch 1880: 12). In short, reformers claimed that they were being forced to municipalize fire service because of the volunteers' bad behaviour. Historians have generally endorsed the view that the degenerating quality of fire service provided by volunteers was a major factor in municipalization (Wilentz 1984: 259, Laurie 1973: 82–3). Indeed, as Steven Riess has written in the 1992 *Encyclopedia of Social History*, 'Fire protection was originally provided by middle-class volunteer fire companies, but by the 1830s they had become lower-class fraternal and athletic clubs, centers of ethnic, occupational or neighborhood gangs more interested in racing or in fighting than in quenching fires' (Riess 1992: 1259–75).

Despite the willingness of many scholars to accept this explanation, it is not wholly convincing. Recent research has shown that, although firemen were reputed to be 'violent', firemen in different cities did not share in a uniformly violent culture, nor did they engage in identical modes of behaviour (Greenberg, 1998b: 159–95). In some cities, including San Francisco, firemen rarely if ever fought, and never rioted. In other cities, including Baltimore, firemen had always been violent, and it was the community's response to violence that changed over time, not the behaviour of the firemen. In Baltimore, changing standards of social decorum and improvements in reporting crime produced the illusion that firefighters were increasingly out of control, when in reality firefighter behaviour remained largely unchanged. Nor is there evidence that over time firemen became markedly less efficient at fighting fires in most American cities. Indeed, by the mid-nineteenth century, volunteer firemen had taken advantage of technological innovations in fire protection which allowed them to protect better both lives and property, and fire damage dramatically decreased through the nineteenth century in both European and American cities.[3]

But if volunteer firemen did not bring municipalization on themselves by behaving badly, why would city governments willingly expend large amounts of money to replace them? After all, paid departments were expensive. That Boston's paid department cost over $138 000 a year was repeatedly marvelled at by San Franciscans in the early 1860s, while the 'exorbitant' cost of Cincinnati's paid department (at $90 000 a year, three times that of the volunteer departments) fuelled support for the status quo in St Louis and Baltimore.[4] Fire companies were among the few widely supported public institutions during a period when the public good was defined in terms of the interests of a very small proportion of urban citizens. Robin Heinhorn, Sam Bass Warner and Michael Frisch have all concluded that, in the 'private city' of the first half of the nineteenth century, services were intended and provided for those who paid for them through taxes on property. If even the limited cost of supporting volunteer companies was unusual, the extensive funding demanded by municipal departments was without precedent (Heinhorn 1991: 15, Warner 1968, Frisch 1972).

A convincing argument as to why city governments eventually agreed to shoulder this expense can be attributed to the combined effects of three nineteenth-century successes. One, the steam fire engine, was technological; another, fire insurance, was organizational; the third, the rise of professionalism, was ideological. The ideal of the service city, that urban communities could increase their growth and financial standing by providing services previously left up to the citizenry, provided justification for adopting the costs of municipalization. The service city ideal was also, of course, supported by the success of these professional departments. Bolstered by a growing faith in expertise, fire insurance and the steam fire engine together formed a seductive and reliable alternative to volunteer firemen, which allowed citizens to transfer their faith away from the heroics of the individual volunteer fireman. The volunteer fireman was not replaced simply by paid firemen, but by a network of financial security gained from insurance, the seductions of technology and the appearance of order and expertise. The first city to employ a fully paid department, Cincinnati, was the home of Alexander Latta, the manufacturer of the first quality steam engines, and also the home of a powerful board of underwriters that funded the manufacture of the first viable American steam engines. In 1852, insurance and steam engine interests offered a firefighting combination, couched in the language of professionalism, that Cincinnati found irresistible. Almost every other American city would likewise be seduced within the next two decades, as the volunteer departments of America's large cities, like dominoes, toppled one after another (Gigierano 1982: 80, White 1973: 166–9, King 1896: 13–18).

Paid firemen were almost superfluous in this equation. Although critics of the volunteer system championed paid forces that would perform in a more sober and orderly fashion than their predecessors, it was rarely argued that they would be more skilful at fighting fires than their volunteer counterparts. Even while strongly in favour of a paid department, a joint committee of Baltimore's city council had to admit to Mayor Thomas Swann that 'your committee are of the opinion that volunteer intelligence, judgment and discretion are superior to hired ignorance', which was all that the city was likely to attract with the proposed $100 a year salaries (Latta and Latta 1860: 14). New men would not easily replicate the skill of the individual volunteer, when he was sober and attentive. Nor could the valour of the individual volunteer be faulted, as even the fiercest critics admitted to their bravery. While nineteenth-century Americans may have accused volunteer firemen of inefficiency and disorder, their replacements had little to do with these factors. Fire insurance, the steam engine and professionalism were the real replacements of the volunteer forces. Before detailing the municipalization of fire services in San Francisco, Baltimore and St Louis, it is worth taking a closer look at each of these three factors.

Fire insurance and the rise of the steam engine

No group championed the steam engine – and paid forces – more vehemently or successfully than did fire insurance companies. They funded pioneering steam engine development in England and America, and English insurance companies contracted the earliest paid fire companies.[5] Before becoming the strongest foes of the volunteer firemen, fire insurance companies were among their staunchest supporters. Originating in the sixteenth-century Low Countries and Germany, these organizations flourished after the great fire of London in 1666 and by the eighteenth century commercial fire insurance had spread throughout Britain. America's first stock insurance company, the Insurance Company of North America, appeared in 1792. By 1820 at least 28 American stock companies were competing with more powerful British companies to insure buildings in East Coast cities against fire. A New York conflagration in 1835 proved a minor setback to this process, and insurance companies continued to multiply and expand during the 1840s and 1850s (Pyne 1982: 495, Goudsblom 1992: 151, Hazen and Hazen 1992: 132–3).

Unfortunately, insurance companies ended up providing much of the financial backing behind the volunteer system. Volunteer companies received only minimal support from municipal governments and constantly needed money for new equipment. It was in the best interests of insurance companies to provide this support, because better-equipped fire companies resulted in smaller fire losses. As the cost of supporting volunteer companies increased over time, insurance found that it had a financial stake in municipalization. Even though a paid system cost taxpayers and the municipality several times that of a volunteer system, the cost to the insurance agents was *less*, as the burden was shifted to the city. Under a paid system, firemen would not look to the insurance companies for support, nor would an insurance company be expected to contribute anything to their upkeep, beyond whatever minor tax the city levied.

Insurance also helped to undermine volunteer firefighting in a more abstract sense. It allowed subscribers to replace their faith in the efforts of men to prevent damage with a new faith in the ability of money to negate the importance of damage. Fire insurance companies could not help but see a kin expression of their driving ideal in the paid department. If fires could be rendered impotent with dollars, should not firemen also be made reliable with money? Ordinary Americans were increasingly integrated into the market by the middle decades of the century and were made aware of the fact in a series of crippling depressions starting in 1837. Insurance represented money without contingency and safety through dollars in a market which, it was increasingly evident, was not itself safe. Insurance offered decreasing risk in a period when other risks became ubiquitous.

As for the first steam fire engine, this was the London-built 'Novelty' of 1829. Named by its inventor, George Braithwaite, it proved to be a mechanical failure, as was the first American steam engine, commissioned by insurance agents in New York. The latter model could throw a stream of water 166 feet, but was so large and ungainly that it was effectively useless. Also it broke down repeatedly even before being sabotaged by the hostile volunteer firemen of New York City.[6] Alexander Latta and his partner Abel Shawk of Cincinnati built the first successful steam engine in 1852. By 1858, these engines had proven effective at fighting fires in several American cities.

Steam engines, like fire insurance, worked to undermine volunteer firefighting. Although a steam engine and paid department were not inseparable, new technology catalysed the development of a paid department in two ways. It reduced both the number of persons needed to man a fire engine and the number of engines required in a department. A hand pump engine required a minimum of 15 men to drag the engine to the fire, pump the water through the engine and control the hose, and 30 men could perform these activities more quickly and effectively than could 15. The average volunteer fire company had at least 40 members (White 1973: 166–7, King 1896: 19). Conversely, one steam engine was commonly believed to pump more water than could three hand engines, in a shorter amount of time, and yet needed only a small fraction of the number of men to operate. Steam engines were too heavy for even 30 men to drag to a fire; they required the use of horses. Once at the fire, men were needed only to set up the machinery and direct the flow of water. These were jobs that 10 men could successfully complete. Cincinnati boosters claimed that between one-third and one-tenth as many firemen could successfully man a department composed of steam engines compared to a department of hand engines. Experts in Baltimore and San Francisco estimated that 100 to 150 paid firemen could operate steam-engine departments in those cities (Latta and Latta 1860: 39).

The steam engine also required specialized and expensive knowledge.

During the 1860s and 1870s, lengthy and technical handbooks covering the 'running, care and management' of the new engines were published to guide firemen (Roper 1876, Lewis 1872). As one source advised:

> The man in charge should be a practical engineer. He should have a thorough knowledge of steam and steam machinery; should be capable, also, of adjusting all the different parts of his engine, and telling whether they are in order or not. He should fully understand the causes of deterioration in the boilers of this kind of machines [sic] ... He should have, if not a thorough, a tolerably good knowledge of hydraulics and hydraulic machines and should be capable of determining their capacity, and understanding the strains to which they are subjected when in use.[7]

Running a steam engine was a technical feat, as a three-page list of instructions to engineers in the same guide reveals. As with an increasing number of jobs in nineteenth-century America, all this demanded *specialized* knowledge of the sort only a professional could acquire. This was no job for the part-time fireman, who left his employment on hearing a fire alarm. A capable fireman would have to devote all of his time to understanding the machinery of the steam engine, and devote himself entirely to its upkeep. If a steam engine was to operate at all, it was necessary that some portion of the fire department should be paid, even if it was not a 'paid' department. Strength and endurance, so celebrated by volunteer firefighters, and central to the ability to operate the heavy but simple machinery of the earlier hand-pump engines, were of relatively little importance in the use of steam engines. The strongest man, if not trained in the intricacies of the machine, would be powerless against the fire. The man who knew how to work a steam engine had to be a professional and his expertise had to be paid for.[8]

What the steam engine replaced was the old method of firefighting. Men could fight fires from a greater distance with a steam engine. The chances of burns were reduced by the greater power of the stream. The need for strength and agility in face of conflagration were to a large degree replaced by a tool with which a few highly trained individuals could extinguish a fire from some way away. The mechanical technology of the steam engine in fact required an entirely different human technology of firefighting.

Insurance agents understood that steam engines really replaced volunteer firemen, not other engines. Firemen were invisible in their descriptions of these successful engines, and instead machines received the praise once accorded to brave individual volunteer firemen. One enthusiastic letter writer described an engine:

> proceeding noiselessly to the scene of the destruction, we find it in a few minutes at work, and in as many moments more mastering the

devouring element, and promptly extinguishing it. But should the
fire be more stubborn from the combustible nature of the material,
with untiring energy it works on, and limits it where it originated.[9]

Steam engine manufacturers also measured their creations against
firemen, rather than other engines. Miles Greenwood of Cincinnati
tersely compared his namesake engine to the violent volunteers: 'It never
gets drunk. It never throws brickbats, and the only drawback connected
with it is that it can't vote'.[10]

   The steam engine and fire insurance were mutually compatible. Both
the steam engine and insurance worked to ward off contingency, to
reduce human intervention in unpredictable processes like fire and the
market. People were not insured by an individual, but by a corporation.
People were not protected from fire by men operating machines, but, it
was increasingly believed, by machines driven and guided by men. The
machine was privileged in this construction, as was the corporation.
Ralph Waldo Emerson's observation that 'things are in the saddle and
ride mankind' accurately assessed the transformations in nineteenth-
century firefighting, as well as in society as a whole. Money, not people,
became the key to security in the mid-nineteenth century, and trust in
professionalism, and expert systems, replaced faith in the bravery of the
individual fireman.[11]

The ideology of professionalism

Insurance agents, politicians and property owners came to agree that
volunteerism was an idealistic concept better suited to an earlier time
than to the dynamic and quick-moving 1850s, when immigration and
industrialization led to a dramatic increase in urbanization and
increasingly anonymous cities. For volunteerism to function as a guiding
principle of interaction, all segments of the population had to believe
that they were bound by ties of common interest. In the decades leading
up to the Civil War, many city dwellers began to doubt that this was
true. The ties that bound the property owner with the fireman he did not
know personally began to appear entirely insufficient to protect
property. By the 1850s, urban elites had internalized an ethic of self-
control and self-discipline, and demanded both stability and order in
their society. According to Burton Bledstein, professionalism became a
value in and of itself: 'Amateurish, a new mid-century word, connoted
faulty and deficient work, perhaps defective, unskilful, superficial,
desultory, less than a serious commitment, the pursuit of an activity for
amusement and distraction. The middle-class person required a more

reliable institutional world in which to liberate individual energy than amateurs had previously known'. Both internal ethic and social vision were incompatible with volunteer firefighting.[12]

Professionalization and payment came to replace selfless volunteerism as the guarantor of service. No doubt the rise of fire insurance, which also promoted payment as assurance against loss, played at least a suggestive role in this process. It is interesting to note, anyhow, how often supporters of paid departments argued that labour should be paid for, even when the volunteers were willing to contribute their labour without payment. Frank McCoppin of the San Francisco State Assembly declared that he was 'in favor of paying for labor generally, and also in favor of the Paid Fire Department', when casting his vote on the new system in 1866. In 1858, the Mayor of Baltimore also declared that it was necessary to pay firemen to fight fires: 'It would hardly be expected that any class of men would bring themselves under the obligations of an oath to do that which they are asked voluntarily to assume, and from which they can hope to derive no manner of profit or emolument.'[13] Neither of these men believed that volunteers received sufficient payment in the return of adulation, sense of community and personal satisfaction for the services they rendered. This was because leadership in society had passed into the hands of professional men, business leaders who were 'modernizers as well as moralizers'. By the 1860s, it is clear that professionalism, and middle-class Christian capitalism, had replaced the republican values which supported volunteer firefighting. For the new leadership, only money could guarantee an oath, and only money could adequately reward.[14]

American industrialization was largely responsible for this shift. Professionalization was increasingly embraced in the USA during the mid-nineteenth century. The rapid expansion and integration of the economy led to new business and commercial activities. The growth of cities, rising volumes of trade and improvements in transport all contributed to the creation of hundreds of specialized and previously unknown firms. New technologies of production and the rise of factories contributed to the transformation of manufacturing. Within cities like San Francisco, St Louis and Baltimore, an entire new class of middle managers was created to coordinate increasing numbers of employees carrying out very particular jobs. The organizational and technical challenges inherent in these management positions encouraged a new sense of professionalization among white-collar employees. This was matched in other professions, such as medicine, which worked to protect and elevate its membership through standardized training. Throughout society during the 1840s and 1850s, employment in America became increasingly specialized, and professionals began self-consciously to identify with others practising their occupation (Chandler 1977: 15–78, 281–3, Wiebe 1967: 111–27, Bledstein 1976).

Volunteer firefighting, which upheld not the skill of the paid expert but selfless sacrifice, thus became suspect. One critic of the Baltimore volunteer department marvelled:

> That a service so important to the welfare of society, so closely allied to the taxable resources of a large city, and so essential to the preservation of the property and the very lives of its people, should have been, for so long a time, performed entirely by volunteers, without fee or reward, save in the applaudings of conscience, and the occasional approval of others, is of itself a fit subject of remark. (Holloway 1860: 96)

The experience of American cities

The combination of fire insurance, the steam fire engine and the ideology of professionalism proved fatal to volunteer firefighting in large cities. The example of Cincinnati, with the first municipal department in the USA, was touted across America by insurance representatives, as were later municipal departments in their turn. In 1857, St Louis moved to a municipal department. The following year Baltimore made the switch and in 1866 San Francisco followed suit. The advantages of St Louis's paid department over volunteer departments like San Francisco's were spelled out by insurance agents to residents of the latter city in 1863, in terms indicating the combined significance of insurance, professionalization and steam engines:

> When a fire breaks out, it creates no particular alarm, for every one feels confident that it will not be permitted to extend beyond the building on fire. As an instance: a large audience, composed of the most respectable ladies and gentlemen, was sitting one evening in the Library Hall, listening to a public lecture. ... The working of the fire engines was heard. Before the lecture was through the fire was seen bursting through the roof of the building, in full view of the audience. So confident was that audience that the fire would be extinguished promptly by those who were employed to put it out ... that not one in ten persons left their seats to concern themselves about the matter. It was felt to be no part of their business to put out the fire, as they knew they could render no assistance, and so kept their seats.[15]

In St Louis, this account claims, safety had been attained through a paid fire department manned by professionals with modern equipment. The final vestiges of volunteerism were gone from St Louis, and supposedly gone as well was fear of fire, the most potent danger of the early nineteenth-century city.

The lecture audience, the reader is told, was confident that 'the fire would be extinguished promptly by those who were employed to put it out.' In clear view of a fire, they remained in their seats, because 'It was felt to be no part of their business to put out the fire'. These ladies and gentlemen were reassured, not only by the steam engines and new telegraph alarm systems (as well as the unspoken probability that the burning building was insured), but also by the fact that the proper people, people who were *employed*, would put out the fire. There was no chance that these firemen might not appear when the firebell rang. Firefighting was their *job*. If they were disorderly they could be fired. If they were inefficient, they could be replaced by the city. They were experts in firefighting, employed, like other Americans, at the job in which they were most skilled.

Fire in St Louis was no longer the business of gentlemen, and so they kept their seats while those who were 'employed' or paid did the work. Fire insurance also played a role in this transformation. As early as 1825, Josiah Quincy, the mayor of Boston, recognized that fire insurance led to alienation of citizens from firefighting. Increasingly, he noted with some worry, neighbours would not turn out to aid the firemen:

> Why is this? If you ask the owner, and he answers truly, nine times in ten it will be, 'I am insured; why should I keep fire-buckets? Why subject myself to the rules and customs of fire clubs: or why turn out to fire at all? I go to the expense of protecting myself. I ask no protection of others, and I mean to incur no voluntary expense, and much more, will not incur the risk of health and life in protecting them.'

But this, Quincy recognized, 'is the practical language of men in all great cities'.[16] The underwriters had the force of expertise and money behind them. They were the professionals in the business of fire. As they grew in capital they also grew in civic influence. On the eve of the replacement of San Francisco's department in 1866, the *Alta California* summed up the underwriter arguments in favour of paid firefighting, and why those arguments could no longer be denied:

> The Underwriters everywhere favor the Paid System. In this city they unanimously passed a resolution in favor of it; they sent representatives to lay facts and figures before the delegation at Sacramento; they have offered to contribute a considerable sum towards the establishment of the Paid System. They are experts in fire matters; they have studied everything connected with the causes, risks and management of fires; they know the experience of other cities and the opinions of men in their business throughout the

world; their opinions in regard to a matter of fire policy or fire risk should be regarded as authoritative. ... Firemen work for excitement, and must keep up to the artificial standard of honor which has been established among them, and which, unfortunately, is entirely inconsistent with the interests of property.[17]

Volunteer standards of honour upheld by firemen in San Francisco could not compete with the expertise and financial stake of the underwriters. The transition process in St Louis and Baltimore was similar to that of San Francisco. In all three cities the introduction of a few steam engines paved the way for the total replacement of the volunteer forces with the financial support of the insurance industry. Once the new technology was introduced, it was impossible to remove. In St Louis, the early purchase of the Union Fire Company engine and a visit from Mr Latta of Cincinnati were followed two years later, in September 1857, by a proposal on the part of the Board of Engineers to order three new and improved Latta engines. After putting a fire-alarm system in place, itself a new technology, the underwriters of the city successfully proposed to supply the rest of the six steam engines necessary to support a paid department (King 1896: 6, 19, 29). As an early history of the transformation recounted,

> With the telegraph completed and the addition of the three new steamers the Department was greatly strengthened, and by its systematic, orderly and effective work rapidly gained the confidence of the general public. The Board of Underwriters of the city took a deep interest in its welfare, and gave it their hearty support from its inception.[18]

The confidence of the general public was gained. The telegraph produced quicker responses by the firemen to alarms. The steam engines performed impressively. The small bands of paid firemen followed the directions of their engineers in an orderly and non-disruptive manner. The firefighting system emerged like a machine itself, systematic, orderly and effective. And the process was repeated across the nation. According to the author of a steam engine handbook in 1876, the transition from volunteer to paid department was almost always made *after* a quorum of steam engines was in place. The technology facilitated the transformation (Roper 1876: 94).

In Baltimore, where in late 1858 there were three steam engines in partial use and two more on order, Mayor Thomas Swann vetoed a proposal for a mixed fire department, with volunteer companies and paid employees working together. He had the backing of the insurance industry, which assured him that a department half-paid and half-volunteer could not function. The conflict of interests between the volunteer and paid firemen would be too great. They assured him that in Cincinnati, 'so great is the attachment of the Insurance Companies, and the mercantile and mechanical interests generally to the Paid Department, that, we doubt not, they would agree to pay the entire expenses of the same rather than permit it in any manner to be seriously affected or interfered with'. He also had a quorum of needed steam engines already in place, and could safely urge a single municipal department, at an initial cost of $50 000 on the city of Baltimore (Holloway 1860: 12–20, 26–7).[19]

The civic influence and authority of the insurance industry would only increase during the second half of the nineteenth century. 'By what right, or under what authority, do the insurance companies attempt to interfere in the management of the Fire Department?' grumbled a St Louis fireman in 1879, as underwriters attempted to depose the department's chief engineer. He had apparently not been following the growth of insurance in his city closely. The rights of the underwriter continued to grow as both firefighting and the business of insurance became increasingly schematized. Fire insurance companies continued to study and fund improvements in fire engines and firefighting itself.[20] Fire underwriters threatened municipal authorities with the withdrawal of their policies if stringent fire codes were not enacted. According to Jon Teaford, 'by the close of the 1890s the national board [of Fire Underwriters] had assumed such authority that it virtually dictated the standards of fire protection and prevention in America's municipalities' (Teaford 1984: 198–202, D'Ambry 1953: 23–30).

Conclusion: the European experience

The municipalization of urban fire service has, in retrospect, an air of inevitability, but the seeming naturalness of paid firefighting should not obscure the contested process of professionalization in the mid-nineteenth century. Simply because the modern municipality depends on paid fire service does not mean that volunteerism was rendered obsolete by progress. The fact that it now seems right and necessary to pay firefighters in large cities proves only how ingrained the ideology of professionalism has come to be.

What the American examples make clear is that a decline in volunteer fire company performance has been overemphasized in contemporary accounts of municipalization as well as in modern historical accounts. Orderly fire departments with excellent records of performance at fires, such as San Francisco's, were dismantled as quickly as violent departments with poor records, such as Baltimore's. What remained constant among cities was not the performance of their volunteers, but the combination of fire insurance, steam fire engines and the ideology of professionalism.

What significance might the American model of municipalization hold for the cities of Europe? Future research into the topic of fire protection in nineteenth-century Europe might consider whether an apparently analogous combination of forces was at work in many of the bigger cities, and to what extent this accounts for the almost simultaneous professionalization of firefighting on both sides of the Atlantic. As in America, steam engines made quick inroads in Europe during the decades after 1850. Berlin's municipal government led the charge in 1832, when it invested in a steam engine (Young 1866: 480). As in America, non-professional forces in London, Amsterdam and elsewhere were accused of inefficiency and disorder, sometimes, it appears, without a great deal of justification. Eyewitnesses at a conflagration in Amsterdam in 1858 blamed firemen for a generalized disorder at the scene of the fire that prevented any sort of concerted effort. As in the USA, calls for reform at mid-century reflected an increased perception of urban criminality and disorder. However, this perception may have reflected changed expectations of order and improvements in the reporting of crime more than it reflected any actual growth in disorder (Douwes 1968: 267–71, Goudsblom 1992: 178–9, Cohen 1998: 100–101, Greenberg 1998b: 159–95).

Finally, in most large European cities accusations against firemen meant that fire brigades were reformed to increase their 'professional' qualities, even if some cities still retained volunteers. Amsterdam, Rotterdam and Copenhagen, for example, all purchased steam engines and switched from volunteer to municipal systems in the 1860s, resulting in increased order and efficiency, according to observers. Hanover retained its volunteer department while adopting the steam engine in 1863, while Paris retained traditional fire engines, but completely reorganized their *Sapeurs Pompiers*, a military firefighting brigade, as a single uniform system in 1845. Even the smaller cities of France followed this model of municipal change. French provincial cities, like similar-sized American cities, first organized fire service in the mid-eighteenth and early nineteenth centuries, and began to professionalize their firefighting forces in the mid-nineteenth century after increasing complaints about lax firefighter performances. Bordeaux established a paid fire service in 1864, and Saint Etienne paid a small professional squad in 1855. Other cities, like Marseilles and Lyons, began to professionalize their fire service in the same period, but did not complete the process for many decades. Notably, these French provincial cities looked not only to Paris, but to other cities in Europe as a model for their actions. As in the USA, municipalization had a domino effect; once one city successfully professionalized, others quickly followed (Young 1866: 465–82, Lussier 1987, Cohen 1998: 100–101, 248, 258).

To varying degrees, the majority of major European cities changed the method, technology and organization of their fire brigades between 1855 and 1870, but all placed new value on professionalism. As Johan Goudsblom writes, the result of such reforms was 'a higher degree of specialization and organization than had existed among their predecessors. The system of recruiting conscripted hosemen was abandoned. Not only did the new brigades have more advanced technical equipment, but their members received a better training and were more highly rewarded' (Goudsblom 1992: 179, Wallington 1989).

In the long run paid fire departments were more effective that volunteer departments. Average losses per fire in America decreased nationwide in the 1880s and 1890s, and steam engines proved to be far more efficient than hand pumps. But it is important to note that an increasing faith in professionalism did not automatically translate into municipal firefighters who were better than volunteers, at least not in the USA. In the provincial cities of France, volunteer firemen never occupied positions of status, but were recruited from the lowest ranks of society and were attracted to the job for the paltry stipend offered by the municipalities. In this context, the higher pay of professional firefighters virtually guaranteed a higher level of service. Yet, in America, payment sometimes had the opposite effect.[21] America's paid firemen did not fulfil the promise of a professional, moral, orderly firefighting force. As one fireman explained, 'Experience seems to show … that without *selection* there is little difference whether the men be volunteers or paid.' Critics continued to complain about firemen who were untrained in the basic skills of their occupation, were morally lax or not committed to firefighting. Selection was limited in new municipal departments because wages paid to the firemen were not particularly high (between 20 and 40 dollars a month) and appointments were regularly made on a political basis.[22] The link between paid departments and professionalism did not prove as natural as reformers had hoped. While insurance agents might promise that paid departments and steam engines would result in orderly firefighting by experts, some knew otherwise. In 1881, the Silsby Steam Engine Company published a testimonial that their engines were so well made that they could not be damaged, even by the drunkest fireman. By 1881, of course, those drunk firemen would have all been municipal employees, and not volunteers.[23]

Notes

1. Background information on volunteer fire department development is taken from Greenberg (1998a).
2. See Cohen (1998), xi. On the historiography of urban services, see Monkkonen (1988), 4, 245–6.
3. See Frost and Jones (1989), 333–47, for an explanation of the 'fire gap' which emerged in the 1840s. On specific fires and fire damage in American cities, see Dana (1858).
4. *Alta California* (San Francisco), 5 January 1862; *Report on the Fire Departments of Cincinnati and St Louis* (1858); *Report of the Special Committee of the Baltimore United Fire Department* (1859); 'Report of the Chief Engineer of the Fire Department of St Louis, to the City Council at their meeting, March 11, 1859', in Latta and Latta (1860), 18–19.
5. On steam engine development, see Gilbert (1966), Goudsblom (1992), 151 and King (1896), 1–3. For most of the eighteenth century, London fire insurance companies funded fire companies. In 1866, The United Fire Brigade was turned over to London, because the level of protection provided by the insurance companies was insufficient for such a large city. See Anderson (1979), 332–5 and Blackstone (1957), 65–77.
6. See King (1896), 1–5, White (1973), 166–7, and Earnest (1979), 108–9. According to Earnest, Braithwaite's engine was a great success when tested in London against hand pumps in 1830, but steamers were not accepted in the metropolis until 1858 owing to opposition from city fire chiefs.
7. William King (1896), ix–x, unfortunately there were few such men in America's paid departments as late as 1896, a misfortune that the author attributed to 'political influence'.
8. 'Professions', as we know them today, came into being in the mid-nineteenth century, according to Burton Bledstein (1976), 90. Professional firefighting fits perfectly into this culture. As Bledstein continues, 'The culture of professionalism required amateurs to trust in the integrity of trained persons, to respect the moral authority of those whose claim to power lay in the sphere of the sacred and charismatic.'
9. Letter from John S. Law to Alexander B. Latta, 1857, and quoted in Latta and Latta (1860), 33.
10. Greenwood's comment about voting relates to the supposed political power of volunteer companies. See Greenberg (1998a), 109–24 and Park (1954), 105.
11. See the 1982 edition of Emerson's *Selected Essays*. On the rise of expertise in society, see Bledstein (1976).
12. On the move from volunteerism to order, see Bledstein (1976), 31–2, and Blumin (1989), 66–107.
13. Report of the Sacramento State Assembly in the *Alta California*, 23 January 1866; 'Mayor's Message' in the Baltimore *Sun*, 17 November 1858.
14. See Smith (1995), 66–9; also Leverenz (1989), 137 and Bledstein (1976).
15. (San Francisco) *Evening Bulletin*, 19 February 1863.
16. Circular distributed by Josiah Quincy to the citizens of Boston, 4 July 1825, quoted in Brayley (1889), 154–5.
17. *Alta California*, 9 February 1866.
18. St Louis Fireman's Fund, 1914: 171–3.
19. Indeed, one historian sees the municipalization of the department as the

natural conclusion to the development of a 'public order' in Baltimore started by the Democrats and Whigs in the 1840s; see Browne (1980), 110–11.

20. Letter from 'Future City,' in the *National Fireman's Journal* (New York), vol. III, 1879: 6. As an example of insurance companies working to improve firefighting technology, see Wheeler (1876).

21. Frost and Jones (1989), 341; *Alta California*, 9 February 1866; Latta and Latta (1860), 19; *California Spirit of the Times and Fireman's Journal* (San Francisco), 23 February 1867; Forrest (1898), 100; Cassedy (1891), 67; Teaford (1984), 243–5; Cohen (1998), 100–101.

22. Young (1866), 485 (emphasis in the original); *Evening Bulletin*, 13 January 1867; Forrest (1898), 108; Lewis (1872), 40.

23. Letter from 'Insurance' to the *National Fireman's Journal*, vol. II, 1878: 399; Silsby Manufacturing Company (1881), 137.

CHAPTER FOUR

The formation of a bureaucratic group between centre and periphery: engineers and local government in Italy from the liberal period to fascism (1861–1939)

Roberto Ferretti

The theme of autonomy and professionalism forms the context of this exploration of engineers in Italian local government between 1861 and 1939. Studies of municipal employees in general and engineers in particular have been relatively rare in recent Italian historiography. From the 1980s, little published research has appeared and, despite the interest of Italian scholars in the middle classes, their work has seldom incorporated the experience of the municipal bureaucracy.[1] Yet, significantly, a pioneering recent book has focused specifically on Italian white-collar workers during the nineteenth and twentieth centuries (Soresina 1998). The contributions to this collected volume generally portray a fragmented group, with diverse work patterns, remunerations and lifestyles. On the other hand, the authors identify a linking characteristic in the important role such workers played in the modernization process, especially as a mediating influence between the centre and periphery. The interaction of modernization and tradition has been interlaced throughout the history of Italian state and society relations, with particular resonance for the conduct of local and national government from the mid-nineteenth century. As this chapter elaborates for municipal engineers, in the local arena the legacy of personal and patronage links combined with the formation of an autonomous and professional bureaucracy, which reflected the steadily growing influence of rational and formalized concepts of public service.

If not a specific subject of analysis, Italy's municipal employees have been included in works on the history of local government during the nineteenth and twentieth centuries. These consider civic personnel as part of local public policy making, which is in turn related to the general question of centre–periphery relations and the evolution of municipal services (Alaimo 1990a, Sorba 1993, Mazzanti Pepe 1998, Balzani 1991). They suggest that, in the years after the formation of the unified Italian state in 1861, municipal employees did not have a defined and distinctive professional identity, owing in part to the lack of national legislation on this matter. Local studies have emphasized the fragmented nature of Italian municipalities as a result of regional distinctiveness, a characteristic which prevailed until the end of nineteenth century (ISAP 1990). During this period, there was a trend towards professionalizing local expertise through the formation of a modern municipal bureaucracy, with formalized training and impersonal selection procedures in line with Weber's sociological model. Yet resistance often slowed down or even halted the process of change. This was due to the persistent intervention of factors such as personal connections, patronage, clientele groups and discretionary practices, which had long governed relations between the municipalities and their employees (Adorno 1998, Musi 1998, Alaimo 1990b).

Specialist studies of the Italian engineering profession lack specific analysis on the personnel employed in local government, with one remarkable exception (Sorba 1998). Technicians in the public sector have been dealt with only in the case of state engineers and their distinctive social profile (Melis 1988, Melis and Varni 1997, 1999). Conversely, in studies of the history of the town planning movement, municipal engineers have been identified as among the first agents of urban change during the late nineteenth and early twentieth centuries (Nicoloso 1987, Ernesti 1988, Zucconi 1989). The transformation of their technical role, which was inextricably connected with urban expansion, had dual consequences. It led to greater autonomy with regard to the representative bodies of local communities and a more conspicuous perception of the engineers' professional identity and institutional function. Municipalities tried to thwart this tendency in an attempt to retain full control over their employees, at the same time as the engineering bureaucracy, in search of legal recognition, demanded the protection of the central state from the discretionary powers of local administrations. The quest for greater autonomy was supported by two developments: the professionalization of their group, the engineers, and the administrative centralization of public institutions. These processes were eventually accomplished during the fascist period, under the guardianship of the totalitarian fascist state.

The slow rise of professionalism: municipal employees in liberal Italy

For many years Italian historiography highlighted the centralist character of the institutional organization of relationships between central power and local collectivity in post-unification Italy (Pavone 1964, Giannini 1967, Zanni Rosiello 1976). Current research, on the other hand, has paid closer attention to the 'administrative praxis', emphasizing the importance of the 'margins of autonomy' made possible by gaps of indecision left free by legislation. According to this perspective, the Italian experience is characterized by '*autonomia contrattata*' (bargained autonomy), which is partly attributable to the absence of national legislative regulations in certain sectors, and to the ability of municipalities, in certain historic circumstances, to establish their authority in new spheres of institutional activity (Romanelli 1995).

The management of bureaucratic personnel was one of the most important features of local administrative authority. It had been sanctioned by the *Legge comunale e provinciale* of 20 March 1865, and reserved for town councils all rights regarding employees, leaving only a purely formal level of control to the prefects (Giannini 1967: 26).[2] Because there was no united national provision in this field, relations between institutions and employees were defined in terms that varied according to local circumstances and historic contingencies. Historians have interpreted this lack of unitary legislation as indicating the reluctance of the national governing classes to choose between affirming the principle of local autonomy and the need to assure stability and provide certain guarantees to employees.

In post-unification Italy the difficulty involved in defining the role of municipal workers translated into a multiplicity of practices relating to the workplace and conditions. The absolute discretionary power of the local political–administrative classes over municipal bureaucracies, at least during the first decade after 1861, led to inconsistency and instability. Employees ultimately had recourse to law in order to challenge the procedures adopted by different local administrations concerning their career paths, promotion and right to a retirement pension (Carpinelli 1997: 61–4). Compounding these personnel problems was the legacy of administrative structures that continued from the pre-unification states. These created ambiguities about the precise remit of the various categories of employees and failed to develop specialist roles within the bureaucracy. During this period the local elected administrations were more interested in selecting a body of employees whose fundamental qualities were demonstrating faith, zeal and loyalty towards the local power-base, and not professional ability.

The *riforma crispina* of 1888 changed the situation.[3] Named after the first minister, Francesco Crispi, the law made local authorities more electorally accountable. Although it also confirmed municipal powers over local bureaucracies, allowing for complete liberty in this field, it framed such powers within the *Tabelle organiche* (Systematic Tables of the municipal staff) and *Regolamenti organici* (Personnel Regulations). As a result, local authorities were forced to respond to staffing issues within the confines of state-sanctioned regulatory activity. At the same time a process of 'nationalization' began for various groups of public sector workers, such as teachers, secretaries and medical officials, which aimed to remove them from local control and place them under the direct protection of the central state administration (Schiera 1971, Romanelli 1989). On the other hand, municipal engineers were without relevant sociopolitical representation, and came to be assimilated with other employees whose systems of professional selection, promotion and activity continued to depend entirely upon the decisions of local authorities.

During the 1890s a potential conflict began to emerge between the continuing influence of local autonomy and the tendency to form a modern professionalized bureaucracy, relatively stable and autonomous, and with a defined profile and formalized relations. Both processes were the consequence of urban expansion and the concomitant extension of municipal activities, and both responded to the demands of the same local administrations. The specialization and professionalization of the bureaucracy encouraged the formation of functionary groups that acquired a strong collective consciousness. Recognizing the growing importance of their role and function, they continually claimed greater security and autonomy from local government. Over time the municipal bureaucracy gained legitimacy as the guarantor of stability and continuity within administrative institutions. It therefore defended the general interests of local collectivity, with greater room for manoeuvre in influencing local affairs, and consequently became less of a passive instrument for transmitting the political will of municipal leaders.

After the *riforma crispina* there was progressive adoption of the competition system for access to bureaucratic careers, coupled with the valorization of qualifications and certificates of a higher level, and the professionalization of the most important figures, such as the secretary, chief engineer, chief accountant and doctor. These were accompanied at the national level by a general process of regulation and the creation of more uniform relations between local authorities and their personnel (Carpinelli 1997: 66–70). Various factors produced this transformation: the need for greater emphasis on expertise as the criterion for appointing personnel, the pressure applied by the organizations of municipal secretaries for increased job security, and the influence of centralizing control authorities, which tended to regulate communal bureaucracy by assimilating it to that of the state.

During the *età giolittiana* (1903–13), the diffusion of *municipalismo* was accompanied by the most important legislative innovations for municipal workers and employees, which extended to recognizing the category within a national statute. As a result of this legislation, and thanks also to ever more decisive intervention by the central state, a legal framework for the employment of municipal workers began to take form.[4] This involved new definitions of municipal liberty, greater service efficiency and the protection and security of personnel. There was also more coherence in the process of centralization and nationalization, which entailed sacrificing the autonomy of local institutions to the needs and demands of uniformity (Schiera 1971: 110, 115–16).

Engineers of municipal technical services in liberal Italy

In the years following Italian unification, engineers employed in local government were very small in number. They did not have an important place within the municipal bureaucracy, compared with other administrative groups such as secretaries or accountants, especially in the smaller and middle-sized cities where the organization of technical services developed slowly after 1861. These municipalities frequently did not afford provision until the 1880s, when there was greater preoccupation with questions of public health and town planning.[5] In Como, for instance, there was only one engineer on the municipal staff until 1882 (Pederzani 1990: 147). The sluggishness of progress was partly due to the social and economic backwardness of Italian cities, even after unification. While industrial take-off began in the 1890s, this was confined to north-western Italy. Up to the twentieth century, urban communities tended to be static, and still retained features associated with the *ancien régime*. This meant that there was generally no urban expansion outside city walls, where public services were yet to be organized and infrastructures developed. In consequence, the municipalities of the smallest cities preferred to employ external experts for public works, such as consultant professional engineers. They also turned to engineers employed in the most important nearby public administrations: for instance, members of the technical services of the largest municipalities and of provincial administrations, or of the corps of *Genio Civile*.

Nevertheless, bodies that represented municipal engineers were formed in the most important cities, and gained importance within the local bureaucracy. They gradually strengthened their position with the local political powers, especially during phases of public works expansion. The leading figure was the *ingegnere capo*, the chief of all technical services in the local administration. He rapidly advanced in the local bureaucratic hierarchy, ultimately achieving the same level as the secretary and the chief accountant. As was shown by the municipal personnel regulations established in the 1880s and 1890s, in the biggest cities the power and responsibilities of the *ingegnere capo* were considerable and important.[6] Firstly, he managed all technical services and was responsible for all the employees within his department, with power to mediate with local government. Secondly, he coordinated the jobs carried out by different technical divisions. Finally, he had control over all of his department's technical and administrative functions. He signed every important project and administrative document and directed relations with external enterprises. As a result, the *ingegnere capo* enjoyed substantial autonomy from local government, which allowed him considerable freedom of action in projecting public works and organizing technical services. He was the first adviser of local executive power, and his professional activity proved to be decisive in many fields, including town planning, architecture and infrastructure development, as well as the general organization of technical services.

In the *Provincia*, too, the chief engineer became a leading protagonist in the institutional life of the administration, both technically and in managing personnel.[7] In selecting candidates for this position, local administrations often looked for a polytechnic engineer with significant leadership experience in the public sector or private enterprise.[8] In relation to urban expansion and the growth of local government, the powers of other municipal engineers also increased after the 1880s, especially for heads of different technical divisions. The responsibilities of these technical employees varied in different fields, from directing building and public works to consolidating a network of municipal services. In this case, specialization in certain technical branches was required for candidates hoping to enter a particular division.

During the years between 1880 and 1914 the tendency towards more precise definition of bureaucratic categories reflected a general trend in municipal employment, as was testified by frequent and continuous modification of personnel regulations. But technical services were afforded more specific attention within the biggest municipalities, which frequently adopted special regulations for these departments. Municipal engineers were often subjected to a particular statutory regime, which provided detailed reports about competencies, functions and responsibilities, especially regarding the problem of relations between their public position and private profession.[9] Technical services were therefore recognized as a special section of municipal administration, part of a local public bureaucracy, but also, in comparative terms, a relatively autonomous department headed by the *ingegnere capo*.

By the early twentieth century the expansion of municipal activity inevitably necessitated the employment of more municipal staff. Local administrators looked for ever more specialized technicians with comprehensive professional experience. The prestige of municipal engineers increased in step with the growing importance of their work for municipalities. The same applied to their power and autonomy in relation to local representative bodies, and in consequence municipalities were hard pressed to maintain control over the operations of these technicians. Some conflicts occurred over the limits that defined and divided the respective roles and functions of bureaucracy and elective bodies (*Giunta* and *Consiglio comunale*). These conflicts were the direct result of the ambiguities arising from the relationship between the political elite and the professional bureaucracy. The latter had to support the objectives of local political classes, yet at the same time they pursued formal recognition of their autonomous identity (Alaimo 1990).

The tendency of local powers to define the municipal engineer as an internal technician, dependent upon the local public administration, was also related to the municipalities' financial needs. Local institutions tried to encompass all aspects of technical activity within the domain of municipal services, from the planning to the execution of public works. Such diversity had the financial advantage of keeping work 'in-house' and avoiding payment of fees for consultancy work by free professional engineers. At the same time local administrations aimed to confine all of their engineers' professional activities to the ordinary work of municipal departments, thereby denying them overtime pay and forbidding them from practising their profession in a private capacity outside the workplace. This limited definition of municipal engineers contrasted with the aims of their professional associations, and partially contrasted even with the policies of central government.

Despite these efforts, the identity of municipal and provincial engineers remained legally undefined for a long time, at least until the fascist period. This was especially true for the *ingegnere capo*. Before unification, he was an expert who lent his services to local administrations, while at the same time maintaining his private practice (Alaimo 1990b). After 1861, the blurring of public service and private professional activities was a continuing bone of contention for the leadership of local administrations, and they were not really able to resolve the dilemma. This was due in part to the problems involved in controlling the engineers. This group claimed the right to practise their profession privately in order to supplement their low municipal salaries, which they deemed inadequate for maintaining the standard of living that their position in the social hierarchy demanded. By the end of the nineteenth century, municipal regulations in the largest cities theoretically prohibited engineers in technical departments from pursuing private activities, but they frequently did so anyway. Relationships in the localities could of course be personalized, according to the character, capability and authority of the chief engineer. In order to restrict the engineers' autonomy, local administrations could resort to the expedient of reorganizing technical offices. In some cases, the power to regulate staff led to the abolition of the post of *ingegnere capo*, in order to resolve conflicts with certain strong-willed and single-minded chief engineers.[10]

In the matter of selecting candidates for engineers' positions, local administrations were determined to maintain their freedom of choice, whatever options were adopted. In general, appointments could be made directly by the *Giunta* (the city executive) or the *Consiglio comunale* (the municipal council), through internal promotion (by seniority), or by public competition. The adoption of the competition system, particularly from the early twentieth century, was not really a linear tendency (Sorba 1998). Similarly, in the choice of *ingegnere capo* posts, various routes were followed. Sometimes a municipal engineer or local professional emerged as a result of his professional prestige and standing; at other times the direct appointment of the *Giunta* was contested by the *Consiglio comunale*, which demanded recourse to public competition. More usually, the selection of municipal engineers was conducted by way of public competition; however, the final choice of applicant could be no less contested than under the appointment system. The local authority, even in the competitive context, was unwilling to renounce its power of nomination. Conflicts with the central state therefore could arise when the candidate preferred by representative local bodies did not correspond to the competition winner, designated by the board of examiners. The state's superior authority represented an effort to affirm the universal values of objective and impersonal competition results, ratified by a neutral board of examiners, which should have strictly limited the power of local institutions. Yet the municipalities and provincial administrations aimed to keep the last word on the subject and defended the principle of liberty of choice. From this perspective, the list compiled by competition committees and its examination process were considered as preliminary and informative activities, almost as a recommendation that should not necessarily be followed.

As far as the choice of candidates was concerned, in the largest cities the board of examiners generally gave credence to a background in municipal and provincial institutions. The candidates' educational qualifications were also important. To enter the higher posts (section chief or *ingegnere capo*) it was crucial that candidates had administrative and management ability, especially previous experience as the head of a local administration. As a result, careers within municipal or provincial staffs became virtually interchangeable, with frequent passages from one administration to another.[11] From the late nineteenth century the increasing number of public competitions for the post of municipal engineer, which became highly formalized with regard to prerequisites and required qualifications, demonstrated the group's high level of mobility (Sorba 1998).

The recognition of municipal engineers' status by local administrations, associated with recruitment formalization, job mobility and extensive professional experience, were factors that led to the embryonic homogenization of the group between the 1910s and 1920s. In the cultural field, they shared a high 'general' technical training which was not very specialized, and reflected the character of the schools of applied engineering where the core of academic disciplines related to techniques of architecture, construction and hydraulics (Guagnini 1993, Minesso 1995). However, in these years and particularly after the First World War, new municipal services, such as lighting, gas supply and tramways, called for specialist technicians in electrical, mechanical and chemical engineering. Additionally, municipalities required 'in-house' engineering expertise for essential utilities and services such as water supply, road maintenance and building construction. With reference to their identity and social function, the engineers tried to define themselves as midway between municipal bureaucracy and free professionalism, serving as a channel of communication and simultaneously as a point of tension between these two professional worlds. The growing sphere of urban organization, notably town planning and infrastructure development, came to be a particular focus for the evolution and definition of the engineers' common identity.

Professional identity between the public sector and free professionalism

The development of town planning between the 1900s and 1920s led to institutional and professional conflicts that were related to the ambiguous identity of municipal technicians. In the particular localities the engineers contributed considerably to the formation of the town planning discipline, and thus strengthened their group identity. At the same time, during the years from 1880 to 1910, municipalities assumed an ever-stronger role in directing urban development. The engineers became leading agents in the expansion of municipal services, and also the key figures of public policy making. They were responsible for town planning, architectural and building control, and reorganized the roadway systems according to the new scientific principles of 'sanitary engineering'. The leading figure of *ingegnere capo* assumed greater importance because of his synthesizing role in specialist engineering disciplines (Zucconi 1989: 58–62). His role was a mediating one between the urban modernization process and the political sphere. Urban history has furnished several examples, such as Chieti, Catania and Bologna (Troilo 1997, Nigrelli 1992, Alaimo 1990b: 266). He was a part of the *urbanesimo municipale politecnico* (polytechnic municipal urban professionalism) during the *giolittiana* era (1903–13). This reflected the activity of various professional figures within the municipal technical departments interested in city problems, such as engineers, physicians, lawyers, hygienists, statisticians, administrators, economists and sociologists (Zucconi 1989: 69–92, Salvati 1993, Ernesti 1988: 166–8). Thus a network of urban experts flourished during the heyday of 'municipal socialism' in the early twentieth century (Rugge 1986).

The expansion of municipal activities during these years led to the modification of the professional identity of municipal engineers. As we have seen, they often exercised their profession outside office hours, in order to augment their salaries. This activity was important even from a symbolic point of view, as the engineers could maintain a sense of belonging to the prestigious 'independent' world of the free professionals and could thus distinguish themselves from other dependent bureaucracies. However, free professional engineers felt this activity to be an invasion of their professional territory, and considered municipal engineers to be unduly favoured in the public services job market. Other conflicts between municipal and free professional engineers were related to the role of the chief engineer in projecting and directing public works during phases of municipal expansion (Alaimo 1990b). Moreover, from the 1890s, several associations emerged that were opposed to the positivist technical culture of municipal engineers (Zucconi 1989: 93–131, Penzo 1994). These associations encompassed a range of professional and creative disciplines, including architects, men of letters, engineers, historians and archaeologists, and they urged greater respect for the artistic and cultural heritage of the historic parts of Italian cities.

The question of professional responsibilities in town planning remained open until the 1920s. It was then that the engineers defined their cultural and institutional standards, in direct consequence of conflict between two opposing tendencies. On the one side was a multidisciplinary idea of town planning as the result of different scientific competencies, linked to local government; on the other side was a more restricted 'artistic' and 'aesthetic' concept, supported by architectural graduates from new *Scuole superiori di architettura* (Superior Schools of Architecture). These latter institutions had been originally created in Rome in 1919, and were then established in the national universities of the most important cities (Nicoloso 1987).[12] During the 1920s, architects rapidly emerged as a new collective group, in search of professional success in developing fields, such as town planning. To legitimize their professional monopoly they tried to establish a distinctive definition of the *Urbanistica*, founded on scientific and aesthetics values, according to the ideas of *architetto integrale* (Zucconi 1989). This conception was opposed to the *Urbanesimo* of municipal functionaries, which was defined as the science of urban development, synthesizing a range of different disciplines and diverse professional figures, such as secretaries, hygienists, engineers, physicians and lawyers.

The creation of the *Istituto Nazionale di Urbanistica* in 1930 indicated that the architects had won the struggle. The project of free professional architects matched the objectives of the fascist political class. The politics of administrative centralization aimed to reduce local autonomy and utilize architecture and town planning for pedagogical purposes in 'mass nationalization' (Ciucci 1989, Falco 1988). Yet this institutional change did not really have a practical effect in managing the development of Italian cities during the 1930s (Franchi 1999). A specific national law was adopted only in 1942, and the municipalities, with their engineers, continued to maintain full control over the process of urban transformation. The fascist professional associations tried to impose a national discipline of town planning and public works upon local municipalities by demanding the recognition of a compulsory system of public competition, which was exclusively open to professional graduates organized in fascist associations of engineers and architects.[13] Nevertheless, local administrations continued to behave as they wished, and municipal engineers still represented their primary agents in these fields, as denounced by the same fascist professional associations. After public competitions for town planning, the winners were almost never called to design and execute the urban development plan and direct the various jobs involved; this remained the responsibility of the technical services.

Associations and the definition of professional groups

During the early twentieth century the development of an associative movement of engineering employees in Italian local government was fundamental to the elaboration of a shared underlying culture, and for promoting the group's common identity. In liberal Italy, despite the requirement of high standards of formal academic and scientific knowledge for engineers, their professionalization process did not really advance during the second half of the nineteenth century because of the group's territorial fragmentation and the strong local roots of the associative networks, the *Collegi di ingegneri ed architetti* (Colleoni 1989, Minesso 1995). The professional movement was strengthened before the First World War because of the increasing number of engineering graduates and the heightened sense of frustration within the engineering profession, which intensified its claims that the state should protect status and professional practice. Various national associations of specialized engineers (railway engineers, land survey engineers, municipal and provincial engineers) were created in these years and contributed towards overcoming the strict local bonds of old engineering associations and ultimately to 'nationalizing' the professional group (Minesso 1995).

From 1883, engineers employed in local administrations made several attempts to create a professional organization. Their common aim was the reorganization of technical services in order to achieve independence from local public powers. A national organization was eventually created in September 1911, when a *Collegio Nazionale degli Ingegneri Provinciali e Comunali* (CNIPC) was established in Turin.[14] During this period, the engineers at the head of the CNIPC tried to lay out the cultural and social boundaries of professional groups, an activity of symbolic definition which one sociologist has described as the passage from a 'probable class' to a 'real class' (Bourdieu 1984). Firstly, they established a clear distinction between themselves and other municipal employees by emphasizing the title of graduate engineer. This identified a highly technical figure trained in Italian universities and belonging to the social national elite. Secondly, they tried to underline their specific character within the engineering world as a whole, pointing to their public function within local administrations, with specific interests and professional ethics. From this perspective it was important to form an integrated identity of municipal and provincial engineers, which was translated into the request for national uniform status for the technical bodies of all local authorities.

The promoters of CNIPC aimed dualistically to create solidarity links between association members in order to form a technical common culture and to bring political visibility to jobs within the local services. The circulation of ideas and the exchange of experiences, the professional improvement of members and the development of local technical services, were the main objectives of the programme established by the association's leaders. Their aim was to create a 'technical scientific circle' in order to study questions that related to their ordinary activities in local government. This moderate and sober image, based on pacific cultural action, was intentionally opposed to the turbulent collective action of more militant organizations. It was an important element of the collective identity of this professional category, and symbolically distinguished it as an elitist social class.

After the constitution of 1912, the CNIPC directed its efforts towards two main objectives. The first was the creation of a social security system, which would allow the movement of engineers between various local administrations and guarantee career continuity.[15] The second and most important objective was reform of the *Legge comunale e provinciale* of 1865. Their intention was to make engineers working in local technical services independent of the municipalities and *Provincie*, instead coming under the superior guardianship of the central state. The project involved the creation of a large national corps of *Provincie* engineers, in charge of road systems and independent of the local authorities.[16] In general the CNIPC tried to assert the principle of job security within local government.

After the First World War, the economic and social anxieties of the postwar Italian *petite bourgeoisie* exacerbated the uneasiness of the engineers, and forced the CNIPC to make its action more decisive regarding economic claims to public institutions. It consequently abandoned its previous moderate character.[17] The crisis of CNIPC organization, demonstrated by its continually diminishing members, was also due to the radical tenor of professionalization conflicts. These absorbed much of the energy and attention of young engineers working in local administrations. In consequence, the hegemony in the associative movement of Italian engineers was rapidly assumed by a new and more radical *Associazione nazionale degli ingegneri italiani* (ANII, National Association of Italian Engineers), created in Milan in 1919. It was the group's first unified and centralized national organization, and the main objective was to secure a law to protect the status and professional practice of engineers. This was effectively granted in 1923 by Mussolini's government (Minesso 1995). The new movement emphasized its academic credentials as a mark of social and professional distinction, and contributed eventually to the group's nationalization.

The hard-pressed CNIPC was absorbed by the ANII in 1920, and re-emerged as a new collective organization, the *Corporazione nazionale degli ingegneri comunali e provinciali*. The local government engineers left the general engineering associations in charge to represent and defend their specific interests with regard to public powers. This increased their propensity to consider themselves more as graduate engineers who belonged to a professional engineering world than employees who belonged to the world of public functionaries. The activity of the *Corporazione nazionale degli ingegneri comunali e provinciali* underlined these attitudes. It sought recognition of a specific *regolamento organico tipo* (model-personnel regulation) for technical services of municipalities and of *provincie*.[18] However, the entry into new engineering associations, which exerted greater collective pressure on public administrations, also exacerbated the problems of professional conflicts with free professional groups, the most numerous and most influential sector within the ANII.

In any case, the expansion of the new association was soon stopped by the politics of fascist penetration to every social institution after the seizure of power by Mussolini in October 1922. In 1925, under increased pressure from fascist professional associations, the free and apolitical engineers' national association was forced to abandon its activity. All Italian engineers were compelled to organize in the *Sindacato Fascista degli Ingegneri* (Fascist Association of Engineers), created in 1923, which claimed exclusive representation of the professional body. The engineers working in local government, however, had to maintain a separate identity from their free professional colleagues, because public employees were prohibited from joining trade unions.

Conclusion: fascism and the ambiguities of nationalization

During the fascist era, tendencies beginning after unification in 1861 were ultimately realized. However, a number of unresolved questions still remained. Along with the process of nationalizing municipal employees came institutional centralization, which radically modified centre–periphery relations by abolishing the representative bodies of local administrations (Schiera 1971).[19] In particular, the limitation of local autonomy in the question of bargaining between local administrations and their employees was intended to impose tighter financial restrictions on municipal activities and introduce national standards of 'bureaucratic efficiency' controlled by central powers. Between 1923 and 1934, central government interfered with numerous laws and conditions regarding municipal employees, which accelerated the tendency towards aligning the local bureaucracy with that of the state, and ultimately nationalizing certain staff.[20] The management of municipal personnel and *provincie*, now fixed at a national level, was almost totally removed from local authorities, which lost their previous autonomy.

This process was completed for the municipal secretaries, who were made state functionaries, but remained unfinished for engineers in the municipalities and *provincie*. If their status and work conditions were effectively even more 'nationalized' and assimilated to those of state bureaucracy than in the past, they retained their dependence on local government and were not metamorphosed into state functionaries, despite expressions from members of professional associations that a national corps of engineers should be formed for local technical services.[21] During these years the engineers' professional identity was increasingly aligned with the world of public functionaries, as opposed to the former tendency to feel themselves as belonging to a community of 'graduate engineers'. That was another consequence of fascist corporative organization, which forbade public employees to enrol in professional associations representing the free professional world, and instead organized them in the *Associazione fascista del pubblico impiego* and in the *Cassa nazionale di previdenza degli impiegati degli enti locali*.

Therefore fascism achieved the process of constructing and consolidating the professional group, organizing it into recognizable institutions and furnishing it with an official identity and visibility in the sphere of public employment. But it could not resolve the ambiguities of the previous period arising from the engineers' relationship with local authorities and the free professional world. Mussolini's regime did not complete the centralization project, and the engineers could not mobilize enough political resources to remove the technical services from their dependence on local government and create a national independent group. Conflicts between engineering employees, particularly the *ingegnere capo*, and local administrations still occurred throughout the 1920s and 1930s. The working conditions of these technicians remained dissatisfying for them, not least because of the lack of financial resources for technical services due to the restrictive policies of the fascist government. In practice, however, municipal engineers maintained an important influence in organizing city services and town planning, and strongly conditioned urban development with their culture, despite the claims of free professional architects and engineers formally supported by the fascist regime.

In terms of relations with the free professional world, there was still a strong continuity with the liberal period. The fascist authorities formally forbade the free professional activity of public employees, according to the propagandist valorization of professions in the corporate state. But this prohibition, which was frequently restated by prefects who tried to satisfy the claims of the fascist professional associations, was not, in practice, respected. Since the government denied local administrations the financial resources necessary to raise the low salaries of their employees, the regime chose to mediate between different needs in tolerating this infringement of corporate rules.

Notes

1. In a recent work on the Italian middle classes, little space is reserved for employees, compared with other social groups of the bourgeois world, because of the scarcity of research on this matter (Banti 1996: 129–33).
2. In liberal Italy the personnel of the *provincie* shared a common statute and identity with municipal employees. The law of 1865 established the *provincia* (province), as an ambiguous institution, representative of local territorial interests, yet at the same time allowing for central government control over municipalities with regard to their assets. The employees of the *provincia* depended directly on the prefect (who presided over the provincial administration), and they were initially considered to be part of the state bureaucracy. With the reforms of 1888–9, however, when all the provincial bodies became elective (*Consiglio provinciale*, *Deputazione provinciale* and the *Presidente*), the local authorities, which already had some responsibility for public health, road systems and education, took full control of their bureaucracy (Schiera 1971: 44, 85–8).
3. Law no. 5865, 20 December 1888, and *Testo Unico* no. 5921, 10 February 1889. It also bestowed on the *Consiglio comunale* of municipalities in the biggest cities the right to elect the mayor. The king had previously nominated this office, according to legislation of 1865.
4. A Law of 1902 (no.144) stated a mandatory requirement on local administrations to endorse a '*regolamento organico*' for its employees and workers. The law no. 88 of 6 March 1904 instituted a retirement scheme for secretaries and for municipal employees with obligatory enrolment. Finally the *Testo Unico della legge comunale e provinciale* (no. 269, 1908 and no. 297, 1911) made access to secretarial and other positions possible only through public competition, in cases where internal promotion was not possible.
5. An inquiry of the *Ministro dell'interno*, in 1897, reported that the proportion of engineers in the municipal bureaucracy was 5.5 per cent; for secretaries the figure was 29.5 per cent (Bigaran 1990: 892–3).
6. See, for example, the regulations of Milan and Turin: Comune di Milano, *Nuovo organico dell'Ufficio tecnico Municipale*, and Città di Torino, *Amministrazione interna. Regolamenti*, Torino, Tip. Municipio, 1887, 84–6, in Archivio Storico del Comune di Bologna (=ASC), Carteggio Amministrativo (= Cart. Amm.), 1895, Titolo II, Rubrica 5, Fasc. *Ufficio edilità ed arte*, Sf *Nuovo ordinamento*.
7. See Archivio storico della Provincia di Bologna (ASP), Ufficio Tecnico (UT), 1927, b. 800.
8. In the competition for the position of *ingegnere capo* of Bologna's provincial technical service in 1911, experience at the top of technical services in other local administrations and the possession of administrative capacities, together with necessary technical competence, were the decisive factors in the choice of candidates. (ASP, Archivio Generale, 1911, VI, 1–2, b. 2125).

9. Municipal engineers often worked as free professionals, with dangerous confusion between their public and private professional activities. Other issues defined by regulations related to the exceptional jobs and salaries of engineers (for services given after hours) and the problem of assigning public work projects to external professionals. See Comune di Milano, *Nuovo organico dell'Ufficio tecnico Municipale*, cit.; Municipio di Firenze, *Regolamento e ruolo normale dell'Uffizio Tecnico Municipale (approvato con deliberazione del Consiglio comunale del di 17 luglio 1889)*, Firenze, Tip. Fratelli Bencini, 1889; Comune di Genova, *Regolamento per l'uffizio tecnico dei lavori pubblici*, Genova, Stab. Fratelli Pagano, 1894. In Bologna a special regulation for technical services had been adopted in 1859: *Regolamento per l'Ufficio degli Ingegneri Comunitativi*, ASC, Atti del Consiglio Comunale, Allegati, 1859, b. 2, sessione del 15 dicembre 1859, All. C.

10. Como's municipality in 1912 abolished the position of *ingegnere capo*, in order to eliminate an undesirable technician. 'La soppressione del capo dell'organico di un Ufficio Tecnico Municipale e la stabilità degli Impiegati Comunali messa a dura prova', *Rivista tecnica del Collegio Nazionale degli Ingegneri Provinciali e Comunali*, 1913, no. 1: 2–5. In Bologna too, in a regulation of 1870, the position of *ingegnere capo* was abolished. The previous chief engineer, Coriolano Monti, had gained too much autonomy from the *Giunta* (Alaimo 1996: 153–5). See also De Pieri in this volume.

11. If we analyse the files of the candidates for the post of *ingegnere capo* of Bologna's *Provincia*, we can see the extent of engineers' mobility in the technical services of municipalities and *provincie*. See ASPB, *Gen.*, VI, 1–2, no. 2125, 1911, fasc: *Concorso al posto di ingegnere capo, Curricula dei candidati*.

12. For the creation of the *Scuole superiori di architettura*, the result of a long fight to emancipate architects from engineering schools, see Calabi 1997, Nicoloso 1999.

13. 'Per la disciplina dei concorsi di Piano regolatore et Bando-tipo per i concorsi di piano regolatore', in *L'ingegnere*, IX, 1935, no. 1, 12–14.

14. The formation of CNIPC in 1911 came at the end of a long gestation period; see 'L'organizzazione degli ingegneri provinciali e comunali', *Rivista CNIPC*, 1917, no. 3–4, 2.

15. The representatives of this group tried to take part in the movement of municipal employees that aimed to reform the *Cassa di previdenza degli impiegati delle amministrazioni locali*. In this conflict, the engineers asserted their specific interests and symbolic distinction in relation to other employees. See Ing. Aldo Servi, 'La riforma della Legge sulla Cassa di Previdenza per gli impiegati dei Comuni, delle Provincie e delle Opere Pie', *Rivista CNIPC*, 1914, no. 4, 59–63.

16. It was a project that could have strengthened the power of the central state and reduced local autonomy: Ing. Pietro Rimondini, 'Lo statuto giuridico degli impiegati degli Uffici Tecnici Provinciali e Comunali', *Rivista CNIPC*, 1917, no. 7–8, 37–40.

17. Amidst the general crisis of the Italian middle classes were the specific grievances of engineers working in local government, who lamented the lack of precise definition of their status and the weakness of their real power in projecting and executing public works. See L. Frosali, 'Gli ingegneri comunali e provinciali nel dopoguerra', *Rivista CNIPC*, 1918, no. 5–6, 27.

18. This regulation could have defined a national statute for engineers working in local administrations, with general rules recognized by the central state, which local administrations had to respect. See 'Le rivendicazione morali ed economiche degli ingegneri provinciali e comunali', *L'ingegnere italiano*, no. 18, 15 September 1925.

19. The law no. 237, 4 February 1926, the Regio Decreto Legge (RDL) no. 1910, 3 September 1926 and the law of 27 December 1928, no. 2962, abolished elective bodies in the municipalities and in the *provincie* (*Consigli comunali* and *Consigli provinciali*) and conferred all powers on a monocratic organ (the *Podestà* for the municipalities and the *Preside* for the *provincie*), chosen by the prefect and nominated by the minister of the interior. Despite this authoritarian project of centralization, aimed at controlling local life on the periphery, recent historiography has underlined the unfinished character of fascist centralization, which could not live up to its principles, and did not really transform the municipal employees into state peripheral functionaries (Rotelli 1973, Romanelli 1995, Baldissara 1998).

20. In 1923, the fascist government compelled local administrations to revise their *pianta organica* and *regolamento organico*, in order to reduce the salaries and number of employees to the bare minimum (RDL no. 1177). In 1926, two legislative provisions (RDL no. 1577 and no. 2108) prohibited local authorities from changing the *pianta organica* and *regolamento organico*, with a view to improving salaries and conditions. In 1928–29, municipal secretaries were transformed into state functionaries, nominated by prefects after public competition, and with a national role (laws no. 1953, 17 August 1928 and no. 371, 21 March 1929). Finally, the *Testo Unico della legge comunale e provinciale* (no. 383 of 3 March 1934) extended to other municipal employees some of the provisions promulgated for secretaries (although not state status), and fixed minimum terms for the local regulations of employees (Schiera 1971: 123–52).

21. These projects were without result. See G. Stellingwerff, 'Uffici tecnici e disoccupazione degli ingegneri', *L'ingegnere*, III, no. 11 November 1929, 724; 'Questioni sindacali, comunicazioni e notizie', *L'ingegnere*, VIII, 1934, no. 5 and 6, 248–9, 356–7.

CHAPTER FIVE

Municipal innovations versus national wait-and-see attitudes: unemployment policies in *Kaiserreich* Germany (1871–1918)

Bénédicte Zimmermann

Towns in *Kaiserreich* Germany were *avant-garde* theatres in matters of social and labour policy. Forced to confront the combined effects of population mobility and industrialization that were generating rapid urbanization, they have been identified as the true 'pillars of Germany's economic and social transformation' at the turn of the twentieth century (Langewiesche 1988: 200). The self-administration charters (*Selbstverwaltung*) that governed the towns conferred a large number of duties upon them, but also guaranteed a substantial degree of autonomy and significant scope for innovation, to the extent that some historians refer to the emergence of local states during the *Kaiserreich* period (Steinmetz 1993).

The recognition of unemployment as a legitimate area of public action was a prime example of this local innovation. The first policies to combat unemployment were produced at the municipal level, whereas at the national level immobility and wait-and-see attitudes were *de rigueur*. In a situation of rapid industrialization and urbanization, their responsibility for poor relief encouraged municipalities to differentiate the unemployed from the indigent with a view to developing specific measures, such as labour exchanges or insurance, which could limit the cost of relief. But the history of Germany's first unemployment policies is also that of the specialization of municipal services and their rationalization, particularly via the establishment of labour exchanges, labour offices and the use of statistics. It is also the history of a process of innovation, which went beyond unemployment and made towns an authentic testing ground for public policy. Finally, it is the history of the confrontation between elected officials and administrative staff from different generations and representing various political perspectives.

The political and administrative changes affecting the conduct of local affairs at the turn of the twentieth century determined the general framework for differentiating unemployment from the problems of poverty. While the rationalization and professionalization of municipal management represented the common features of the process under review, their pace, changing personnel practices, the politicization of elected officials, the intensity and effectiveness of social democratic pressure on assemblies, along with the nature of the economic fabric, led to a great diversity of local experience.

Confronted by the limitations of municipal unemployment strategies, protagonists at the local level were quick to locate their action in the national sphere of public policies, and extend the impact of their initiatives beyond the solely municipal scene. Yet the growing differentiation between place of work and place of residence was a significant curb on the effectiveness of local policies. The bonds that rooted individuals did not necessarily converge; there was a disjunction between the world of work, within which the reality of employment was assessed, and the limited territorial remit of townships, which were politically competent in matters of policy implementation. The township framework was circumscribed by the administrative definition of municipality, and proved inadequate to cover the much larger and unstable economic terrain whose contours were shaped by employment patterns. Citing this inadequacy, municipal and trade union leaders lobbied to place unemployment within the national sphere of intervention. Until 1914, however, the action of voluntary associations and the nationwide reforming network they tried to create came up against the inaccessibility of the state sphere. This inaccessibility reflected a profound political deadlock between the predominantly liberal local arenas and the national arena, which remained a bastion of conservatism in imperial Germany.

The changing role of municipal administration

The principle of self-administration (*Selbstverwaltung*), which had been legally codified in township charters by the various German states during the early nineteenth century, gave municipalities a substantial degree of autonomy in fiscal matters as well as in public policy.[1] Up to the mid-nineteenth century, the exercise of autonomy was confined to an administrative policing role and the maintenance of order. The recognition of the social sphere as an autonomous field of action only came onto the agenda at the end of the century, bringing a new impetus to the *Selbstverwaltung*. Introduced in Prussia during the 1848 revolution, but subsequently consigned to oblivion by the reactionary backlash, the economic and social functions of local self-administration only began to blossom from the 1880s onwards. The demographic explosion of the urban centres and the critical approach taken in intellectual and political circles towards laissez-faire liberalism contributed to this reorientation of municipal policy (Heffter 1950: 331 and following).

During the last quarter of the nineteenth century, urbanization underwent spectacular acceleration, stimulated by robust demographic growth and changing patterns of mobility. Until the late 1850s, population movement had been mainly due to the search for arable land, but it was driven latterly by the search for industrial employment. Migration thus changed in orientation, from being intrarural or transatlantic to being predominantly urban (Bade 1984). Between 1873 and 1913, towns had to meet the challenge of absorbing some of the most substantial population movements in German history. By the 1900s, 48 per cent of the total population was living somewhere other than their place of birth. Urbanization became a complementary feature of the industrialization process. Medium-sized and large urban areas were particularly affected, and their overall population tripled between 1871 and 1910 (Köllmann 1974: 126). Coming mainly from agricultural regions in the east, migrants focused on Berlin and the industrial centres of the Rhineland and Westphalia.

Urban growth was a major challenge to the *Selbstverwaltung*. From the 1880s, municipal policies underwent unprecedented development through the 'municipalization' of a whole array of activities relating to the public interest. Among the services entrusted to municipal enterprise were gas and electricity supplies, sewerage, slaughterhouses, transport and street lighting. Established programmes, such as relief schemes, were reformulated, while new policies for housing, legal and financial aid, emergency works and labour exchanges were introduced (Krabbe 1989). Service-providing administrations (*Leistungsverwaltung*) burgeoned alongside the more traditional areas of regulation (*Ordnungsverwaltung*), in order to assume what contemporaries described as the 'social duties' of the townships (Adickes and Beutler 1903). Others saw it as the expression of 'municipal socialism', which the *Verein für Sozialpolitik* conservatives theorized as the local counterpart to state socialism (Krabbe 1979). Although inspired by the British experience, the German concept of municipal socialism was not a project to reform the whole of society such as that developed by the Fabian Society. Nor was it linked to the socialists' strategies to take power, characteristic of the French experience. For the members of the *Verein*, municipal socialism was associated with a firm belief in the irreversibility of the economic changes taking place and the necessity of extending the state's area of competence to public well-being.

The notion that municipal socialism managed to establish itself as part of the administrative and political practice of German towns, most of them run by liberal majorities, might seem surprising. Dieter Langewiesche has seen in this a conception of the township as a 'protective communitarian unit', on the laissez-faire principle (Langewiesche 1988: 203). This distortion of Manchester liberalism was the result of an alchemic process that transmuted the weight of tradition, the framework of action and economic and political dogma. Yet its establishment was uneven and depended on a wide range of circumstances. The heterogeneity of economic and social changes, the identity of those in charge of municipal administrations and the influence of tradition on the latter contributed towards shaping many variants. But whatever the specific situation, urban administrations everywhere had common characteristics that related to the growth and diversification of service provision. This extension of the field of application of *Selbstverwaltung* also coincided with a general process of differentiation within municipal governments, internally, through the proliferation of administrative services, and externally, through the professionalization of personnel.

The reform of public relief and the promotion of new labour policies were revealing indicators of this specialization process. Departments of social affairs, employment agencies, and labour and statistics offices were services that came to proliferate during the 1890s, and which generally defined a space for dealing with labour issues that was distinct from the traditional prerogatives of the police. Administrative reorganization, which allowed for greater autonomy within the sphere of social action, reflected practical changes that were affecting the sciences of government during the nineteenth century. Police science (*Polizeiwissenschaften*) and cameral studies (*Kameralistik*) thus gave way to political economy (*Volkswirtschaftspolitik*) and the administrative and legal sciences (*Verwaltungslehre, Rechtswissenschaft*) (Maier 1980). Far from being solely an intellectual matter, this shift in disciplines brought into play different forms of practical organization. The concept of 'good police' in an ordered society progressively lost ground to a developing 'social' discourse of integration, associated with new definitions of society in terms of class. Thus the Department of Social Affairs was created in Strasbourg in 1892 and federated a range of programmes, among them the fight against poverty, which had hitherto been under the supervision of the police. This new department, responsible for relief and public welfare, aimed to substitute more selective policies, such as labour exchanges, for measures that hitherto had smacked of repression. The fact that specialists replaced local notables who had until then taken unpaid responsibility for the conduct of public affairs also contributed to the changing role of municipal employees.[2]

Themselves students of *Verein für Socialpolitik* masters such as Schmoller, Engel and Brentano, most of the specialists in this new administrative sector usually held doctorates in law or, sometimes, from the second generation onwards, in political economy. This shift in the traditional recruitment norms for administrative personnel reflected the economic and social vocation of these professionals and, beyond that, the changing intellectual climate of the time. Because these new attitudes had difficulty penetrating the positivist-dominated legal discipline, which prevailed until the First World War, from the 1890s political economy became a breeding ground for intellectual and political dissidence (Dilcher 1976: 58). The most active and innovative municipal professionals in the social services emerged from such a background. Their espousal of the reformist cause generally went along with a liberal left political commitment, which, more readily than elsewhere, found a platform in the towns, most of them with liberal majorities. In this respect, the municipal arena represented fruitful ground for testing and implementing reformist ideas, which, in the *Kaiserreich* context, could not materialize in practical systems of action elsewhere. But the corollary of such a profile was restricted professional upward mobility. These men were undoubtedly able to consolidate their experience within the municipal services and move from one town to another. However, access to responsibilities at federated or *Reich* state administrative level was made difficult by their intellectual and political dissidence in relation to the dominant national conservatism.

Thus, in Strasbourg, it was a young team, united by a shared commitment to leftist democratic liberalism, who took over the reins of institutions established during the late nineteenth century (Zimmermann 1994). Their action was guided by a concept of social intervention that rejected both Manchester liberalism and Bismarckian conservatism. The old liberal school dealt with the entirety of social ills in an undifferentiated manner according to the canons of individual responsibility and relief. On the other hand, Bismarck, faced by the labour movement's growing power, tried to integrate the working classes into the German state through his social policy in a bid to divert them away from trade unionism. Rejecting these two options, Strasbourg's professional administrators sought a third way. Its main ingredients were recognizing the labour movement and its involvement in dealing with social matters; its expression was the institution of joint labour exchanges in 1895 and unemployment insurance in 1907.

Each of these three strategies offered a different response to the issues of poverty and unemployment. More than a political choice, from the turn of the twentieth century the development of a third way represented a change in the way the governing elites viewed society. However, the majority of municipal officials did not share the democratic values attached to the reformist option of collaborating with the labour organizations. While generational change and the professionalization of the public administration contributed to disseminating these values, the system and distribution of political representation held them back. Strasbourg was atypical in this respect. There, the right to vote for men was more egalitarian than in Germany as a whole, and from the start of the century the electoral context favoured the socialists and democrats. In the majority of other German towns the unevenness of voting rights, for instance three-class suffrage in Prussia, slowed down the democratization process.[3] Yet, despite its specificity, Strasbourg gives an exemplary view of the trend towards the bureaucratization, professionalization and politicization of the management of local affairs that, in the long run, affected all German urban administrations (Sheehan 1971: 126 and following).

According to Max Weber's analysis, in the response of the township administrations to social challenges, bureaucratic specialization combined with the professionalization of their employees. These ultimately became the essential criteria of modernization within German society (Weber 1964: 697–738). This notion seems to have been shared by several public servants of the period, especially those of the new generation who ardently promoted their modernizing mission (Zimmermann 1994). In consequence, and despite the democratic deadlock that characterized them, urban municipalities became the loci of the strongest changes and social innovations of the *Kaiserreich*. Proximity, the major asset for municipal action, made the town a privileged focal point of worker integration and dialogue between work and capital. The townships became favoured environments for progressive liberal public servants and consequently were recognized as ideal units for implementing social policy.[4]

The creation of municipal statistic offices was indicative of this specialization and professionalization process. The reports that towns were responsible for sending to the State Statistics Office served as the basis of local statistics. These reports were originally intended to create an overview of state resources and attested to the towns' proper use of the *Selbstverwaltung* charter. Until the mid-nineteenth century, the duty of compiling these reports was entrusted to a non-specialized municipal agent, who incorporated this along with his other tasks. It was only from the 1860s that some large towns began to set up bodies specializing in the statistical monitoring of their administrative activities.

Both the consequence and the expression of the expansionism then characteristic of the management of urban centres, this specialization encouraged the development of a new mission for municipal statistics, which was to produce empirical material intended to support local political action. Invested with this twofold function of assessing progress, in the traditional sense, and producing tools for political intervention, municipal statistics offices proliferated rapidly. The impetus to establish these offices did not as a general rule come from elected assemblies, but from the executive committees (*Magistrat*), composed of professional administrators. As the cases of Berlin and Strasbourg illustrate, their establishment was mainly a product of internal administrative rationalization. Berlin's statistics office was created as a result of a resolution addressed to the town's executive committee in 1856 by the Poor Department. This resolution demanded the creation of a statistics office to gather all information relating to poverty, which had hitherto been scattered around the various municipal departments (Silbergleit 1912: 1–3). Similarly, setting up a statistics office in Strasbourg in 1895 was part of an attempt to rationalize relief policy.

The question of poverty, far more than that of workers' status, was a driving force in the deployment of these permanent statistical services. It was during a second phase in the 1890s, at a time of considerable debate over unemployment, that work and non-work were to become the unavoidable focus of attention in municipal statistics. The *raison d'être* of the workers' parties and their main crusade in the late nineteenth century, work became a political issue in its own right. Erfurt and Magdebourg were the first towns to begin recording unemployment statistics in 1892 (Schikowski 1895: 17). The practice then spread according to the experience and intensity of recession. Still limited in 1902 to 1904, it was rapidly expanding by 1908. But, more than in other areas, in the matter of unemployment the measure turned out to be a precarious exercise.

The debate in Berlin over the municipal statistics for 1908 to 1909 was particularly revealing. Municipal statisticians and social democrats disagreed over survey methodology, as well as over the extent of 'real' unemployment. The social democrats accused the municipality of favouring self-declaration to produce what they claimed to be the partisan nature of its results, which were used to justify the town's lack of action in combating unemployment.[5] Waiting for people to present themselves spontaneously presupposed not only that individuals determined their own unemployed status, but also that they grasped the importance of doing so. This was not self-evident in cases of straightforward enquiry where declarants could not expect any direct return for their action.

Without going into the controversy over the figures brandished by the workers' opposition, this polemic illustrates the extent to which statistics could shift political antagonisms directly to the sphere of socioeconomic data. Far from contributing to 'social peace' as some had hoped, labour statistics created a new power focus, as control of their production allowed the producer to control the articulation of 'social truth.' The example of Berlin also sheds light on the position of municipal statisticians within the local municipal administration. To some extent they were circumscribed, because the activities of statistics offices were subject to political decision and monitoring. However, the statisticians had considerable power of influence through their working expertise. In relation to the growing interaction between statistics and reformist action, the local statisticians of the *Kaiserreich* were credited within the municipal team with a legitimacy which often went beyond their purely technical competence. Asked to develop the empirical tools necessary to resolve social questions, they participated, via their surveys, in constructing new categories of public intervention such as unemployment (Zimmermann 1994).

But neither the statistical debate nor innovations necessarily developed into new municipal policies. Using the example of unemployment, two scenarios can be distinguished that illustrate the substantial latitude for action that existed at the municipal level within the imposed rules of the game. While traditional left liberal municipalities, such as Berlin, used statistics as legitimate justification for non-intervention, the democrats and progressive left liberals used them, conversely, to support the development of new policies, such as joint labour exchanges and unemployment insurance.

The town 'laboratory'

In the matter of employment policy, the towns were like experimental laboratories for the *Reich*. The local programmes of emergency works, labour exchanges, unemployment insurance, *Gewerbegerichte* (industrial tribunals) and joint commissions were all experiments that fuelled the national debate.[6] Thus the 1890 law for establishing joint *Gewerbegerichte* was largely inspired by the model developed in Frankfurt by the reformer, Karl Flesch (Weitensteiner 1976: 20). Conversely, in other cases, such as that of unemployment, imperial officials justified their non-interventionist, wait-and-see position on the grounds of incomplete information drawn from municipal practices. Whether concerning labour exchanges or unemployment insurance, the recurrence of this argument exposes the *Reich* government's strategy of delegation and avoidance, while reinforcing the towns' propensity to become social laboratories whose initiatives would eventually inform national policies.

The first unemployment policies were indeed devised and tested at the municipal level, their development reflecting a desire to free public funds for relief. In accordance with the law on the place of settlement, the municipalities were responsible for relief to any individual residing in their district for over two years; a period that was reduced to one year in 1908.[7] Like town charters, this law left it up to the townships to determine the conditions and forms of relief. During the second half of the nineteenth century, most large towns embarked on a relief reform programme in order to improve efficiency and reduce costs, following pioneer experiments conducted by the municipality of Elberfeld in 1853. This reform, which specified relief measures depending on the causes of poverty, marked the beginning of municipal attempts to differentiate unemployment from other sources of indigence. It initiated a shift in the debate over poverty from the issue of subsistence to that of work, while eventually differentiating between the issue of work and that of poverty (Weisbrod 1981: 346). The Strasbourg case-study is illuminating in this respect. The labour institutions created at the turn of the twentieth century, as in most other German towns, originated from ideas about how to rationalize the management of poverty. But they rapidly went on to achieve administrative autonomy.

In 1888, the attention of Strasbourg leaders was drawn to the functioning of poor relief. This followed an investigation revealing a particularly high number of people receiving relief from various institutions of the town. In consequence, there was a reorganization of public aid, which represented a recognizable prelude to the emergence of municipal labour institutions. From 1889, a labour exchange was created within the charity department, in the hope of eradicating the cases of indigence attributable to poor organization of the labour market. But very soon labour exchanges and the labour market were to become the object of policies and administrations distinct from poor relief, as illustrated by the creation in 1895 of a joint labour exchange.

Generally, it was over the course of the economic crisis of 1892–94 that municipal labour exchanges came to proliferate, as the result of an attempt to match supply and demand and organize the labour market. During this period the most innovative arrangements were those involving the joint cooperation of labour and employers' organizations. But joint labour exchange remained experimental until the turn of the century, in contrast with the rapid development of other forms of municipal labour exchanges. Despite federal state government recommendations from 1894, their establishment came up against the requirement for cooperation between the administration, the labour movement and the employers. The municipalities of Esslingen, Strasbourg, Erfurt and Heilbronn opened the first joint offices in 1894, but their proliferation dates only from the following decade. Although in 1910, 54 per cent of the *Reich*'s public labour exchanges were joint, there were substantial regional disparities. In 1904, all public labour exchange was jointly organized in Wurtemberg, over two-thirds in Baden and half in Bavaria, as against only 20 per cent in Prussia (Faust 1986: 66).

Joint labour exchange developed particularly strongly in the southern German states. An array of factors combined to favour this development: the involvement of governments in launching inter-local trade networks, an economic structure mainly composed of small and medium-sized businesses with diversified activity, and finally, for some regions, the importance of Catholic culture, charged with a 'social peace' mission by the *Rerum Novarum* papal encyclical. On the other hand, in the specialized industrial centres of Prussia and Saxony, the big industrial employers, organized in the *Zentralverband Deutscher Industrieller* and the *Bund der Industriellen*, had their own labour exchanges and remained fiercely opposed to any form of cooperation with labour organizations until the First World War.[8] Thus, until 1914, joint labour exchange was mainly the province of towns of small and medium-sized industry with a strong craft orientation, where the poorly organized employers and the unionized workforce found mutual advantage in maintaining labour market stability.

Based on the supposition that municipal, union and employers' interests could intersect, joint labour exchange was a cornerstone of the 'third way' social reforms promoted by the progressive professionals who were running several municipal administrations from the end of the nineteenth century. For progressives such as Karl Flesch, who between 1884 and 1914 devised an audacious labour policy in Frankfurt, and Alexander Dominicus in Strasbourg, all social and employment policy proceeded from the objective of integrating workers into society and hence should not be confused with poor relief, which involved suppressing their civil rights. As evidence of their influence, the first joint offices were not created in consequence of social democrat demand, but at the behest of professionals concerned as much with administrative rationalization and social reform as with the organization of the local labour market. More fundamentally, the adoption of the joint project depended on the nature of power politics that were specific to each town. Thus, in Strasbourg, where the liberals had to compromise with the Catholic party and the democrats, it met with great success. Conversely, in Berlin, where the upholders of traditional liberalism reigned supreme, in 1893 elected officials excluded the possibility of joint labour exchange, on the grounds that it would amount to proclaiming the right to work for all (Hirsch 1908: 206). Depending on local circumstances, the spectres of public interventionism and socialism met with varying degrees of success.

These innovative policies of labour exchange had their counterparts in insurance terms through the adoption of the Ghent system by a number of towns. Named after the Belgian municipality that inaugurated it, this system granted union organizations a municipal subsidy proportionate to the amounts paid in unemployment allocation. With a ceiling, and limited in time to one year per person, this aid was provided to the unemployed on an individual basis, in addition to the compensation allocated by the unions. In return, the latter undertook to advance the total amount to their members, to assume monitoring of the unemployed and to ensure transparent accountability for unemployment benefits. Yet, unlike the rapid development of public labour exchange, the municipalities proved to be more hostile to unemployment insurance. Because allocation depended on the accumulation of benefits rather than employment circumstances, it did not fit in with the municipalities' favoured policy of organizing the labour market. According to a hierarchical system of priorities, insurance was seen as a last resort, to be invoked only when labour exchange and emergency works were deemed inadequate to deal with the lack of work. But as a point of principle, most municipal leaders excluded it from their remit, thus setting themselves against the federal state and *Reich* governments. Indeed, although the latter delegated handling of the problem to the local authorities, only a *Reich* law could authorize the municipalities to establish compulsory insurance.

And yet, in the opinion of specialists of the period, compulsion was an essential condition for making any kind of unemployment insurance viable. If this were not the case, only the most exposed populations would choose to pay into it, compromising the fund's financial stability. But beyond this functional impracticality, local leaders, whether elected officials or professional administrators, proclaimed their powerlessness in the face of an unemployment problem caused by economic issues over which they had no control. Assembled at the Congress of German Towns, the *Deutscher Städtetag*, the mayors and representatives of the largest towns declared their opinion in a joint resolution addressed to the *Bundesrat* in 1911. This resolution called for compulsory *Reich* insurance, restricted to the winter months and the most exposed trades, especially the building trade, along the lines of the British model established the same year (*Verhandlungen des dritten Deutschen Städtetages ...* 1911: 68–9).

On the eve of the First World War, only around 20 German towns offered unemployment benefits, and most were based on the Ghent model. Strasbourg was the first to adopt it in 1907. But outside

Strasbourg and Schöneberg, it was, as with joint labour exchange, mainly towns in southern Germany that were committed to such a policy of cooperation with the unions. Beyond the various factors favourable to joint policies, their diversified socioeconomic structure gave them reason to hope for less vulnerability and a balance of risks in the event of recession, unlike the large, specialized industrial centres of the Saar, Rhineland, Saxony or Silesia. But unlike joint labour exchange, the adoption of the Ghent system was never the result of administrative initiative. Instead, it was always a result of a social democrat demand. Thus, from 1910, the Ghent system featured in the municipal programme of the Prussian SPD (*Sozialdemokratische Partei Deutschlands*) alongside demands for labour statistics, joint labour exchanges, emergency works and labour offices centralizing all municipal employment policy (Hirsch 1911).

The *Städtetag* collective of mayors had rejected comprehensive unemployment insurance for reasons of its elitist and non-egalitarian nature and the infringement of the duty of administrative neutrality that it would introduce. Because it was addressed only to workers already enjoying cover for unemployment and excluded seasonal workers who, even when they were organized like those in the building trade, did not receive union benefits, it was denounced as an illusory solution to the problem of unemployment. Added to this was fear that the system would encourage trade union membership and thus contribute to strengthening organizations of class struggle. This fear was combined with suspicion of the social democrat definition of unemployment and the unions' capacity to respect the terms of the agreement at the basis of coordination. How could the truly unemployed be distinguished from those who were not? This was the question that haunted municipal officials and only mutual trust between administrative and workers' elites seemed able to resolve this.

Trust between administrative, political and workers' leaders was in fact an essential ingredient of these innovative arrangements. Some municipalities seem to have been able to use the proximity of those they administered to cultivate this trust and open up a new avenue to social policy, at the instigation of a small number of reformers. As the example of Strasbourg shows, the strategic reasons for the integration and domestication of the SPD were not unrelated to the adoption of joint labour exchange or the Ghent system, but proved insufficient without some basis of confidence in the social democrats' capacity to channel conflict and respect the established rules. In this context, innovation in matters of policies for work and non-work can be seen as largely dependent on the nature of interactions between urban elites and workers' representatives. While in some cases, such as Berlin, the social democrats' appeal to the municipalities for coordination provoked stalemate, elsewhere it gave rise to forms of cooperation with local officials. Yet, even where the political conditions for coordination came together, the measures adopted came up against structural limitations. In effect, most municipal policies used the place of settlement and means of subsistence to identify their beneficiaries. For their part, the unions made membership of the organized work sector the determining criterion. This resulted in the necessity to compromise with the dual imperatives of employment circumstances and territorial residence.

When unemployment statistics were undertaken by Stuttgart in 1902, for example, representatives from the social democratic unions protested against using place of residence to identify those jobless who were entitled to relief. Because it eliminated those workers employed in the city but who, because of high rents in the urban perimeter, were forced to take lodgings in neighbouring townships, they maintained that there were inadequacies in recording the 'real unemployment' currently afflicting Stuttgart. Union statistics from 1900 indicated in particular that 52 per cent of bricklayers and 29 per cent of masons employed in the city were obliged to commute. The trade unionists took this as proof that it was preposterous to base policies to combat unemployment on the place of settlement.[9] But for the municipality, 'real unemployment' was restricted to residents to whom it owed relief. This territorial cleavage between civic and employment identity was particularly noticeable in the application of the Ghent system. Whereas the local union provided relief to claimants who worked in the town, regardless of their place of residence, the municipality provided for the needs of those who had their place of settlement there, regardless of their place of work. As for the Ghent system, this was intended exclusively for those who fulfilled both conditions; that is, those who worked and lived in the town. Inevitably, this excluded a substantial number of people.

Provoked by job mobility and the concentration of activities in urban centres in a state of demographic saturation, the growing differentiation between place of work and place of residence raised the issue of the social link that could cover all the unemployed. To the extent that the bonds that tied the individuals to their work and those that tied them to a place no longer necessarily coincided, public policies to combat unemployment came up against the dissociation between new arenas of economic action, within which unemployment appeared, and the areas where public action was implemented, within which unemployment could be addressed.

Although trade unionists and municipal leaders were the first to denounce the relevance of the place of settlement as a basis for public unemployment policy, they nevertheless used it as a last resort in coordinating their actions. Illustrating the possible incongruity between the defence of general principles and forms of action, the implementation of the Ghent system involved concessions to the structural and institutional constraints inherent in the framework of intervention. Exploring an alternative to the repression strategy of the labour movement, the policy of coordinating municipal and union unemployment actions relied on integration through dialogue and cooperation that would be characteristic of Weimar Republic policy. From this standpoint, joint labour exchange and the Ghent system can be seen as the expression of a 'positive integration' of social democratic organizations, contrary to the analysis of 'negative integration' suggested by Dieter Groh (1973). Reflecting social democracy's mode of entry into the national political system of the *Kaiserreich*, Groh's analysis disregards experiments in situated integration. Despite their limited character, these were reshaping the dominant political culture on the eve of the First World War.

Situated practices and national generalizations

As the first significant public policies to combat unemployment, municipal initiatives were characterized by their heterogeneity. This was despite underlying common practices relating to professionalization of the administration and the means of differentiating the unemployed from the poor. Using the laboratory analogy, they were also experiments that determined the direction of national debates. The means of identifying the unemployed activated by municipal policies helped to pave the way for formalizing unemployment at the national level. Thus, beginning in 1903, statistics from local labour exchanges were aggregated by the Statistics Office of the *Reich*, while the municipal surveys of unemployment that flourished from the early twentieth century were subject to attempts to standardize them by the *Reich* interior ministry between 1908 and 1909. However the main means of structuring the national debate were not administrative in origin, but came from voluntary associations. The *Reich* administration, characterized by immobility and wait-and-see attitudes, was confronted by a range of local experts who felt restricted by the limited scope of township opportunities and who sought to establish unemployment as a national sphere of interest. To do so, they were ready to embark on collective mobilization, using the associational network as a means of access to the national arena, which was otherwise inaccessible through the democratic play of institutions under the *Kaiserreich*.

In Germany at the end of the nineteenth century, the grouping of local activists in national associations was their preferred means of mitigating the limitations and relative isolation of the municipalities. Thus constituted as a collective entity, they set out to defend causes neglected by the *Reich* leaders. Once again, unemployment was an exemplary case. Based on local experience, collective mobilization in favour of a national policy to combat unemployment proceeded in two stages. At first it was developed within specialized groups built around a specific professional activity, such as, the association of municipal statisticians and the association of public labour exchanges. The first organization provides a particularly good illustration of the tension that could arise from attempts to forge a national movement based on coordinating experiences at the local level. Municipal statisticians were the classic example of the local practitioner with wider reformist aspirations, who combined the practical imperatives of municipal intervention with the cognitive requirements of statistical generality (Zimmermann 1994). Expressing a particular political rationale and a more general scientific rationale, they became architects of an interrelated articulation that reflected both the local and national interests. Theie Conference, and later the *Verband Deutscher Städtestatistiker* (VDSS), within which they were associated from 1888, was where their demands were collectively shaped. Their efforts on unemployment were to be characterized by the internal debate in the pursuit of scientific generality and professional legitimacy in the national domain.

The principal features of the new competence for which they sought recognition were the locally situated background to their action and the use of this knowledge to produce statistical categories. Emphasizing their localism, municipal statisticians felt that they had the authority to inform their national counterparts of new statistical objectives, which before then had been only of local relevance. Notwithstanding the practical justifications that the municipal statisticians publicly proclaimed, exporting statistical knowledge in this way enabled them to reconcile the dilemma arising from the need to correlate the globalizing aims of VDSS and the local and specific programmes carried out on the ground by each VDSS member. Seeking to combine the statistician's demands for generality with the local expert's experience of plurality, the municipal statisticians tried to show the national statistics community the value of the situated nature of their action, which they also identified as an obstacle to their claims to generality. Through this change of scale, they tried to convert what restricted their action at the municipal level into a resource.

The same kind of analysis can be applied to the Association of German Labour Exchanges, the *Verband Deutscher Arbeitsnachweise* (VDA) established in 1898 (Jastrow 1898). This association aimed to federate all the public labour exchanges in the *Reich*. Its main objectives were to standardize local practices and to develop inter-local networks in order to reach beyond the restrictive township framework of adjusting supply and demand. Labour exchange was, like statistics, a technique for territorial unification of the nation and a vehicle for placing unemployment on a national level of generality.

This work of mobilization within small groups was an important lever for placing unemployment in the national domain, but there were limitations because of local roots and specialist interests. Consequently, the connection between these various arenas constituted a second stage in the trend toward generalization.[10] This new phase saw the networking of various local specialists and an enlargement of the mobilization platform by involving new militants, particularly those with a national status. The creation of the Association for Social Reform (*Gesellschaft für Sozialreform* – GfSR) in 1901, then in 1911 of the Association to Combat Unemployment (*Gesellschaft zur Bekämpfung der Arbeitslosigkeit* – GzBA) offered opportunities for such expansion.[11] Seeking to federate all the defenders of a national unemployment policy, these associations created a forum for the exchange and circulation of ideas among political, administrative and academic professionals, as well as allowing for dialogue between the local and national experts.

A stage for multiple interactions, the network of associations reflects the image of a Wilhelmine pluralist society, far from the society of subjects described by Heinrich Mann in *Der Untertan* (1918). It reveals the strong potential for local innovation that found expression at the margins of an authoritarian and conservative state. Associations provided the means for channelling reform into the national domain.[12] As vehicles for collective mobilization, they helped to create a public arena around the cause of unemployment, while at the same time remaining dependent on state intervention to convert this space into an effective frame of action. The associational network revealed the interdependency of an array of entangled relationships, which structured the reformist network and conditioned its strengths and weaknesses. Within this network, municipal statisticians and public labour exchange officers looked to national reformers to legitimize their generalizing aims, whereas the latter needed the support of the former to promote the model of social regulation they championed. Although this play of interdependencies governed an alliance of complementary resources in support of the demand for state intervention over unemployment, reformers were nevertheless limited by their external dependence on political resources that were inaccessible to them. The incapacity to mobilize activists with influence over the government marked the limits of the political efficacy of their action before 1914.

The principle of subsidiarity, designed to regulate relations between local and central administrations, lay at the heart of the debate on unemployment. Invoked by municipal leaders on the one hand in their demands for national intervention, it was used on the other by representatives of the *Reich* executive to shift responsibility for the problem onto the townships. These contrasting approaches revealed a real conflict of jurisdiction between administrative authorities. The rules of subsidiarity were in effect constantly activated at the governmental level, but only as a rationale to justify action or, more precisely, non-intervention, while the aspirations and local potentialities for innovation were systematically repressed outside the state arena. Although Bismarck's unemployment insurance scheme relied on local bodies to implement it, and although government representatives continually invoked the jurisdictional competence of the township in unemployment matters, the exercise of subsidiarity was strictly a one-way process, from the state to the intermediary, professional or territorial authorities. This unilateral implementation of downward subsidiarity to the detriment of any upward dynamic was one of the many expressions of the weakness of political democracy under the *Kaiserreich*.

Central government policy makers, as guarantors for preserving internal state coherence, were unavoidable intermediaries for any national strategy on unemployment, yet they fitted within a context that was fundamentally different from those of their local counterparts. The latter, trade union and municipal leaders whose understanding of the national arena was based on the interconnection of local differentiated spaces, adjusted their action in relation to the short-term time frame of periods of recession. On the other hand, the former were rooted in a perspective of national transcendence and determined their action according to a long-term time frame of state consolidation. The divergence of space–time referents and registers of action specific to these two groups reflected profound disagreement about the terms and objectives of social reform, leaving the question of unemployment before the First World War with no prospect of resolution in the national domain.

Conclusion

Although elected officials and professional municipal administrators failed to mobilize *Reich* intervention successfully in the area of unemployment prior to 1914, they nonetheless succeeded, through the associational network, in federating the majority of reformist aims around an insurance project linked to public organization of the labour market in the national arena. On the basis of their local foothold, they achieved substantial gains in placing unemployment in concrete realities, and in discursive and practical arrangements. In short, by 1914, a prerequisite for achieving the reform programme was in place, save for the political conditions. The Weimar Republic was to invent nothing new in terms of defining unemployment or insurance, but changes in the rules of the political game and the enlargement of alliances, and even more significantly the reconfiguration of the German state, allowed for its formalization as a national category of public policy.

But when a national structure dealing with unemployment finally became effective under the Weimar Republic, the municipalities, which had been the first to demand it, were also among the first to contest it. The national treatment of the problem took a turn that was little to their liking. In particular, they disputed the autonomy of local labour offices created at this time and which, being joint, came under a national administration of labour. Although the geographical delimitation of their field of action often coincided with township boundaries, these offices enjoyed complete independence with regard to the municipal administrations. The *Städtetag* denounced this autonomy as an attack on the principle of municipal self-administration (*Selbstverwaltung*) and called for powers to oversee the implementation of unemployment policies in the interests of ensuring the consistency of local policies (Lewek 1992: 323). Illustrating the subtle mix of local autonomy and national policy that characterized the *Selbstverwaltung*, this reversal of the situation attested to the fluctuating interpretation of the self-administration principle according to circumstances and situations. Whereas under the *Kaiserreich* the towns demanded that the nation state assume its responsibilities, under the Weimar Republic they complained about an assault on their local state prerogatives.

Translated from the French by Cynthia Schoch.

Notes

1. Rural towns and townships had their own distinct charters, the *Städteordnungen* and the *Landgemeindeordnungen*, respectively. They were not initially differentiated on the basis of the number of inhabitants, but, rather vaguely, on type of activity. However, from the end of the nineteenth century, a town was described as having over 2000 inhabitants. The first charter for towns was the Prussian *Städteordnung* of 1808, redrafted in 1853. The Constitution of the *Reich* of 1871 left the determination of township law to the prerogative of the federated states, so that in 1912

there were 30 different town charters. Prussia alone had eight, distributed by geographical area (Most 1912, vol. 2: 6, 19 and following). The most important charters are reproduced in Engeli and Haus (1975).

2. German towns were run by a *Magistrat*, an executive body composed of the mayor and executive advisers, half of them unpaid. All members of the *Magistrat*, including the mayor, were designated by the elected municipal assembly, but were not necessarily from it. The executive was assisted in its action by an administrative team whose specialization and professionalization accelerated at the end of the nineteenth century. On the professionalization of municipal leaders, at the political level as much as the administrative level, see Hofmann (1983), 613 and following, Scarpa (1992), Sheehan (1971). For a more general approach to professionalization in German history, see MacClelland (1991).

3. Apart from Alsace-Lorraine, where it was democratic and egalitarian, male electoral suffrage was limited across the German states. The right to vote was conditional on age, municipal citizenship and payment of tax, according to conditions fixed by each federated state.

4. The adjective 'progressive liberal' does not refer to particular partisan membership, but designates all those who sought to make their reformist voluntarism part of the values of political liberalism. Although most of them saw themselves in the early twentieth century as generally affiliated to parties of the *Freisinnige Vereinigung* and the *Freisinnige Fortschrittliche Partei*, some, placed themselves in the orbit of the national–liberal party.

5. See 'Die Arbeitslosenzählung', *Vorwärts*, 18 November 1908.

6. The *Gewerbegericht* was an industrial tribunal some of whose powers were similar to those of the French *Conseil des Prud'hommes* (a sort of labour relations board). But, unlike the latter, its jurisdiction was not restricted to dealing with individual cases. It could, indeed, intervene at times of collective conflicts such as strikes. Another distinctive feature was the fact that it was presided over by a municipal leader.

7. On the place of settlement (*Unterstützungswohnsitz*) and the successive laws regulating it, see Tennstedt (1981), 92 and following.

8. The *Zentralverband Deutscher Industrieller* represented heavy industry, whereas the *Bund der Industriellen*, created in 1895, represented the manufactured goods sector. In 1913, the two organizations merged in the *Vereinigung Deutscher Arbeitgeberverbände* (Führer 1990: 82).

9. 'Amtliche und gewerkschaftliche Arbeitslosenzählung in Stuttgart' (1902), 46.

10. On the trend toward generalization in public action, see in particular Boltanski and Thévenot (1991).

11. The *Gesellschaft für Sozialreform* is the German section of the international Association for the legal protection of workers, founded in 1900 during the Paris universal exposition. The *Gesellschaft zur Bekämpfung der Arbeitslosigkeit* is the German section of the international Association to combat Unemployment, founded in 1910 in Paris by the Belgian Louis Varlez and the Frenchman Max Lazard, to develop an international anti-unemployment platform (Topalov 1994: 59–115).

12. Refuting the thesis of a society of subjects, Blackbourn and Eley (1984: 195 and following) give a more global analysis of the associational movement as one of the main means of affirming the bourgeoisie and its aspirations within the *Kaiserreich*.

CHAPTER SIX

Town clerks in the Paris region: the design of a professional identity in the late nineteenth and early twentieth centuries

Emmanuel Bellanger

The typology and statutory diversity of municipal jobs reveal professional worlds that can be difficult to identify, and where outlines and definitions are uncertain, even porous. The written traces repose in hundreds of square metres of archival shelves, where the space reserved for personnel files seems to be the most substantial and imposing. Under these circumstances, research constraints are hardly due to the limited availability of the records. Instead, the researcher is confronted by their sheer depth and density, and the elaborate methods necessary to work with them.[1] Yet the effort involved in constructing and analysing these life records can ultimately contribute towards a better understanding of municipal employees and work practices as they developed over time. In this way, the records highlight the nature of professional progression and career advancement, the distinctiveness of the workforce and, conversely, the degree of their dependency on the municipal power-base.

This introduction may seem out of place. At first sight, the formation of the French *secrétaires de mairie* or *secrétaires généraux* corps, which broadly represented the equivalent of town clerks in British local government, differs significantly from the broader experience of the municipal workforce.[2] Their social position and limited number suggest that they came from more exclusive and specialized backgrounds. However, the study of their career path reveals that this was not the case. For all that they represented the administrative keystone of the municipalities, the *secrétaires de mairie* of the Paris region were not specialists or technicians, holding prestigious university degrees. In general, they first settled into the municipal bureaucracy as clerical workers or even, less frequently, as stenographers. Following the same trajectory as other municipal staff, they benefited from the dominant mode of career advancement, which was internal promotion.

Conscious of the limits of their formal academic achievements, the *secrétaires généraux* tended to identify themselves within the bureaucratic hierarchy as 'a lower elite, trained in the school of diplomacy'.[3] This reflected the experience of the Paris region. More than other senior municipal employees, such as the heads of surveying, architecture, tax collection and *octrois* (municipal customs), the *secrétaires de mairie* justified their pivotal social position by claiming expert knowledge of the local terrain and the urban, social and institutional transformations that affected it. With an entrenched position in the community, the *secrétaires de mairie* were important principally because of their practical experience in the workings of municipal organization. This knowledge, acquired 'on the job', was augmented from 1922 by training at a university-level institution, which in 1929 became the National School of Municipal Administration (*l'Ecole nationale d'administration municipale*, ENAM) (Bellanger 2001).

Yet until the 1940s any comparison with higher-ranking public servants was debatable. For the nineteenth-century *secrétaires de mairie*, as for their successors, the golden age was identified with the *secrétaire greffier* of the *Ancien Régime*. This position related back to a lost heroic period, with overtones of '*honours*' and '*office*' that still had considerable resonance (Martineau 1906). Although of humbler status when compared with their technical colleagues or prefectoral and ministerial civil servants, the *secrétaires de mairie* successfully established and protected their localized field of skill and investigation throughout the second half of the nineteenth century. As the *mairies*, or town halls, became conspicuous theatres for the display of municipal activity, visibly implanting themselves in the monumental landscape of French towns and cities, so these public servants consolidated their position in the Paris region. Well before the adoption of the municipal charter of 5 April 1884, the *secrétaires de mairie* knew how to play their intermediary role between local power legitimized by universal male suffrage and the maintenance of the centralist tradition of French administration.

From the second half of the nineteenth century to the end of the Fourth Republic in 1958, the outlines of this profession took form and became an integral component of French administration. This chapter will examine the process of professionalization and how the *secrétaires généraux* maintained their position, even during the period of radical political change after the First World War. Over time, the forms of recruitment and selection expanded and a collective identity emerged, built upon the role that the *secrétaires généraux* had assumed between municipal power and prefectoral authority, and between the municipal workforce and the mayor. As will be elaborated, this decisive position became particularly significant for administering the territory of the *Seine-banlieue*, the area of the département of the Seine surrounding Paris.

The *Seine-banlieue*: specificity of a territory

According to their own definition, *secrétaires de mairie* represent a social grouping rooted in a municipal structure, the product of a territory, a local history and a privileged, even personal relationship with municipal power. This image, based on the first-hand testimony of eye-witnesses, reflects a shared feeling of identity with a 'community', a 'small family' or 'local patriotism'.[4] Thus *secrétaires de mairie*, steeped in a 'city culture', often expressed attachment to their community within the framework of a distinctive civic history.[5] Yet studies of the organizational archives of the *secrétaires de mairie* suggest little about these local ties and sensibilities. Instead they show how this group was able to transcend municipal borders by developing common administrative practices and building networks. At the same time they reveal that such decompartmentalization was limited geographically to the *Seine-banlieue* and its 80 municipalities, described by provincial *secrétaires généraux* as territories that seemed to be the exclusive preserve of their regional colleagues.

In the general history of French municipal employees, this suburban territory occupies an atypical place.[6] The municipalities of the *Seine-banlieue*, of which the number shifted from 69 to 80 between 1860 and 1964, reflected a plurality of sociological, political and urban profiles. As pointed out by Jean-Claude Farcy (1991), these communities were 'at the same time agricultural, working-class, bourgeois and tourist'. Their jurisdiction distinguished them by statute from the city of Paris. Subordinate to the double guardianship of the prefect of the Seine and the prefect of police, they were nevertheless subject to uniform rule by the municipal law of 1884.

The distinctiveness of the Paris region is evident from the size of its municipal workforce. In 1937, an inquiry made at the behest of the Ministry of the Interior (Orsoni 1938) revealed that the department's 81 municipalities, including Paris, had 94 109 employees out of the national total of 296 938 (Table 6.1). The department thus employed 31.7 per cent of the national municipal workforce, almost a third of the total. This represented a ratio of 19 employees for every 1000 inhabitants, compared with just over five employees for the rest of metropolitan France. The nature of employment in the provincial municipalities also contrasted with that of the Paris region. The inquiry showed that, in the

Table 6.1   Comparison of municipal employees in the Department of the Seine and French provinces, 1937

	Number of municipal employees	Number of municipal employees per 1000 inhabitants	Number of employees holding two jobs	% of employees holding two jobs
Seine	94 109 (31.7%)	19.0	4 933	5.2
Provinces	202 829 (68.3%)	5.5	75 144	37.0
Total	296 938		80 077	

Source: Orsoni (1938).

provinces, 37 per cent of municipal employees occupied a second job, against only 5.2 per cent in the department of the Seine.

The quantitative disproportion and difference of status revealed by these figures can be explained in part by urban and demographic expansion in Paris and the territory of the *Seine-banlieue*. In consequence, municipal power had to redefine and expand the organizational structure of its workforce, while at the same time reorganizing administrative departments. At stake was satisfying the heightened expectations of a fast-growing population and responding to the emergence of new social needs.

Intercommunality was one of the original responses to this agglomerated space, and ultimately stimulated a general movement that helped to harmonize local public interventionism. Throughout the first half of the twentieth century the municipalities of the *Seine-banlieue* had effectively delegated part of their authority to joint management boards (*syndicats de communes*) that crossed spheres of local activity. At the prompting of the professional association of mayors of the department of the Seine (*Amicale des maires de la Seine*), these boards represented a collective response to the administration of services hitherto under individual municipal management. Such boards for funeral and gas services emerged in 1903, and for water and electricity supply in 1922 and 1924, respectively. A board for municipal staffing matters followed in 1937 and for *octrois* in 1939. Reflecting the same coordinating trends, the municipalities of the Paris region were able to join with the refuse collection service of the city of Paris from 1934, and the responsibility thus became department-wide. On a smaller scale, numerous municipalities combined their resources to create hospitals, community clinics and cemeteries.

Research by Jean-Luc Pinol (1999) on inter-war municipal finance has further emphasized the specificity of the territory, revealing the essential contribution of state and departmental subventions in the budgets of communities of the *Seine-banlieue*. According to the 1934 statement of revenue and expenditure carried out by the Ministry of Finance, 40 of the communities were listed as among the richest towns in France. Not only did the municipalities collect considerable income, such as tolls and local taxes, but they also benefited from a financial contribution made by the state and *conseil général*, which was distinctive of the *Seine-banlieue* and which covered on average 46 per cent of municipal revenue. The partial interventionism of public power consequently increased the territorial particularity of the region, and served to differentiate the role and function of the municipalities even more from the rest of France.

Secrétaires de mairies: a socio-historical sketch

In the *Seine-banlieue* there were generally four forms of recruitment for municipal employees, depending on different circumstances: these were local, familial, social and personal.[7] They coexisted continually throughout the nineteenth and twentieth centuries, often overlapped and were mutually reinforcing. It was only staff appointed by qualifications, emerging in the 1920s at the time when training programmes for municipal staff were created, who were able to distinguish themselves from this seemingly closed system, founded on ties of territory, residency and kinship, and extending into clientele networks. The personnel files of *mairie* staff from the early twentieth century shed intriguing light on some of these recruitment practices.[8]

Closely associated with the selection of candidates, *secrétaires généraux* benefited from and reproduced these traditional modes of appointment. For applicants for municipal jobs, living in the city or, better still, being born there, was a major asset. The application forms of new recruits reveal the keen interest taken by mayors in the domicile and seniority of applicants. Following the example of their subordinates, the place of residence of *secrétaires de mairie* was always linked to their place of activity. Up to the 1940s, when mayors made appointments, their insistence upon local residency was indispensable to the continuous offer of employment and the needs of political representation. Similarly, family ties had long been a legitimate criterion for recruitment. This system was more widespread during periods of economic crisis, as it provided the advantage, when a large number of jobs remained unoccupied, of retaining employees liable to opt for a more lucrative professional career in the private sector. The appeal of belonging to a closed circle of intimate acquaintances served as a stabilizing factor and professional heredity became present within all levels of the municipal hierarchy. For instance, the municipalities of Suresnes, Saint-Denis, Stains, Vincennes and Montreuil all witnessed the promotion of *secrétaires généraux* who were the sons or daughters of *mairie* employees.

Municipalities also had a social commitment to people who to some extent depended on the community or became isolated from their professional milieu. The redeployment of invalided-out soldiers, elderly men, widows and housewives illustrates this mission of integration. During the first half of the nineteenth century, discharged army officers had often occupied the position of *secrétaire de mairie*, and the dislocation of the First World War rapidly accelerated this process. In 1923, the municipalities were obliged by central government to place war invalids in reserved jobs, and around 10 *mairie* employees who became *secrétaires généraux* and *secrétaires de mairie* during the 1930s and 1940s had originally been beneficiaries of this legislation.

Personal recruitment was based on different configurations of connections and sponsorship. These could be linked to national solidarity, professional networks, political allegiance or union membership as well as various associational commitments, notably Masonic affiliation. Up to the Second World War, Masonic lodges in the *Seine-banlieue* built a personal network that was influential, yet operated at a shadowy level. The silence surrounding the identity of their members was broken by the implementation of the Vichy government's repressive and discriminatory legislation against 'secret societies'. The law of 11 August 1941 had the effect of revealing the active role of certain Freemasons in leading *secrétaires de mairie* to suspend their work, following the example of the *secrétaires généraux* of Suresnes and Saint-Maur-des-Fossés.

Although difficult to quantify, the politicization of municipal administration did not generally affect *secrétaires généraux* until the 1970s. Hitherto this group had an entrenched position as collaborators with municipal power and did not feel the need to resort to political activism. However, there were some incidences of politically based recruitment. At the beginning of the 1920s, partisan appointments in municipalities under left-wing control focused principally on the industrial public enterprises. In the words of former socialist and communist elected representatives, this mode of recruitment reflected 'a political preoccupation of the time', that of gathering together a nucleus of sympathizers in order to influence particular municipal policies.[9] Yet, in practice, the slow turnover of existing municipal staff and the controlling power held by the prefectoral authorities considerably limited opportunities for creating new jobs with underlying political objectives. Additionally, at a time of sometimes radical political changeover in the *mairies*, the prudent 'wait-and-see' strategy of municipal employees undoubtedly facilitated smooth transitions and administrative continuity.

Recruitment by qualifications, especially university degrees, represented one of the last routes of access to *mairie* jobs in the *Seine-banlieue*. At the turn of the twentieth century, municipal employment was conspicuous by the absence of such personnel, with the exception of a few qualified staff among the *secrétaires de mairie*. The formal education level of *mairie* staff rarely exceeded the *certificat d'étude complémentaire* or the *brevet élémentaire*. For instance, during the 1920s and 1930s in Pantin, only one employee out of more than 2000 held a higher education degree: the assistant *secrétaire*, who had passed the first half of the *baccalauréat*. At the same time, the mayors of the Paris region encountered considerable difficulty in appointing engineers to head their technical services. The dearth of qualified staff aroused alarmist reactions not only from superior authority, but also from municipal officers themselves. Particularly outspoken was Aimé Malvardi, the assistant legal officer for the city of Toulon, who witheringly likened the *mairie* to a 'refuge for incompetents' (Malvardi 1928).

However, in the aftermath of the First World War, the feminization of administrative services enhanced the educational qualifications of municipal workers. A particular stimulus was managerial concern to rationalize the municipal machine, notably with the introduction of typewriters. The entry of female stenographers symbolized the political will to promote new technical know-how sanctioned by vocational training certificates. The formal recognition of Pigier school training permitted a generation of women born at the turn of the twentieth century to rise rapidly through the internal promotion structures and even achieve the elevated positions of assistant head and head of office. Yet the development of women's careers struggled against the ingrained hierarchical constraints of the municipal administration. Among these former '*sténo*', only two reached management level within the *secrétariat general*: in Bobigny in 1928 and in Pantin in 1936. Moreover, until 1945, only one was tenured in the post of *secrétaire général* and the terms '*femme d'autorité*' and '*maitresse-femme*' used to describe her were clearly discriminatory.[10] Even the recognition in 1944 of women as full French citizens did not change their prospects of professional advancement. By 1960, as in 1950, out of the 84 *secrétariats de mairie*, women managed only three.

Confronted by territorial transformations, the inter-war municipal leaders of the *Seine-banlieue* sought to surround themselves with educated and competent personnel. In 1922, the opening of a department of administrative improvement (*section de perfectionnement administratif*) by the *conseil général* of the Seine was tangible evidence of the growing training needs of municipal management with ever-expanding prerogatives. Henri Sellier, mayor of Suresnes and *conseiller général* of the Seine, was the promoter of the school for administrative training, rebaptized ENAM (*Ecole nationale d'administration municipale*) in 1929 and adjoined to the Institute of Urban Planning (*Institut d'Urbanisme*) at the University of Paris. The programme was at first open only to employees of the *département* of the Seine, but from 1925 it was extended to those in provincial cities, thanks to the inauguration of correspondence courses. According to the judgment of Malvardi (1928), ENAM trained 'true city administrators', and it was recognized by the prefectoral corps of the Ministry of the Interior as providing the best professional instruction for local administration. During the 1930s, the number of *secrétaires généraux* graduating from ENAM increased from 17 to 43.[11] Students were recommended or chosen by the *secrétaires de mairie*, and for 50 years thereafter the school accommodated three successive generations of municipal employees. ENAM was therefore not a general means of access to municipal service, but rather a higher level of training for a select number of deserving staff already in service.

At the more general level, competitive examination was introduced in all municipalities of more than 5000 inhabitants by legislation of 23 October 1919. However, this did not radically modify methods of recruitment. Indeed, until the 1960s, the appointment of applicants who passed the examination and were listed as qualified continued to reflect the traditional appointment criteria, based on kinship, local roots, social position and personal and associational affiliations. This continuity even contributed to the organization of the examinations. Usually taking place within the *mairies*, they were judged by municipal representatives in the presence of *secrétaires généraux* and, from the early 1920s, prefectoral representatives. By the end of the 1930s, the establishment of the first intercommunal examinations of the department of the Seine had not helped to eradicate these entrenched modes of selection. Qualified local applicants frequently remained privileged, whatever their rank after the examination process.

Subject to the requirements of being a French citizen, in good health and of a mature age, *mairie* administrative positions represented the only means of access to managerial responsibility.[12] From the perspective of promotion opportunities, employment within municipal accountancy offices, the welfare department or the *secrétariat général* was an obligatory route for aspirants to the post of *secrétaire général*.[13] On the other hand, certain public services, such as customs, repair services, refuse collection, food markets and workshops (for men), along with schools, nurseries and community clinics (for women), were unfruitful ground for aspiring managers. As for 'external' managerial posts, the municipal tax collector's job, before its nationalization in 1941, was especially coveted. This was often given to former *mairie* employees who went on to become *secrétaires généraux*. Conversely, the post of chief architect and surveyor was invariably given to those from the liberal professions or to state engineers.

From the 1900s to the 1960s, three generations of *secrétaires généraux* succeeded each other. The generation operating before the First World War sought status recognition, the inter-war generation sought to strengthen its social position and the subsequent generation consolidated its professional identity. For all of these groups, municipal employment represented a conscious and planned professional choice with an anticipated long duration. Of course, alongside these career-minded personnel were other staff in the municipal bureaucracy, more difficult to quantify because they have left fewer traces. They were distinguished by transitory service in a range of jobs, from street-sweepers to school cleaners. Unlike these manual workers, who had a less stable social position and limited scope for career mobility, administrative staff were, by the end of the nineteenth century, far more secure and motivated. It was from this section of the workforce that the *secrétaires généraux* were recruited. Their stability was reinforced around three pivotal factors: the perennial and essential nature of municipal work, the possibility of advancement offered by internal promotion, and the development of a collective identity.

Collective identity and professional recognition

In the face of local power, the profession of *secrétaires de mairie* was consolidated through an associational network that transcended partisan and trade union divisions. As far back as 1862, the *secrétaires* of large cities had first combined to create a pension fund, following the example set by state workers.[14] It was from this early organization that the first professional association was structured, *l'Association amicale des secrétaires de mairie de la Seine*. Two other important dates mark the progress of this professional 'fraternity': 1922, when the programme of professional training was founded, and 1931, with the birth of ASSENAM, an association that, as its initials suggest, was dedicated to organizing erstwhile students of ENAM. All of these groups, from the professional association to mutual relief associations, knew how to compromise with their different negotiators, the representatives of state and local authorities. They thus placed themselves under the protection not only of the prefect of the Seine, of the head of the *préfecture* administrative services and of its director of departmental affairs, but also of the *conseil général* of the Seine, on which sat numerous mayors.

At the turn of the twentieth century, the professional advance of the *secrétaires de mairie* was achieved at the expense of another group within the municipal workforce, the *secrétaires de mairie-instituteurs* (SMI). These were staff placed in smaller towns, generally of a rural nature, and who held dual responsibility for teaching in public schools and assisting the mayor in his administrative tasks. During the 1840s and 1850s, the two main districts of the Seine had about 40 SMI, while the suburban municipalities had 70. Yet by 1906 their presence had dwindled to only seven in municipalities with a population of less than 900. The decline of the SMI in the Paris region contrasts with their national position. In 1911, they still numbered more than 24 000 and represented a significant 61 per cent of France's *secrétaires de mairie*. However, after the First World War, the cohesion of 'professional' *secrétaires généraux*, based in larger municipalities and who came to conceive of their job as heading municipal administrations, contributed to the definitive disappearance of the SMI. Although organized in union associations, they lacked specific administrative training and above all did not have prefectoral support. The SMI were thus abandoned by *mairies* in favour of full-time municipal employees, who were thought to represent a more solid basis for implementing policy and enforcing regulations.

The growing influence of professional *secrétaires de mairie* had derived considerable impetus from the success of the mutualist movement, based on two 'insurance' structures founded under the auspices of this group, and open to *mairie* employees. These were the pension fund, created in 1865, and the mutual aid fund, founded in 1867. This pioneering mutualist expression had forged itself from the pension fund organizing commission of 1862, comprising 12 *secrétaires de mairie* who represented colleagues from the eight cantons of the *Seine-banlieue*. Dismayed by the lack of enthusiasm from mayors in response to their original petition, the *secrétaires de mairie* called directly upon the Ministry of the Interior. The Duke of Persigny, Secretary of State for the Department of the Interior, and Baron Haussmann, prefect of the Seine, eventually gave them their support. From that time onwards, they received the support of 43 out of 69 municipal councils and the decree creating the pension fund was promulgated on 24 June 1865. Its statutes excluded manual workers, who had to wait for the decree of 21 August 1923 to achieve parity with administrative staff. Yet the second fund came into existence thanks largely to the efforts of the *secrétaires de mairie* professional association, which played a decisive mediating role between the different sides involved in the negotiation.

In the long term the pension fund was a crucial factor in extending the authority of the association of *secrétaires de mairie* of the Seine, made up exclusively of professional *secrétaires*. After several years of apparent dormancy in the late nineteenth century, this organization was decisively restructured towards the end of 1893. Thereafter, growth was rapid. In 1862, there had been 12 active members in the pension fund organizing commission; in the revitalized body of 1893 there were 29. Numbers subsequently reached 43 in 1895, 55 in 1908 and 78 in 1923. Significantly, in 1893 its honorary chairman was the head of personnel of the prefecture of the Seine, who took on this role in accordance with the tradition of prefectoral sponsorship. Paternalistic attitudes also featured prominently in the association's rhetoric; for instance, 'the senior members [must hand down] their experience to the younger'.[15] However, the objective of mutual support was practically expressed in the inauguration of a job exchange system for *secrétaires* who had been marginalized following the election of a new mayor, and were consequently seeking posts in a more congenial work environment.

Faced with the changing profile of political parties and the uncertain impact on the careers of its members, the professional association sought to maintain its privileged connection with the prefectoral corps. As a sign of this entrenched relationship, successive directors of departmental affairs occupied the position of honorary chair of the association. Nevertheless, ties to the prefecture were not wholly exclusive. Over 1896 the association adopted a position that reconciled both the protection and stability of municipal employment and the principle of local autonomy. In February of that year it had supported a national petition in favour of modifying article 88 of the 1884 municipal legislation, in a move intended to give the prefect the power to appoint and dismiss *secrétaires généraux*. However, by December it had come round to advocating a different position: 'The corporation runs the risk of failure, since the change to the law [article 88] is in complete opposition to the ideas of decentralization that are advancing every day.'[16] The association, while defending the specificity of the *mairie* employees of the *Seine-banlieue*, equally recognized the power of mayors in appointment and dismissal.

The history of the relationship between the professional association and trade unionism was more complex, inevitably marked by the tumultuous history of the French labour movement. However, even in this climate of conflict, the association played an essential intermediary role. From the beginning of the twentieth century, municipal trade unions had been divided among the 'confederate', the 'unitary' and the 'autonomous' trends, and the association of *secrétaires de mairie* continued to gather within itself this diversity of union sympathies. The context altered in 1947, when serious tensions threatened the unity of the association. Under pressure from leaders of the public services' federation of the CGT (*Confédération générale du travail*), who asked for the 'immediate abandonment of the term *amicale*', the association had to state its position on modifying its statutes and renouncing its associational structures. The attitude of senior members was clearly opposed to that of their union colleagues, but the latter's position ultimately prevailed. The protection of professional interests had from then on to be examined by the union sub-commission of *secrétaires généraux*. The change of statutes was adopted and the association altered its title from '*Amicale*' to '*Conférence*' in March 1947.[17] Yet the preservation of its motto, 'to harm no one and be useful to all', maintained the original spirit of fraternity.[18]

Legitimized by the early success of their lobbying, from the 1860s to the eve of the Second World War these *secrétaires de mairie* – the 'founding fathers' of municipal mutuality – retained their influence over the administration of the corporate funds of the municipal workforce. The statutes of these funds prohibited geographic mobility between places of work and largely contributed towards locking employees into a *mairie*. In consequence, job transfers in larger municipalities were practically always limited to the department of the Seine, and over the century between 1850 and 1950 only three *secrétaires généraux* of the *Seine-banlieue* moved to posts outside the Paris region, in Mulhouse, Reims and Tours.

The association of *secrétaires de mairie* reflected a broader movement from the end of the nineteenth century, when other associations that organized municipal staff came into existence. For instance, the associations of customs officers and municipal tax collectors became flourishing collective organizations that single-mindedly focused on their professional development and were compartmentalized into their place of work. This movement accelerated as the twentieth century progressed, and was marked particularly by the creation of two new organizations serving the interests of specific groups of workers. The first was the association of city engineers of France (IVF); the second was ASSENAM, founded in July 1931 as a direct outcome of the teaching of ENAM. The latter shared common values with the professional association of the *secrétaires de mairie*, to the extent that there was dual membership. Thus former students of ENAM who became *secrétaires* were still able to associate with their professors, who were often high-ranking civil servants at the *préfécture*, and contributed to the construction of a prestigious administrative network. Moreover, ASSENAM not only maintained a near monopoly of professional authority, but also wielded a certain influence on the choice of candidates for *secrétaire* posts.

Despite sometimes divergent interests, the different forms of professional associations had in common the promotion of unity and cohesion within their specific sphere of identity. The fundamental principles of these associations were summarized by a few key words: mutual aid, acquisition of new knowledge and professional practices, and independence from the various trade unions looking to federalize, horizontally and vertically, the diverse municipal workforce. Owing to this asserted independence, these associations received encouragement from elected representatives' organizations, *conseils généraux* and ministers of the interior. The mayors of large cities, where the majority of municipal staff were concentrated, were particularly supportive, including those of a radical and leftist orientation.[19]

As other lines of convergence, these associations could take the form of pressure groups. Thus, in 1934, Georges Décamps, *secrétaire général* of Saint-Denis from 1933 to 1944 and a spokesperson for both ASSENAM and the professional association of *secrétaires de mairie*, urged that state intervention should determine staff pay scales. This was despite the expressed objection of a number of mayors for whom governmental intrusion was seen as undermining civic liberties and 'the spirit of particularism that leads the smallest municipalities in our country'.[20] In this quest for emancipation, and in order to justify state interference in municipal affairs, professional organizations attempted to draw upon the legal obligation that mayors should recruit 'war victims' for certain reserved jobs. The coexistence of these different organizations, composed of distinctive professional groupings, suggests that the interests of the municipal workforce were fragmented. Yet *secrétaires de mairie*, bearers of specific values that were based on professional culture and collective solidarity, sought to federalize other administrative colleagues in order to promote a common base of demands. In this context, the profession of *secrétaires de mairie* assumed, until the Second World War, a linking role between mutualism, confederate trade unionism, local associations, municipal power and supervisory authorities.

In 1917, one representative of the administrative elite, certainly in the minority, was present at the creation of the federal union of municipal workers of the department of the Seine (*Fédération syndicale des travailleurs municipaux de la Seine*). Michel Verrier, the *secrétaire de mairie* of Pavillons-sous-Bois, was in fact the trade union's principal founder. Of confirmed socialist convictions, Verrier radicalized the professional association's position, while at the same time legitimizing union action in an effort to reconcile the entire municipal workforce. In the wake of the First World War, the need for national status in pay and conditions was seized upon as an instrument of cohesion that could transcend sectional differences. In September 1919, Verrier successfully organized a major strike of municipal workers in the *Seine-banlieue*, achieving for the first time the federal organization of substantial numbers of staff. According to the local press, notably the conservative *Le Journal de Saint-Denis*, this display of strength paralysed local municipal activity in the Paris region. The strike led to the law of 23 October 1919 that instituted uniform status in all municipalities larger than 5000 inhabitants and compelled municipal leaders to recognize union representation and accept the establishment of *paritarisme*, a co-management system of the workforce with an equal representation of town councillors and staff representatives.

However, despite the gains of 1919, the slow penetration of municipal trade unionism – more reformist than revolutionary, and created late – reflected the reluctance of certain *mairie* staff to participate in new forms of protest. Even at the time of the massively attended strike of September 1919, solidarity was undermined by the resistance of office workers, who did not endorse militant action. The backlash to the strike, aligning certain employees with the employers, is explained to a large extent by the perpetuation of 'wait-and-see' attitudes. These exposed the principle of loyal collaboration that lay at the heart of municipal administration, and which left little room for action that was based on trade union commitment. For all this, the unions, as with the association of *secrétaires de mairie*, were divided between supporting the greater integration of municipal workers with their state colleagues or defending municipal autonomy and the distinctiveness of municipal work.

After the 'dark years' associated with the Vichy regime, which unsuccessfully tried to bring the *secrétaires de mairie* under state control, the years 1944 and 1945 marked a definitive end to attempts at integrating municipal staff and the national civil service. The principle of municipal autonomy was then protected by the overwhelming support of *secrétaires généraux*. Nevertheless, two significant attitudes persisted within the profession. The first adopted absolute neutrality in the exercise of its functions. The second, evident in 1947 when the *amicaliste* structure of the association was abandoned, defended a more political concept of the profession. For those advocating the first approach, *secrétaires de mairies* were considered to be municipal

administrators, responsible for implementing policy whatever the
political orientation of the municipality. The loyalty of these *secrétaires
généraux* to the mayor was deemed indispensable, but, as far as politics
were concerned, they defended an independent and clearly defined
domain of intervention. As for the second approach, the *secrétaire
général* was considered not to be a neutral collaborator, but a counsellor
to the mayor, and thus part of the political power-base. The origin of
this movement went back to 1919, and Verrier was its precursor in the
department of the Seine. His example was followed during the
Liberation by the rare communist *secrétaires de mairie*.

Whatever the personal or collective position of *secrétaires généraux*,
as Jean-Yves Nevers has emphasized, the reconciliation within *mairies* of
three power groups – representing administrative hierarchy, political
authority and the dominant trade union – undoubtedly helped to pacify
social relationships.[21] In communist municipalities, trade unions much
more specifically expressed strategies in tune with the politicization of
administrative responsibilities.

Secrétaires de mairie and municipal power: converging histories

The collective identity of *secrétaires de mairie* inevitably depended upon
the close relationships existing between elected representatives and their
staff. Written into the municipal charter of 1884, this relationship
always permeated the recruitment, stability and reorganization of the
municipal workforce. From these legal definitions emerged a simplified
vision of staff at the mercy of mayors' discretionary power. Originally
perpetuated by professional organizations dominated by *secrétaires de
mairie*, this dark picture needs clarification.

In comparative terms, the respective histories of *secrétaires de mairie*
and municipal politicians display similarities, especially relating to the
long struggle of both groups for legal recognition.[22] While the social
position of the workforce was strengthened at the turn of the twentieth
century, as a result of statutory recognition, that of municipal power had
been fully recognized only a few years earlier, with election of mayors by
town councils in 1882. Yet another point of similarity was the impact of
professionalization. Administrators and politicians initially had been
trained 'on the job', in touch with local needs and responsive to the
changing urban environment. Over time this encouraged a more
politicized administration, especially after labour movement militants
acceded to municipal power. Reflecting their political interest, mayors
were able to create 'jobs of refuge', or, in a contrary movement,
'springboard' or transitional jobs. The porous borders that separated the

administrative and political worlds were accordingly revealed, as former elected representatives were appointed to work within the *mairie*. For instance, Michel Georgen, the first socialist mayor of Aubervilliers from 1919 to 1923, later became assistant accountant in his city of election.[23]

Conversely, while working in a *mairie* permitted certain municipal administrators to construct networks, their social position could also be associated with professional skills exploited by political parties. Michel Verrier, once retired from his post as *secrétaire de mairie* at Pavillons-sous-Bois, went on to consolidate a political career as deputy mayor, before becoming mayor of a Paris *arrondissement*. Georges Bathélémy, the former chief arbitrator for the *mairie* of Puteaux, followed a similar route by becoming mayor of that town. Gaston Chardin, municipal collector of Puteaux, was socialist mayor of Champigny during the 1930s, while another socialist, Alphonse Le Gallo, moved from municipal employment in Boulogne-Billancourt during the 1920s to a long career as mayor between 1945 and 1965. From the 1930s, the career path of communist *secrétaires généraux*, although a very small group, reveals that they could be useful human resources for the party. Legitimized by their professional experience and municipal background, the communists promoted the *secrétaires* in order to break the barrier between policy and politics. This was the case for the deputy mayors of Bagnolet and Bobigny during the 1930s. Fernand Roussel, former municipal employee at the socialist *mairie* of Suresnes, became deputy mayor of the same municipality at the time of the Liberation. He thus concurrently held two offices, as he was *secrétaire général* of Saint-Denis between 1944 and 1964.

Communists did not operate in isolation, and bridges existed on matters of municipal interest even with political adversaries. For example, during the 1950s communist *secrétaires généraux* presided over the French section of the technical committee of the International Union of Local Authorities, while its general committee was composed of socialist mayors, Christian democrats and the representatives of the Gaullist *Rassemblement du peuple français* (RPF). Nor were bridges between administrators and political activists a monopoly of so-called 'leftist' municipalities. Charles Deutschmann, a former municipal collector, was elected RPF mayor of Levallois-Perret from 1947 to 1965. Of the same political persuasion, Jean-Claude Caron, *secrétaire général* of several suburban *mairies*, later embarked on a political career as deputy mayor and *conseiller général* of Rueil, just as Charles Jobelin, *secrétaire général* of Nogent-sur-Marne from 1907 to 1929, was elected mayor of the municipality from 1947 to 1954.

The history of the *secrétaires généraux* was punctuated by brief periods of political radicalism, notably after the First World War and during the post-Liberation period of 1944–45. Yet, taken as whole, the politicization of managerial jobs was limited and late in coming. Accordingly, in 1919, a year of concerted action for the socialists of SFIO (*Section française de l'Internationale ouvrière*) in 24 of the 80 municipalities that made up the *Seine-banlieue*, electoral representation was altered considerably, but did not impinge on administrative stability and continuity. The spoils system or sanctions that could have affected *secrétaires* at this time of transition were completely non-systematic. Similarly, the municipal elections of 1935 were characterized by gains for the French communist party, which increased its number of mayors from nine to 26. However, political change did not upset the careers of the *secrétaires de mairie*. From the 1920s to the 1970s, the *secrétaires généraux* of communist-dominated Montreuil, Ivry, Aubervilliers, Drancy, Colombes, Bobigny and Pantin were never party members. Deriving strength from their ENAM training, these high-ranking officers benefited from internal promotion, priding themselves on their professional skills, their political neutrality and their loyal collaboration.

In the militant municipalities of the *Seine-banlieue*, comparing the role of *secrétaires de mairie* to classic forms of 'clientary politicization' appears to be ill-founded, at least until the 1970s. Instead, the common history of the *secrétaires* and politicians derived from 'divided legitimacy'. Universal suffrage legitimized elected representatives, professionalization legitimized municipal administrators, and the two processes were intertwined. Following the First World War, the achievements of Henri Sellier in Suresnes, especially his distinctive brand of 'municipal socialism', were sources of recognition and cohesion not just for the socialists but also for the administration (Burlen 1987). In the same way, the success of 'municipal communism' during the postwar period, exemplified in the municipality of Saint-Denis by Auguste Gillot, was inseparable from the professionalism of its *secrétaire général*, Fernand Roussel (Gillot 1986). More generally, the Saint-Denis workforce was committed to the municipal project. The authoritative position of communist and socialist mayors in the municipalities of Aubervilliers, Saint-Denis and Suresnes depended largely on the acquisition of administrative experience and knowledge. Elected office and municipal intervention thus legitimized the professional qualities of the administrator. Moreover, this convergence was reinforced by the considerable longevity of local decision makers, *secrétaires généraux* and mayors combined.

In this climate of harmony, only the purging of collaborationist municipal administrations after the Second World War constituted a rupture. The political sanctions affected only a minority of municipal workers. Sanctions rarely exceeded 5 per cent of the total, with the exception of Saint-Denis, where the municipality had been under the rule of the fascist PPF (*Parti populaire français*). Here 131 workers out of 700 were affected.[24] Nor did they destabilize the profession of *secrétaires généraux*, as only 27 out of 80 in the *Seine-banlieue* had cause for concern. Yet, after the Liberation, the principle of 'loyal collaboration' between mayor and *secrétaire de mairie* became highly suspect. Between 1940 and 1944, numerous *secrétaires* agreed to 'collaborate' with the leaders of *délégations spéciales*, the Vichy appointed committees that replaced many mayors who had been elected in 1935. The appointment of three retired *secrétaires de mairie* to head the delegations further discredited the profession. In this climate of mistrust, the professional association of *secrétaires de mairie* intervened. Its new president was Pierre Sasseau of Saint-Maur, himself a victim of Vichy oppression as a Freemason. In October 1944 he pleaded to the association of patriot mayors of the Seine, the CGT union and the prefecture of the Seine for the 'reclassification or reintegration' of disgraced colleagues.[25] But the relationship remained difficult with the communist-dominated patriot mayors. These tensions focused on the wartime duties of *secrétaires de mairie*, which had, according to the communists, led them to 'professional deformation, in following prefectoral instructions'.

Yet, for the duration of the twentieth century, the purging of the municipal workforce, and *secrétaires de mairie* in particular, remained exceptionally rare. The stability of municipal officers, who represented continuity of action in public services, was the dominant model of management. Also, at times of political changeover, elected representatives coming from the left, devoid of sufficient municipal administrative knowledge and without contacts of supervisory authority, valued administrative continuity and internal promotion. However, the 1970s were a period of leftist political dynamics that finally put paid to this constant. In Epinay-sur-Seine, Bobigny and Drancy, as in the majority of communist and socialist *mairies* of the Paris region, a new development ocurred. This was the recruitment of *secrétaires généraux* belonging to a younger generation, and who consciously asserted their political convictions and partisan ties.

Conclusion

Although advancing through internal promotion, the *secrétaires de mairie* occupied a unique place in French municipal administration. Their social status, working conditions and professional associations distinguished them from their subordinates, who seemed doomed to anonymous, undifferentiated and interchangeable tasks. Their attributes expanded relentlessly with the development of municipal services and helped to make this social group a skilled and homogeneous body unlike, in the words of Yves Lequin, 'those to whom one can do anything because they don't know how to do anything' (1992). In consequence, the *secrétaires de mairie* drew nearer to the management of municipal affairs and consolidated their position at the head of various departments.

This social category, characterized by strong disparities according to size of municipality, the number of staff and modes of management, experienced continuous professionalization. From the mid-nineteenth century, *secrétaires de mairie*, far from being destabilized by urban development, relied upon these social changes to make themselves indispensable. In this context, the recognition of their profession was a key factor in the disappearance of the *secrétaires de mairie-instituteurs* in the Seine region at the beginning of the twentieth century. Thereafter the professional *secrétaires* orchestrated the rationalization of municipal services and the specialization of *mairie* jobs. Under the protection of the prefecture of the Seine, which sought full-time municipal officers, they proved capable of implementing policy and working harmoniously with mayors.

To become an essential administrative link, the *secrétaires de mairie* of the Seine drew upon their interest organizations. These 'fraternities', concerned with maintaining their distance from trade unions and parties, not only demanded and defended the statutory guarantees of their profession, but also looked after recruitment procedures, with a considerable degree of success. This 'social reproduction' rested upon 'a family mentality', in the words of Edmond Podeur, a former *secrétaire general*.[26] The members of this 'family' were eventually trained in the same school, ENAM, and perpetuated their ties in its offshoot, ASSENAM.

Yet, within the context of these modes of reproduction, it is perhaps worth questioning the solidarity of this elite, its limited mobility, its divided legitimacy and commitment to reinforce the selection and promotion of municipal duties. Could these qualities not, equally, generate forms of inertia? Conversely, the relationship between mayors and their *secrétaires* was not reduced to a history of dependence often described as 'clientelism' or 'participatory or militant indebtedness'.[27] Analyses of these complex connections, often harmonious, sometimes tumultuous, expose the 'wait-and-see' policy, even mistrust, of *secrétaires généraux* towards political parties. For all this, the convergences and bridges linking these two legally distinctive categories did exist. The borders separating the sphere of administration from that of policy were permeable.

Notes

1. This chapter is based on work for a doctoral thesis on the municipal history of the Paris region from the end of the nineteenth to the mid-twentieth century, with particular reference to the employees. Jean-Paul Brunet and Michel Margairaz directed the research.
2. In France, *secrétaires de mairie* and *sécrétaires généraux* are both used to designate the person known as a town clerk in the United Kingdom. From the end of the nineteenth century the term *secrétaires généraux* tended to be used more frequently in larger cities, where the *secrétaire* was responsible for substantial administrative, personnel and service functions.
3. From an interview with Marcel Bietry, retired *secrétaire général*, working in the town hall of Levallois-Perret at the end of the 1920s.
4. The descriptions are taken from the author's oral source material, which consists, at the time of writing, of interviews with over 50 contributors.
5. From an interview with Geneviève Cahour, former assistant general secretary and assistant director general of the centre for training municipal staff (*Centre de formation des personnels communaux*, CFPC).
6. From the Revolution to the adoption of the law of 10 July 1964, which divided the Paris region into six new departments, this territory occupied a central place in the administrative fabric of France. Along with the city of Paris, it constituted an administrative entity, the department of the Seine, which was divided into three zones: the capital and the districts (*arrondissements*) of Saint-Denis and Sceaux.
7. In the wake of central government legislation during the 1920s, individual personnel files of French *mairie* staff have been particularly well preserved, hence their illuminating qualities in areas like recruitment.
8. During the early period of the Third Republic, the term 'is elector' was frequently added to job application letters. But municipal workers only represented (until the 1960s) a small part of the voting population, on average 1.8 per cent of those registered at the beginning of the twentieth century.
9. As expressed in an interview with Adrienne Maire, who had worked in the *mairie* of Montreuil from 1935.
10. She was Mlle. Gérain, *secrétaire général* of Pantin between 1936 and 1966.
11. Information about ENAM comes from the records of ASSENAM and archives of the Institute of Urban Planning at the University of Paris XII (now at Créteil), which include the matriculation details of ENAM diploma students.
12. In the early twentieth century, younger people in post and working towards a municipal career were few in number. Thus, in Pantin between 1880 and 1914, out of 107 employees recruited, only two were not of 'mature age', and their careers did not go beyond two consecutive years. The average age of municipal employees on appointment was 35 years. During a period of growth, generational change barely preoccupied municipal leaders, who remained committed to protecting their older employees.

13. These were notably welfare and social services, which created opportunities for women to become assistant *secrétaires généraux* during the 1960s and 1970s.
14. See the municipal archives of Pantin for information relating to the origins of municipal pension funds.
15. Municipal archives of Pantin, files of the professional association of *secrétaires généraux* of the department of the Seine.
16. Ibid.
17. Ibid. The term '*Conférence*' was more neutral than '*Amicale*'. The latter emphasized the corporatist tradition of the *secrétaires généraux*, the majority of whom were hostile to trade unionism up to the Liberation.
18. Municipal archives of Bois-Colombes, *secrétaires généraux* files.
19. For instance, Édouard Herriot, *radical* mayor of Lyons, Henri Sellier, socialist mayor of Suresnes, and Georges Marrane, communist mayor of Ivry.
20. According to Georges Décamps, *secrétaire général* of Saint-Denis.
21. See Chapter 9 of the present volume.
22. Information about *secrétaires généraux* and political activism was taken from the *Maitron*, the biographical dictionary of the French labour movement from 1789 to 1939 (*Dictionnaire biographique du mouvement ouvrier*, Paris: l'Atelier, 44 volumes). Additionally, much material was gathered from interviews, whether with former *mairie* employees or with elected representatives. Individual municipal archives further augmented biographical and oral sources, notably about career and employment patterns.
23. From the nineteenth century it was prohibited for elected representatives to hold a job paid out of the budget of their city of election.
24. Sanctions affected Saint-Denis principally in terms of demotion and termination of service. Between 1940 and 1944, under the Vichy regime, such strictures principally affected active communists. In Saint-Denis, 43 workers were dismissed.
25. Municipal archives of Bois-Colombes, *secrétaires généraux* files.
26. From an interview with Edmond Podeur. The Vichy government had made him mayor of a communist municipality, whose existing mayor had been proscribed.
27. These expressions come from a research seminar (University of Paris I, 1999–2000) and refer specifically to the political allegiances of municipal employees and their relationship to power structures within the *mairie*. Especially in communist and socialist-controlled municipalities, this frequently meant more than collaboration: it reflected conscious political commitment.

CHAPTER SEVEN

A model for the emerging welfare state? Municipal management in Montreal during the 1930s

Michèle Dagenais

From the last decades of the nineteenth century to the 1910s, North American reformers were responsible for the adoption of a multitude of measures aimed at transforming urban life, and, in so doing, greatly enriched future thinking on local governments and their activities. It would be difficult today to imagine such an array of technicians, architects, urbanists, social workers, activists, militants, economists or simple citizens interested in determining road widths, planning neighbourhood parks and linking up sewer networks (Monkkonen 1988: 220–22). Nevertheless, this was the case one century ago. The active involvement of all these groups spoke of the importance and visibility of local government. Yet starting from the 1920s and increasingly in the 1930s almost all these apostles of modern management would abandon local institutions to turn their attention to upper-level governments.[1] Could this explain why historians and social scientists studying the 1930s have also chosen to concentrate on national governments at the expense of their municipal counterparts?

In his synthesis of American municipal history, Eric Monkkonen also stresses that local governments, having experienced a sort of golden age at the end of the nineteenth century and the beginning of the twentieth, fell into oblivion not long after. Monkkonen lays the blame for this fate on the very success of the reformers who had fought to bureaucratize and professionalize the management of municipal services. Municipal authorities, which had often tried to curb the harmful effects of urban growth with makeshift measures at the end of the nineteenth century, were for the most part able to control the situation by the beginning of the twentieth. In so doing, many of the questions linked to urban development, which had previously sparked impassioned debates, no longer generated much interest; they were now considered and treated as administrative issues. These changes were matched by shifts at upper levels of government, which took charge of public services and developed social policy by the end of the Depression. Therefore, just as contemporary reformers turned their attention primarily to national governments from the 1920s and especially from the 1930s onwards, so do the present-day historians, a fact confirmed by a recent survey of the literature in the field (Bender 1999: 214–15). The rare studies that look at local governments depict them as paralysed by the economic slump (Copp 1979: 119, Larivière 1977). In fact, so much space is taken up in describing the troubles plaguing municipal governments and their struggles to keep afloat under the great weight of their responsibilities that very little is left over for exploring the dynamics of local politics.

To what extent has the negative image of municipalities during the 1930s masked developments on the North American local scene during this period? Have existing studies concluded too hastily that local governments deferred to their national counterparts at the first sign of trouble? In the end, despite claims to the contrary (Mabileau 1993: 27), very few studies on local government exist to document the period. So what was really happening at the municipal level during the 1930s? It is with these questions in mind that this chapter focuses on Montreal during the Depression. Of course, the results of this study alone cannot change the history of local governments in North America, or in Canada itself for that matter. But that is not the aim of this chapter, which is to provide some of the elements which may eventually contribute to a (re)interpretation of this overlooked period in local government history.

The 1930s seem to be one of the most important decades in the transformation of Montreal's local government (Dagenais 2000a). Although the decade did not provoke the intense debates of the turn of the century, the Depression did give rise to new thinking about municipal governance and the direction in which it should go. Of course, the situation was quite different from the days when reformers dominated the local scene. Instead of a city hall with indistinct institutional contours, Montreal now benefited from relatively numerous and well-defined services. Like most North American cities of its size, it had undergone a period of reform and its administration had been partly modernized. After the extensive inquiries undertaken on its internal working at the beginning and end of the 1910s, and the adoption of a new charter defining its services in a functional manner and clearly establishing the division of formal power between the various authorities, the city's leaders felt that they had the situation in hand. This view seemed to be confirmed by Montreal's relatively smooth ride through the 1920s.

The economic crisis was particularly acute in North America and would provide a rude awakening. While dealing with its share of tensions and problems, Montreal also confronted a whole series of questions concerning the health of the city's government on the political, financial and administrative fronts. Worried, the business milieu rushed to its bedside and formulated recommendations to allow the city to climb out of the slump in which it found itself and, especially, to improve its management. If many of the suggestions put forward were not new, particularly concerning the electoral regime, others proved to be completely novel and sufficiently important to merit talk of a new period of reform in the history of Montreal's government. In spite of this, the historiography in the field, with few exceptions (Collin 1997, Nevers 1984), has not noted the changes taking place at the local level.

What was the nature of these changes? Certain reforms to municipal accounting and to the management of city employees' careers were reminiscent of those adopted during the preceding period and subsequently abandoned. Others fell into line with the existing movement to professionalize certain categories of employees, including the establishment of administrative personnel to serve elected representatives.[2] These reforms mark an important development in the way that local leaders conceived of the role of municipal institutions. For example, new services were created to respond, not only to municipal problems (Dagenais 2000b, Magnusson 1983),[3] but also to largely urban problems of a social and public nature. In addition, the introduction of a new and strikingly original fiscal policy (Collin 1994) helped Montreal to diversify its sources of revenue and call on those living in the suburbs as well as Montreal proper to contribute to the municipal services they received.

It is likely that these changes derived not only from immediate concerns, but also from transformations both in elected officials' leadership and inside City Hall. Elected representatives had in previous decades been very cautious with regard to administrative reform, believing that these reforms, once enacted, would reduce their political prerogatives. By the 1930s, however, municipal politicians began to position themselves differently. By supporting the rationalization of municipal government, local elites sought to promote their capacity to govern despite the difficult economic situation. In contrast with their attempts to delay rationalization as much as possible in the 1920s, leaders now sought to legitimize their authority and control over the crisis by referring to the concept. Rather than placing themselves in opposition to the administrative sphere, they therefore chose to team up with highly placed bureaucrats and look to them for support. The appointment of strong personalities to the key posts of treasurer and chief of police, which had been vacant throughout the 1920s,[4] testified to this new position, as did the adoption of more modern and rigorous accounting procedures. The end result of the elected officials' attempts to renew legitimacy with reference to the administrative sphere was a rise in political importance for the latter.[5]

The elected representatives' new strategy was not sufficient in itself to transform municipal management; they desperately needed the collaboration of highly placed municipal employees. In fact, the bureaucrats themselves often stressed the desire for reform in public debates when they felt its presence too faintly. This is why it is important to be sensitive to the 'internal logic' of government (Joana 1998: 172), to understand the dynamics that lay behind the transformation of the Montreal municipality during this period.

City Hall at the start of the 1930s

Like other important Canadian and Quebec municipalities, Montreal held a certain number of powers enabling it to manage local problems. These powers were contained in a charter whose content could not be modified without the approval of the provincial government upon whom the existence of municipalities depended (Collin and Dagenais 1997). Thus Canadian municipal governments were not governments in the full sense of the word, as they had no constitutional autonomy. Nonetheless, in order to fulfil their duties, they were equipped with powers that they could exercise at their discretion. Rather than setting out a series of obligations, municipal charters (in the case of large cities) or blueprint laws (in the case of other towns) contained an abundance of optional responsibilities. Consequently, municipal governments enjoyed a certain amount of political autonomy.

During the Depression, 25 members led the municipal council of Montreal, each representing a city district. This body, which held legislative power, was dissolved and reconstituted at each biannual election. At the same time, voters chose a mayor to preside over the council. From 1921, however, it was in fact the executive committee that truly held the reins of powers. The committee was composed of five municipal councillors, one of whom presided.[6] A veritable decision-making body, the executive committee prepared the annual budget and, after submitting it for approval to the municipal council, managed the allocated credits. The committee was responsible for all initiatives regarding bylaws and all decisions had to receive its support. In addition, the body had the power to nominate and manage all municipal employees, with the exception of the director of departments.

After the adoption of the 1921 Charter, municipal departments replaced commissions led by elected officials in ensuring the functioning of the Montreal government. From this point on, the administrative sphere was endowed with a specific legal existence. With the onset of the Depression, seven important municipal departments divided the following responsibilities: finances, the secretariat, legal issues, health, public works, fire protection and policing. The heads of these departments could appoint and remove city employees, as well as regulate salary increases and promotions. Yet in all these cases department heads had first to receive the approval of the executive committee, to which they were responsible. A director of departments, who reported to the municipal council, facilitated communications between all these bodies and coordinated their activities. He attended all executive committee meetings and therefore constituted the principal means by which the municipal council asserted its administrative control. The position of director of departments was thus a key post in the Montreal municipal government.

As a product of the different reforms which took place between 1899 and 1921, this type of regime represents a compromise between, on the one hand, the demands of reformers at the beginning of the twentieth century and several department heads and, on the other hand, the desire of elected officials to continue to have a hand in the administrative sphere. This system marked the beginning of a major change in municipal government, of which the separation of powers, the recognition of the administrative sphere and a reorganization of municipal services constituted the most visible elements. But these official reforms were not sufficient in themselves to substantially modify the working of the Montreal government over the course of the 1920s. In essence, old practices simply continued within the contours of new structures, especially regarding elected officials' politically advantageous authority over personnel management (Dagenais 2000a).

The advent of the economic crisis, which hit the largest North American cities particularly hard, highlighted the limitations of the previous decade's reforms. Even more than during the important period of urban growth at the turn of the twentieth century, the Montreal government saw its responsibilities increase as its resources diminished (Linteau 1992: 415–16). Because the cities assumed the lion's share of social spending, Montreal had to lay out considerable sums to finance aid programmes for the unemployed and the public works it initiated. In 1933, for example, the city distributed assistance to 30 per cent of its population. At the same time, the Depression brought with it a fall in municipal revenues as many property owners could not pay their taxes.

Financial institutions suggested that poor management and exceedingly high administrative spending had placed Montreal in this delicate position. Although these criticisms were not without foundation, it is also true that City Hall manifested a real desire for change and decisively altered its way of operating. Nonetheless, over and above administrative reform, organizations such as the City Improvement League, *La Ligue des propriétaires* (The Proprietors' League), Montreal Real Estate and the *Association des marchands détaillants* (the Retail Merchants' Association) called for a reorganization of the electoral regime to strengthen the voice of property owners at the expense of renters. They also sought to restrict the number of officials elected to the municipal council, as had been proposed by reformers at the turn of the twentieth century (Gagnon-Lacasse 1965: 175–9).

The reform of municipal finances

From the 1932 election onwards, the question of municipal finances and management of the economic crisis became substantive issues, moving to the forefront of political debate (Rumilly 1974: 175–9). The Liberal deputy Fernand Rinfret, a representative of one of the two major national parties in the federal legislature, won a hotly contested battle against the incumbent mayor, Camillien Houde. Acting as an intermediary between the big banks and the business community and local government, Rinfret promised to reorganize the city's finances and exert more control on administrative spending. His election as mayor in April 1932 was rapidly translated into the adoption of crucial reforms, a trend that would continue throughout the decade. In fact, despite the reconstitution of the executive committee after each election and Houde's return to office in 1934, elected officials remained very receptive to the introduction of reforms. Although it is true that the actions of elected officials can be explained in part by the pressure exerted on them by financiers, it is also important to understand how they benefited from the changes. While the reform of budgetary procedures limited the officials' discretionary powers, it also allowed them a better grasp of the financial situation of City Hall. Thus informed, they could easily project an image of authority and competence, which was especially useful in times of crisis (Kahn 1997: 63). This explains why elected representatives, who up to that point had jealously guarded control over municipal finances, approved the project of practical budgetary restructuring.

Certain high-ranking bureaucrats were also very sympathetic to reforms. Throughout the changes in political personnel over the course of the decade, these employees were very important in ensuring the success of the reforms that they promoted. The lawyer Honoré Parent was truly a central figure in the Montreal government from 1930.

Having entered the service of the city in the law department in 1922, he was named the director of departments in 1930, at the beginning of Camillien Houde's second term as mayor.[7] He thus became only the second municipal employee to occupy this position since its creation in 1921. In his position as intermediary between the political, executive and administrative spheres, he found himself at the heart of municipal government. With close ties to the Liberal party, he seemed to enjoy the esteem and respect of many, especially businessmen and financiers (Rumilly 1974: 244, 1975: 14). Contrary to his predecessor who, having started as a humble messenger was able to reach the position of director of departments after 31 years working at City Hall,[8] Parent received this promotion less than 10 years after his arrival. Having the benefit of a university education and a good deal of important professional experience, and having taught at the *École des hautes études commerciales*, this influential lawyer conceived of his role differently from his predecessor. Moreover, he was better prepared to occupy such a post and to undertake reforms.

Louis Fabien Philie was the second dominant figure in the municipal government in this period. In 1929, this former assistant general manager of the *Banque provinciale*, an important financial institution, obtained the prestigious position of city treasurer, which had been vacant for almost 10 years.[9] He was thus one of the first highly ranked bureaucrats to occupy a management post without first having made his way through the internal hierarchy. As soon as he arrived on the job, he began his first reorganization of certain divisions placed under his control.[10] But it was mostly through his highly visible role in the major restructuring of the Department of Finance and of municipal fiscal policy undertaken between 1932 and 1936 that he distinguished himself. He was a fervent supporter of the modernization of methods used in his department and contributed to this modernization through his reorganization and centralization efforts.

Under the influence of these men, the Montreal municipality hired two consulting firms and mandated them to start an enquiry into the municipal government's accounting methods.[11] This enquiry took place over the course of almost seven months, at the end of which the firms handed in a withering report about the methods that were currently being used.[12] The accounting system, they claimed, was completely inadequate and out of date and could no longer respond to the needs of a government the size of Montreal's. This was why it was impossible to exert effective control over spending and revenues. The consultants made four major recommendations in order to rectify the situation. The municipal government needed to reorganize general accounting following the principle of expenditures and revenues; completely centralize control over spending; combine the functions of controller and treasurer into a new position as head of the Finance Department, henceforth concurrently responsible for revenue, the treasury and the city's accounting; and finally to make the fiscal year correspond to the tax year, with both starting on the first of May. Despite the considerable array of changes it implied, in December 1932 the executive committee approved the consultants' report in its entirety, thus confirming the municipal leaders' desire for change.

Over the course of the following year, the consulting firms would also reorganize the system of tax collection and put into place a general accounting division. Instead of the old invoices, consisting of a single copy written by hand, new ones would be produced by invoicing machines, which could make as many copies as necessary. The consultants also instituted an alphabetic index of all property owners on perforated cards containing a wealth of information on every individual. And, instead of sending separate invoices for each tax imposed on a property, it would now be possible to group them together onto a single bill.

As with the large private companies of the same period, the reorganization of accounting methods in the municipal government brought with it the complete mechanization of several tasks, with important repercussions for the organization of work. If the preparation and writing of bills by hand were monotonous and repetitive tasks, they became even more so after the introduction of invoicing machines, which made it possible to produce invoices at an increased speed. The changes wrought by mechanization had the potential to be much more disruptive, though. While the invoicing machines were simply grafted onto an existing system of work without transforming it, the same could not be said of the Hollerith machines that transferred information to perforated cards. Because these machines made it possible to manipulate information in an entirely new way, they completely revolutionized work practices.

Numerous city employees had trouble accepting the upheaval of the almost century-old operating system and resisted attempts to remedy the system's many troubles through the introduction of new procedures. More important, many saw their opportunity for advancement reduced by changes made in the existing divisions and even more by the creation of new ones. Certain individuals heaped blame on the consultants who made changes in personnel without taking into account the existing hierarchy or levels of seniority.[13] Municipal employees also reproached the experts for having taken advantage of their position to place some of their own employees in the most prominent administrative positions, thus violating the fundamental rules of equity.

These grievances were not without foundation. In 1935, the municipal government hired Lactance Roberge, one of the accountants working for the consulting firms, and right away offered him the position of assistant head of finance.[14] At the age of barely 30 years, this 'ardent supporter of the use of office machines and new methods of conducting business', was charged first with organizing the new Department of Sales and Income Tax.[15] Then, following the departure of treasurer Philie and less than two years after his arrival at City Hall, Roberge was promoted to the prestigious post of head of the Department of Finance. Roberge would occupy this new position, created in the reorganization of the department, without interruption until his retirement in 1968. His first assistant, himself a chartered accountant, worked in a consulting firm prior to his employment in local government.[16] Then, at the age of 25, he was appointed assistant to the municipal head accountant and two years later was promoted to the position of head accountant. When Roberge was named as director, this man became his first deputy. This assistant's quick success at City Hall testifies, just like Roberge's own, to the adoption of new criteria in the selection of high-ranking bureaucrats in finance: education and youth.

The move to professionalize highly ranked bureaucrats in the financial sector also spread to certain other job categories in the new divisions created by the reorganization of the Department of Finance. Thus, just as other municipal services at this time benefited from the arrival of highly qualified technical personnel to respond to the growing demands of the city (notably in the areas of health and public works), the Department of Finance also tended to recruit personnel who possessed particular competencies and specialized training in the context of the modernization of municipal accounting (Gagnon 1991: 178–81). The city therefore increasingly valued training over experience and maturity in the recruitment of its staff.

A new taxation system

As important as it was, the reorganization of municipal finances was not sufficient in itself to resolve all of Montreal's budgetary problems. Despite the fact that it was forbidden by the municipal charter, the city repeatedly finished its fiscal year with a deficit. The constant fall in its revenues during the Depression, coupled with the need to provide a large portion of assistance to the unemployed, revealed the rigidity of habitual sources of revenue. The city thus had to seek substantial loans to finance its new responsibilities, placing it in a position of dependency *vis-à-vis* financial institutions.

Unable to count on the provincial government, which had remained very conservative in the area of social policy and was concerned about keeping its budget balanced, the city was forced to find other solutions. In this context, Camillien Houde, who was elected mayor again in 1934, forged links to the business community and set out to transform Montreal's taxation system (Pick 1939: 143–5). Approved by the provincial government, the fiscal pact that resulted included a rise in the existing tax rate and the addition of two new sources of revenue: a retail sales tax and an individual income tax.[17] These taxes would soon constitute a significant contribution to the city's coffers, representing 10 per cent of the municipal budget.

These new sources of revenue were major innovations in the taxation system. First, they had the effect of enlarging the body of taxpayers while at the same time keeping the individual tax rate relatively low. Sales tax was added to all purchases, with the exception of basic necessities, while income tax was established on a progressive basis and applied to all individuals, whether they resided in the city of Montreal or not. Therefore the fiscal reforms were also innovative in a geographical sense. In order to prevent commercial activity, industries and high-income households from moving to the suburbs, Montreal obtained the right to collect the new taxes in eleven municipalities on the island of Montreal. The revenues derived from the taxes would subsequently be redistributed between municipalities proportionately, according to population. In this period, Montreal, New York and New Orleans were the only cities in North America to impose sales tax. As for income tax, Philadelphia and Montreal were the only cities to introduce it before the end of the 1930s.

Montreal's fiscal reform must also be understood in terms of the development of municipal spending. As Montreal enlarged its fiscal base, its spending also evolved towards a larger redistribution. Thus services to property (policing, fire protection and urban infrastructure), which tied up 66.9 per cent of budgetary resources in 1932, represented only 64.1 per cent in 1940–41. At the same time, spending on services destined for individuals (welfare, health, parks and recreation) jumped from 17.9 per cent in 1932 to 25.7 per cent in 1940–41. Although these changes were certainly not revolutionary, they clearly indicate that the municipal government increasingly concerned itself with urban problems by offering services, not only in the areas of housing and recreation, but also in city planning.

This growth in municipal activities was translated into the appearance of several new divisions and departments. In 1933, Montreal organized an unemployment commission to administer all municipal assistance programmes to the unemployed on its own;

previously these had been entrusted to philanthropic organizations (Copp 1979: 117, 124, Larivière 1977).[18] That same year, the city founded an economic development section to produce studies on certain aspects of Montreal's recent development, notably on the growth of the industrial sector.[19] In addition, four new departments were created after 1928: the stores and sales department, the estimates department (both of which were previously part of the Department of Finance), the welfare department (the former unemployment commission) and the city planning department, which was responsible for questions linked to traffic, housing, zoning and green spaces (Léonard 1973). By 1941, there were 11 departments altogether. The government thus began to turn towards political planning and away from the ad hoc measures it had previously adopted.

In short, far from being paralysed by the economic crisis and powerlessly enduring its effects, the city adopted fiscal tools and enlarged its field of action to include public welfare and urban planning. When we realize that, during the same period, upper levels of government still held a very non-interventionist vision of their role, the importance of the changes made by City Hall becomes even more evident.

New tools for managing the workforce

The Depression made municipal leaders more sensitive to the need to rationalize their management by tightly circumscribing various aspects of bureaucratic careers. Having lain dormant throughout the 1920s, essentially due to the lack of support on the part of elected officials, concerns about personnel resurfaced in the 1930s. One after the other, arrangements concerning retirement plans and salary scales were adopted and, more importantly, applied.

First envisioned at the end of the nineteenth century, a permanent retirement plan for city employees was created in 1932. It therefore took over 30 years to resolve the problem of the retirement of ageing bureaucrats. Of course, in the meantime, the municipal government adopted other regulations in this area, but these were makeshift measures that satisfied neither department heads nor their employees. In 1929, the arrival of a new treasurer and, the following year, the nomination of a new Director of Departments paved the way for the adoption of the new retirement plan. As neither of the new appointees had experienced much contact with city employees, it was much easier for them to deal with the latter at retirement time. For their part, employees responded when the Depression hit by calling for the adoption of a retirement plan that promised greater security for their golden years. In this context, a comprehensive bylaw was passed in 1931,[20] and received the approval of the majority of municipal employees a few months later.[21] Twelve pages long and containing over 30 articles, the new bylaw left nothing to chance. The municipal government could forthwith hide behind a legal text to force its older unproductive employees to retire without having to assume the unpleasant responsibility for the decisions it made.

Personnel classifications and wage scales for determining salaries were also updated in the 1930s. The remuneration principle was out of date shortly after it was adopted for the first time in 1920, not only as a result of a change in government at City Hall, but also because it proved inadequate.[22] Over the course of the next decade, the executive committee's stated desire to restrict administrative spending made it possible for the government to enact reform. Here again, the adoption of reforms benefited from the support of a number of upper-level bureaucrats. Restructuring established the municipal government's hierarchy on a radically different basis, in that it substituted employment categories for individual assessment. In the long run, government structure came to mirror management models presented in graphs and diagrams. These models even seemed to ensure the efficient functioning of local government and to soothe the discontent of city employees who saw in the reforms the promise of more equitable remuneration.

Through these measures, the government established crucial aspects of bureaucratic careers on a new basis. Instead of determining retirements and salary on an individual basis through interpersonal contact, the administration turned to a method of allocating resources based on pre-established criteria that, at least in principle, no longer took account of each person's particular situation. Were all these new measures truly effective? Did they really make it possible to reduce the cost of running the Montreal government? Only an exhaustive study of the budgets passed over the course of these years could answer these questions. However, from the point of view of control exerted over municipal employees, the reforms were a great success. Thus, in systematically keeping personnel files that were linked to the new retirement plan, the government was able to follow closely the careers of its employees and to obtain information on multiple facets of their professional or even personal lives at any moment. In the same vein, centralizing the pay system and keeping data cards on each employee made it possible to monitor the personnel's movements and salary deductions due to absence. In short, thanks to all these methods and many others, the municipal government established the principle of control as a common management technique. The introduction of rules to define the multiple facets of municipal employment also contributed to limiting the intervention of elected officials in this domain. The transfer of competencies that resulted from this introduction accentuated the weight of the administrative sphere to the detriment of the political and, in this way, increased the power of bureaucrats.

Conclusion

While the current interpretation of the 1930s presents a stormy municipal context in which politicians combated both the recession and accusations of poor management, analysing the inner workings of the Montreal government suggests the need for a more nuanced approach. Contrary to the business world's widely accepted idea that city management was anarchic and disorganized, the government was, in many ways, run from the Depression on as a modern bureaucracy. Its accounting methods were entirely restructured to keep track of the financial situation of the city at all times. Even the provincial and federal government could not boast of such a feat at this point (Gow 1986: 147–51, Hodgetts et al. 1975, chapter 7, Kahn 1997).[23] In addition, the adoption of a retirement plan and the reintroduction of pay scales gave rise to a certain uniformity in work conditions and made it possible to determine remuneration and promotions on the basis of merit. Finally, Montreal adopted new fiscal measures that allowed it to diversify its sources of revenue; these measures would soon inspire upper levels of government to follow suit.

But who and what should be credited for the radical transformation of the way municipal government worked? As has been mentioned previously, the context of the Depression greatly favoured the process of rationalizing municipal management. The budgetary constraints that administrators faced were powerful incentives in this regard and, in fact, were partly responsible for the enquiry into the city's accounting system, the reorganization of the Department of Finance and the adoption of the new taxation system. Pressure exerted by the business milieu over the course of the decade also encouraged elected officials to better control the direction of municipal affairs and the costs associated with it.

Even if his mandate was brief, mayor Rinfret also breathed life into the movement towards change, most notably through his role in establishing the 1932 enquiry. He was not the only one, however. The years in which Camillien Houde acted as mayor were marked by the adoption of important reforms. In addition, the executive committee played a determining role in this area. It showed itself to be particularly receptive to reforms, in spite of the changes in its composition from one election to another.

Highly ranked bureaucrats also made reform possible. The successful transformation of city government can be attributed first and foremost to the dynamism of certain department heads and their deputies and the notable presence of Honoré Parent, who was involved in all the projects. Parent was asked to step into a leadership role on many occasions and he sought to control the direction of the changes adopted. Reforms can also be explained by the ambition of certain bureaucrats. These men tried to impose their will and to shape the daily workings of government through the adoption of new work methods, which ultimately had the effect of reinforcing their hold over the administrative sphere. Even more important than the goal of improving the internal workings of the Montreal government, it was essential that the new reforms increased the power of bureaucrats over the entire administrative machine, including other municipal employees. At the same time, the transfer of competencies resulting from these changes accentuated the power of the administrative sphere at the expense of the political one.

Therefore, in the case of Montreal at least, the 1930s appear to be particularly decisive in establishing new methods of municipal management. Certainly, many of the ideas circulating at the time were not entirely new. Inspired in part by the solutions proposed during the period of reform at the turn of the twentieth century, they aimed at resolving the numerous problems caused by urban growth and the concomitant growth of local institutions.[24] In this sense, the 1930s can be considered as the outcome of a process of reform begun some decades before. Nonetheless, this did not signal the end of changes to municipal and urban management or to City Hall.

Confronted by problems of unrivalled proportion and lacking the assistance of upper levels of governments, the Montreal municipality was forced to find solutions to confront the crisis on its own. Local actors therefore forged new paths out of the Depression, some of which even led the transition towards a new style of managing economic and social questions. This study, although restricted in scope and by space, suggests that other municipalities, rather than following in the footsteps of the federal and provincial governments, may also have experimented with new solutions. In the process, they may well have provided a model for the changes about to take place at upper levels of government.

Notes

1. This is clearly demonstrated in Rodgers' important study of reformers (1998).
2. This is how the secretariats of the mayor, to the municipal councillors and to the director of departments were created in turn. Although they were not strong numerically – the number of employees ran in the low twenties – the nature of their duties conferred an undeniable importance on the administrative branch. In lieu of the almost total absence of organization that was the norm two decades previously, when all employees were indiscriminately grouped together in one secretariat, the 1920s marked a push towards a progressive structuring of these bodies and the increasingly precise division of political and administrative functions.
3. For example, those linked to the management of real property and which were thus in keeping with the initial mandate of cities as they were defined at the origin of the Canadian municipal system in the mid-nineteenth century.
4. In fact, elected officials did not appoint anyone to these posts, which remained vacant until 1929. In these circumstances, it was much easier for them to maintain strict control of key administrative sectors such as finance and security (Dagenais 2000a: 67).
5. This was also true in the case of Lyons during an earlier period. See Dumons and Pollet (1992).
6. The mayor was therefore not in charge of this important body. In fact, he could not even sit on the executive committee, which considerably reduced his ability to lead the municipal government. This arrangement, adopted under pressure exerted by reformers during the period of the municipal charter's introduction in 1921, was only relaxed in 1949, when the mayor became a member of the executive committee. He was granted the power to lead the committee in 1962 (Dagenais 1992: 27, 38).
7. See Ville de Montréal, Division de la gestion de documents et des archives (DGDA), personnel file of Honoré Parent.
8. DGDA, personnel file of Jules Crépeau.
9. DGDA, personnel file of Louis Fabien Philie.
10. DGDA, Rapports et dossiers de résolution du Conseil municipal et du Comité exécutif (Rapports), 3e série, no. 36498, report submitted to the Director of Departments, 24 February 1930.
11. DGDA, Rapports, 3e série, no. 43834-1, excerpt from the minutes of a special meeting of the Municipal Council, 22 April 1932.
12. DGDA, *État financier de Montréal*, report on the enquiry undertaken by Ross and Sons, Larue et Trudel in 1932.
13. *The Gazette*, 16 September 1936.
14. DGDA, personnel file of Lactance Roberge. Included in the file are numerous articles on his career. See in particular a clipping from the *Concordia* magazine, dated May 1951, which recounts his entry into municipal politics.
15. Our translation. DGDA, personnel file of Lactance Roberge, *Concordia*, May 1951.
16. DGDA, personnel file of the municipal employee, *La voix populaire*, 5 February 1947.
17. This section is based on Collin (1994).

18. See especially chapter 7 of Larivière (1977), which deals also with the question of assistance during the Depression in Montreal.
19. DGDA, *Mémoire concernant l'établissement de l'Office d'initiative économique de Montréal*, Montréal, 1938; Rapports, 3e série, no. 54468.
20. DGDA, *By-law no. 1149 to establish a pension fund for the officials of the City*.
21. DGDA, Rapports, 3e série, no. 41225-3, 'Résultat du scrutin tenu entre le 21 et le 24 novembre 1932'. Out of 1485 permanent municipal employees, 1280 were in favour of the new bylaw.
22. DGDA, Rapports, 3e série, no. 85655, Honoré Parent to the executive committee, 18 January 1946.
23. With reference to Kahn (1997), this work clearly demonstrates that it was following innovations adopted at the local level that the notion of budgeting spread to the United States.
24. This is also shown in the work of Rodgers (1998), 413, and following, where he demonstrates that several of the measures adopted as part of the New Deal were the result, not so much of innovations, but rather of reformist thinking from the turn of the twentieth century.

CHAPTER EIGHT

Municipal employees and the construction of social identity in São Paulo, Brazil, in the 1930s

Cristina Mehrtens

In 1936, a delay in the work to extend the Avenida Brasil in São Paulo prevented several municipal works department (DOP) employees from doing their job.[1] The avenue ended in a cabbage patch 20 metres short of a path already opened further ahead. Visiting the site, Mayor Fábio da Silva Prado talked to the cabbage patch's owner, a *chacareiro* (subsistence farmer).[2] The Portuguese immigrant explained to the mayor that the prefecture offered seven *contos* for the land he believed was worth more than 12 *contos*. Even if the prefecture agreed to his terms, the humble man thought it still might not be a good deal. It was common knowledge that the prefecture took a long time to reimburse people, and nobody would cover for him until he could settle the compensation.

Prado paused, considered for a moment, and offered to pay him the 12 *contos* immediately. Sceptical, the *chacareiro* nevertheless agreed. Though it was a significant amount of money, the mayor quickly gathered it from his personal account.[3] In half an hour, Prado had paid the *chacareiro* and instructed DOP employees to take down the fence around the land, prepare the site and resume their work. In 48 hours, the avenue was opened to the public. In a further wrinkle to the story, Prado officially donated that money to a children's park programme run by the culture department, with instructions that it be retrieved from the DOP. It took more than a year for the park programme to receive the money from the municipal bureaucracy.

São Paulo's urban evolution differed from that of most Latin American cities, which originally developed as bureaucratic, trading, political and cultural centres little shaped by the demands of industry. By contrast, São Paulo, although originally anchored in an agrarian landscape, underwent a process of rapid technological change and economic development after the mid-nineteenth century. With its improvised solution and overtones of cultural and socioeconomic change, the story above expresses some of the transitional ambiguities of a period that was marked by extraordinary rates of urban growth. This process gave birth to a new generation of elites, who oversaw the restructuring of professions and businesses and the reorganization of the workplace. Along with these social changes, elite groups negotiated their own specific circumstances by importing North American and European models of modernization and development into the urban space. Scholarship on this subject has reiterated the classic thesis of a disorderly society that developed without a comprehensive sociopolitical and urban plan, under ineffectual municipal governments. This chapter, by contrast, suggests that the gradual evolution of a central authority for São Paulo was not simply the inevitable result of the city's growth and the proliferation of its problems. In fact, technical firms, private companies and local public agencies all took on diverse and overlapping roles after the advent of the republic.

In this process, the development of strong government agencies such as the DOP became necessary for the formation of professional activities. This chapter focuses on the ambivalent spaces and social identities shared by municipal intellectual and technical groups in São Paulo during the 1930s. Although bureaucrats might not constitute a social class, in liminal moments they may form a powerful group whose interests stem from their origins and positions in the technical administrative apparatus and from characteristics acquired in their political experiences. Usually seen as expressing well-defined social identities, municipal bureaucrats share a variety of imprints and values from transitional contexts that orient their practices and attitudes. In São Paulo, this group ranged along a social spectrum between Mayor Prado, a representative of the vanishing turn-of-the-century farmer–engineer, and the *chacareiro*, the expression of a fading rural informal sector still very strong at that time. Municipal officials were responsible for part of the work-in-progress city depicted in that account. The city that emerged from the technical engineers' maps and the social engineers' studies reflected urban policies that contributed to a grammar of identity. These urban interventions interpreted and defined São Paulo not only territorially, but also within the minds of its people. The technical work and urban interpretations of municipal officials offer a window onto the construction of social identity in São Paulo during the 1930s.

The DOP employees: recruitment, administration and status

We lack specific studies on the history of bureaucracy in the Brazilian political system during the first republican period (1898–1930).

Nonetheless, there is a consensus that this bureaucracy developed under a centralized political system and survived with very few variations throughout different political circumstances (Barros 1992, Scherer 1987, Osello 1983, Terallori 1981). According to the dictates of local politics, private nomination was the principal method used to obtain staff. A network of relatives (*parentela*) and friends were often appointed to the highest positions. This patronage system was never entirely modified.

Even if the distinctions between those who had education and those who did not were clear, such criteria were porous in relation to professional competence, since formal education was not the only path available. After 1924, different construction professionals held a licence issued by the agriculture, trading and public works' state secretary, permitting them to work as engineers. There were three categories of construction professionals: the self-made professionals (plasterers, *fachadistas* or *frentistas*) coming mainly from the School of Arts and Crafts; the grand professionals (engineers and architects) from acknowledged universities; and the professionals with a licence (*licenciados práticos*).

In 1935, college education became a national requirement for any job within the municipal apparatus. Members of all municipal departments raced to get the obligatory diploma, a *coup de grâce* for most professionals. All São Paulo Polytechnic School (POLI) student files contained letters written in 1935 requesting diplomas from those students who became municipal officers. Departments within the municipal machine had to adapt and create new political strategies to enforce, or finesse, meritocratic policies. In this sense, the notion of meritocracy came to be negotiated by officers who knew that the world in which they lived did not work in meritocratic ways. The diploma was supposed to build a 'modern' bridge between merit and patronage. Nonetheless, authorized state institutions issued diplomas, and the forms of opportunity it created were to give patronage a new meritocratic wardrobe.

In the climate of national educational change of the 1930s, São Paulo underwent significant reforms that led to the creation of new universities. These universities – the Free School of Sociology and Political Science (*Escola Livre de Sociologia e Política*, ELSP, 1933) and the Department of Philosophy, Sciences and Arts of the University of São Paulo (*Faculdade de Filosofia, Ciências e Letras*, FFCL/USP, 1934) – provided both the intellectual and technical workforce and the assistance for different public entities. Municipal departments and institutes that were linked or formed part of the political administration kept recruiting engineers mainly from POLI/USP and researchers from the new USP colleges. The reorganization of the public apparatus was closely linked to and affected by changes in the educational structure. The change in the local administrative apparatus expressed both the processes by which office holders were placed and the institutions within which they operated.

In 1934, under Mayor Antonio Assumpção, the prefecture comprised 14 departments. The DOP, divided into nine vital divisions, was the core of the administrative apparatus and had disproportional weight in relation to the others in the structure. The DOP chart (including technical and professional occupations) maintained a confusing arrangement in which for each occupation there were several sub-divisions, categories and wages. Of all occupations, engineering enjoyed the most important place in the hierarchy, since a 'first engineer' received a better wage than the chief of registry employees, who was not an engineer. All the different wage categories reflected particular negotiations developed during the hiring process. The criteria followed the patronage logic of the period, with professionals hired according to both sociopolitical capital and professional competence.

Prado's new administrative reorganization, initiated in September 1934, resulted in seven departments directly linked to the mayor.[4] Under this arrangement, the DOP divisions were redesignated as registry of employees, urbanism, public works, roadways and additional tax on profits. These sections and their engineers performed a central role both in structuring the administration's policies and in enforcing these policies. The reorganization was set in motion in May 1935, after the retirement of the oldest and most influential DOP official, director Arthur Saboya.[5] Prado reorganized these sections and subordinated them to a director cabinet, which was directly linked to his own. This process culminated in the July 1936 Reform Act, when the DOP's procedures were modified to follow more completely the practices of Weber-style modern bureaucracy. The Act crystallized the changes relating to all municipal services.

According to the 1935 reorganization, engineers working at the DOP were divided into four main categories: the chiefs of division, the chiefs of sub-divisions or seniors, the juniors and assistants. The mayor had conceded permanent status to those in the latter two categories. There were also other engineers working under different regimes, such as on commission, substitutes and interim professionals, who were not included here. The DOP technical apparatus was usually recruited from three schools, POLI, the American Presbyterian Mackenzie and the São Paulo Academy of Fine Arts, of which POLI (established 1894) was the historically preferred institution. Of the permanent DOP engineers, more than 60 per cent were from POLI, 20 per cent from Mackenzie and 20 per cent from other schools.[6] Hence analysis of POLI and Mackenzie students who became DOP municipal officials can shed light on the formation of this group. Recent research by the present author has done so as part of a broader exploration of the origins and composition of DOP staff.[7]

Most of the DOP engineers from POLI and Mackenzie went to the few select preparatory schools in the capital.[8] Among these schools were the Catholic Diocesan and São Bento, the public state school *Ginásio do Estado*, the Italian Institute Dante Alighieri and Mackenzie. There were also a few engineers who had attended schools in England, Belgium, Portugal and the United States. POLI might not have expressed an explicit policy of recruiting students from a specific social class, but the school required of its students a strong educational background, the payment of expensive fees and full-time attendance. As a formality, their fathers or some other influential person introduced engineering students to the school. The few files with complete information about the fathers' occupations show them to be from the liberal professions (lawyers, pharmacists, engineers and educators), holding higher military posts (colonel) or possessing distinguished titles (one baron and one judge of the High Court, *desembargador*).

The fact that the majority of files displayed only the father's name gives reason to speculate about their humble origins, not only because occupational information was lacking, but also because of their foreign surnames and places of residence shown on their birth certificates. For instance, the DOP assistant engineers Horácio Marassa and Américo Bove were identified as sons of Italian immigrants who succeeded in small business as owners of a bakery and a small family beverage industry, located in modest neighbourhoods (author interviews, January 1999). Yet, during the 1930s, the majority of these parents could afford to pay fees, and there were very few students with scholarships. According to POLI's regulations, eligible students for full scholarship were divided into four categories: those whose father was a federal employee (*funcionário público federal*), those who worked to pay for their studies, those who were outstanding students, and those who had never committed a serious infringement of school laws. Invariably those scholarships that were awarded went to outstanding poor students or the sons of public officers.

Fit, proper and modern: the DOP engineer

Outstanding POLI students were able to choose an internship in public institutions, of which the DOP was the preferred selection. This was because the DOP had always enjoyed privileged status within the municipal apparatus. In 1935, at least 14 engineers had been outstanding students and all of them had access to their municipal jobs through the granting of an internship. For example, engineer Américo Bove requested the DOP's first section, the directorate of works of art, whose chief was engineer Nestor Ayrosa. As with most of the older engineers, Ayrosa (born in the early 1890s) had a history of working for railways that penetrated the edges of the state's hinterlands (*sertão*) and collaborating in private companies such as the São Paulo Tramway, Light and Power Company and Votorantim. In 1934, the age gap between a chief engineer and an assistant engineer was more than 30 years; however, in 1935 the gap dropped by more than 10 years. From this it can be concluded that, among other factors, Prado's administrative reforms had reinvigorated the engineering chart with a younger generation. From 1935, those working at the DOP had been born, by and large, around the turn of the century, and came of age after the 1920s. It was a young generation that experienced neither the initial paulista coffee boom nor the railway expansion, but instead was mainly experiencing the consequences of urban and industrial growth.

To cope with these transformations, engineers typically held two or more jobs, one with a small private firm, usually with just one partner, and another job in government. Alternatively, they sometimes hired themselves out on a consultancy basis to private enterprises. Another common practice was to buy a piece of land with relatives or friends, and then build houses to sell. These engineers became responsible for most of the middle-class two-storey houses (*sobrados*) constructed in different neighbourhoods in the city. Most permanent municipal engineers therefore did not have full-time commitment to their public job, and those who did so were officials who came to represent a solid symbol of continuity. Part of this group went from DOP internships to the post of DOP director. Others spent their whole professional life working as both municipal officials and professional engineers. Some of these municipal engineers commingled their jobs by entering DOP public tenders. Through their firms, some undertook to build schools for the children's park programme of the municipal culture department (DC) or public prisons or professional schools in the state's hinterlands.

As mentioned above, nepotism continued to exist, but it was not pursued to the detriment of the institution's work; instead it became part of its functional network. It also reflected the maintenance of certain social practices, such as the common tendency for sons to follow their fathers into the same successful profession, and the needs of urban, intellectual and industrial elites. Traditional practices survived mainly through the many employees who could simultaneously keep their private jobs and their public occupations. Reliance on sociopolitical connections continued to be an important strategy for entering the job market but, as evidence from POLI archives suggests, merit (a great number of outstanding students) and civic connections (participation in the 1932 movement) played equal or sometimes greater weight. The ideas of merit, loyalty and civic commitment intertwined and became embedded in the public institutions' hiring strategies. The examination of these practices enhances our understanding of the conditions of white-collar professionals, engineers and technical employees with a diploma in São Paulo in the 1930s. Some of these professionals became bureaucrats, others technicians and yet others politicians; all of them represented a salaried middle class.

São Paulo's public administrative apparatus had been radically transformed in 1930 by the coup that ended the coffee oligarchy's hegemony. Thereafter, the years that President Getúlio Vargas was in power formed an authoritarian drama in two acts: the informal Provisional government (1930–34) and the formal *Estado Novo* (1937–45). Here we focus on the vital, elusive intermezzo between the two acts. During this period, São Paulo captured the national market for industrial goods, as Brazilians substituted paulista manufactures for foreign products. The state consolidated its dominant position in the national economy and its militia rivalled the national army. With those assets at its disposal, São Paulo revolted against the Vargas regime in July 1932, with hostilities ending almost three months later. The insurgent movement had arisen from the paulista coffee growers' and manufacturers' unhappiness with the government coffee control programme (Davis 1935: 6). The growing subordination of the local and regional powers to the federal level was an additional reason for hostility between paulistas and the new regime. In their struggle for autonomy, the leaders demanded the return to a democratic, constitutional order and 'a civil and paulista government' (Bastos 1969: 263). Though neither the longest nor the bloodiest, this conflict proved to be the most extensive civil war the country ever had.

When the revolution broke out, a municipal Act demanded that POLI and its laboratories engage in the production of war material. This effort united the school and the state army in the same production, beginning a strong link between the technical engineering and state military spheres. Another crucial outcome was the technical development the engineering work brought to various needs of the state, such as bridges and communication. The last issue, published in 1932, of the *Revista Polytechnica* emphasized the important role that engineers still retained in São Paulo politics. Among other accounts, the journal referred to the exile and imprisonment in Rio de Janeiro of several engineers' leaders and provided biographies of 12 young engineers who died in the 'heroic revolution'. Some state and municipal leaders went into exile in Portugal or Argentina, but were replaced by counterparts who stayed behind. The presence of municipal engineer Saboya as mayor immediately after the revolution was symptomatic of the DOP's strength, as the municipal department was a bulwark and stronghold of 1932 ideals.

Politically, therefore, the 1932 constitutionalist ideals united this generation. In 1934, Paulo Duarte acknowledged that he had brought to the prefecture 'all [his] soldiers from the *blindado* who needed employment' (1976b: 175). From the lowest to the highest ranks, this pattern pervaded the local government structure. The DOP chart confirms that social capital related to 1932 had its payoff after August 1933 with the arrival of Governor Armando de Salles Oliveira. If the 1930 revolution had been the *tenentes* rebellion, 1932 belonged to the *majores*. All the engineers in Prado's administration had held important positions in 1932, most of them as majors.

The majority of DOP engineers in influential positions had headed inspection commissions of technical delegations (CIDT) during the 1932 revolution. Colonel Alexandre Albuquerque was responsible for the CIDT scheme and organization. After the revolution, he became a principal link between POLI graduates and positions in state and municipal government. In 1935, DOP director Saboya commanded seven chief engineers, of whom five had performed key roles in the revolution. Following the hierarchy, five senior engineers commanded or participated in CIDTs. Of these, two were considered 1932 revolution heroes: França Pinto and Adriano Marchini, who lost his right hand during grenade experiments in the POLI materials testing laboratory (POLI file 2101, Morgan 1934). Three junior engineers headed CIDTs and two others were collaborators. The military hierarchy was not repeated in the municipal chart, where commanders and subordinates worked together for the same wage, or subordinates were in a higher position. The revolution had the effect of provoking a status improvement, from the 1930 humble *tenentes* to dynamic *major* engineers. In turn, these engineers set an example and led the younger generation coming into public service. Though there were two engineer assistants who headed CIDTs, the majority of them provided a homogeneous example of professionals who were from São Paulo state, studied at POLI, and were, throughout their professional life, affected by the ideals of the 1932 movement.[9]

Another revealing aspect about this group relates to its residential profile. The neighbourhood where the engineers were raised usually set the general parameters for location, reinforcing a correlation between income and social status. Nonetheless, it is noteworthy that a project of

1935 stated that the city hall (*Paço Municipal*) was to be located in the northern region of the city, close to the river Tietê. The idea was to follow the examples of Paris and London, whose municipal headquarters were situated close to the rivers Seine and Thames (Duarte 1976a: 68). Perhaps this was the reason why so many senior engineers lived close to the riverside area in 1935. It had a key position between downtown and middle-class developments in the western region, the home of a disciplined occupational group comprising middle-class employees and professionals (Andrade 1996). Judging from this assessment, the archetype for being fit, proper and modern seemed to be a person who had moderate political leanings, strong belief in the 1932 ideals, immigrant descent (especially Italian) and lived in the disciplined middle-class district.

The DOP staff shared different backgrounds and expectations that nevertheless unfolded in the disciplined way municipal engineers were supposed to live and work. The effects that Prado's administration had on its officials' work and lives marked the transition between the old municipal system and the modern one. During this transition, technical competence provided a crucial alternative to active political engagement via the professionals' private and public roles in the job market, backed by their participation in old and newly created associations and councils. Moreover, the process of administrative reform made it possible for the new social engineers hired by the culture department (DC) to enjoy the same social and financial status already bestowed upon the DOP engineers. By 1935, the staff composition of both the DOP and DC suggested that varying sociocultural hierarchies coexisted in work practices. In the municipality, these boundaries were more related to an employee's role in the 1932 movement, and they gave privileged status to education rather than origins, residency or salary. This fact helped to create a mind-set conferring on professionals a status different from that held by the state military, bureaucratic positions or jobs in the tertiary sector.

From engineers to scholars, technicians and intellectuals: the *RAM* contributors

The municipal archives' journal (*RAM*) was created in June 1934 to publish historical documents of civic importance. In May 1935 the journal became the responsibility of the newly created municipal culture department, a vital part of the administrative structure directed by Mário de Andrade, the well-known modernist writer. *RAM* achieved national distribution and took the place previously occupied by the

Revista do Brasil. At the same time, *RAM* reached a huge technical group attracted to its 'public' nature and the scope of its articles. Its audience ranged from those who were interested in all aspects of Brazilian culture, such as students, intellectuals and scholars, to bureaucratic officials, liberal professionals, technicians and business people working in construction, trading and industrial companies. The journal was divided into four main sections, broadly categorized as archival documents and social research, book reviews and headlines, municipal organization and technical research, and official legislation.

Between 1934 and 1938, *RAM* had more than a hundred different contributors. Although most of them had no formal ties with the municipality, to some extent all of them maintained informal links, whether as professors at the Department of Philosophy, Sciences and Arts (FFCL/USP) and the Free School of Sociology and Political Science (ELSP), or as members of learned societies such as the São Paulo Historical and Geographical Institute (IHGSP), the Brazilian Academy of Arts (*Academia Brasileira de Letras*, ABL), and the Institute of Genealogical Studies (IEG/USP). The quest for social identity pervaded the discourse of the period, and was present in topics concerned with local, regional and national history. The main sources of information were the official regional registries controlled by farmers, judges and politicians. In a period when municipalities were being founded each day, their reports became intermeshed with the history of the community itself.

Most of the foreign intellectuals who lived and worked in São Paulo during the 1930s became involved in the creation of the social sciences in Brazil. Many were *RAM* collaborators, such as the Germans Herbert Baldus and Emilio Willems, French scholars Roger Bastide, Claude Lévi-Strauss and Pierre Monbeig, and the Americans Samuel Lowrie, Horace Bancroft Davis and Donald Pierson. All of them were part and parcel of the 1930s political context, which permitted transitions within different cultural institutions and built an influential professional network developed around the triad formed by ELSP, FFCL/USP and the DC.[10]

The DC influenced and was in turn deeply influenced by its foreign supporters. *RAM* presented an extended section under the headline 'The DC Abroad', which included supportive letters from representatives of foreign institutions. Among these were letters from North American officials, which reflected a significant network in São Paulo of professionals from Columbia University and various New York municipal institutions. Those who sent such letters included Jay Nash, associate professor from the New York Education Institute, Paul Vanorden Shaw, member of the New York Municipal Recreation Institute, Samuel Lowrie (given here as a University of Texas professor),

Joseph Lee, National Recreation Association (NRA) president, Howard S. Braucher, NRA secretary, and Lois Marietta Williams.[11] A former San Francisco playgrounds director, Williams became the physical education, recreation and games supervisor of the Brazilian federal culture and education department. Such links expressed the strength of the North American model and its impact on São Paulo's municipality in the 1930s. Although the ELSP did not have a North American mission equivalent to the powerful French mission at USP, its influence was still strong.[12] North American ideas permeated all practices in the municipal machine in the same manner that the French mission exerted its influence at the academic level.

Immersed in a process of cultural interchange, most of these professionals embraced new occupations as part of Brazil's immense middle class of foreign origin. The professionals' translations of their training were interwoven with contingent local practices. From New York to São Paulo, connections criss-crossed with appropriations and imitations.[13] Connections, saturated with concepts of identity, were often enmeshed in debates over domestic social politics. In this system of exchange, North Americans were deeply involved, not only in working in the socioeconomic administration (Lowrie) or academia (Davis), but in different professional spheres such as banks, schools, hospitals and trade. The North Americans and French came to Brazil either invited by powerful paulista entrepreneurs, or hired by the Brazilian government, or supported by American institutions. Additionally, there were other foreign intellectuals who were immigrants, but who exerted immense influence. For instance, Emilio Willems, later a prominent intellectual, had come to Brazil in 1931, 'anxious to escape a profound economic crisis in Germany' (Corrêa 1987: 118).[14]

However, even in Willems's refuge of early 1930s São Paulo, if economic prospects were bleak in the private sector, they were almost impossible in the municipal sphere. Before 1934, educators or writers chose the status of official, not as a professional option, but as a source of income. For instance, Paulo Duarte remarked upon the difficult situation of an ailing 70-year-old poet and municipal official. In 1936, the poet had petitioned the nationally known writer Monteiro Lobato to ask Duarte to improve his work conditions. Duarte was amazed to learn that this intellectual was a municipal functionary in the treasury division and wondered why he was not more appropriately working in the library division (1976b: 226). This account reveals a municipal apparatus whose leaders were oblivious to the experience of their professional workforce. Indeed, 'middle-class' professions, such as teachers and librarians, found their place in the public market only after

1935 as a result of initiatives such as the administrative reform and the creation of the DC.

One intellectual who had a decisive influence on academia and public administration in São Paulo was Samuel Harman Lowrie.[15] One of ELSP's first foreign professors, Lowrie was born in the USA in 1894 and received his PhD from Columbia University in 1932. He was hired by ELSP in May 1933 after being nominated by the American Society of Universities and the International Institute of Education. During his first year at ELSP, he taught sociology and had Sérgio Milliet as an assistant professor. In 1935, Lowrie was hired as a municipal officer (*funcionário por contrato*). His specific remit was to serve as a research expert in population analysis, a new position described in the municipal gazette as a social research technician (*técnico de pesquisas sociais*).[16] Lowrie reported to the chief of division, who happened to be Milliet. Thus Milliet, who was Lowrie's assistant in the academic environment of ELSP, became Lowrie's supervisor in municipal government.[17] Part of a blossoming intellectual network, Lowrie was also an active member of newly created learned societies and a member of the DC award committee. This body confirmed the contemporary quest for historical identity by fostering works that dealt with the creation of urban traditions. In 1937, together with Mário de Andrade, Dina Lévi-Strauss, Plínio Ayrosa and Artur Ramos, Lowrie awarded the first DC history contest prize to the biographer of São Paulo's first mayor, Antonio Prado (Fábio Prado's uncle).

In 1936, Professor Lowrie and his ELSP students developed a survey of the economic and social conditions of workers. Meanwhile, in the municipality, social technician Lowrie researched the origins and composition of the paulistana population and its urban community through immigration and the process of cultural assimilation. His conclusions followed the intellectual and methodological procedures of his time, but his studies were notably innovative in the use of survey techniques, particularly in the context of municipal government in São Paulo. Such surveys showed that population, urbanization and industrial growth were not solely quantitative problems, but were also marked by qualitative shifts of relevance to local governance.

For instance, municipal research traced the immigrant background of children enrolled in three elementary schools of the DC park programme.[18] Though this group could not be considered representative of the whole city, the report revealed that a very low percentage of blacks were enrolled, an approximation of contemporary working wage patterns, and that preference was given to boys in education. These first results, added to other works being developed at ELSP and the DC, were presented by São Paulo's municipal representative, Milliet, at the 1937

Population Congress in Paris. The theme he addressed was 'distribution of groups according to their national origins'. This and other pioneering research at the DC came to identify São Paulo's population as a society composed mainly of immigrants, with very few blacks.[19] Notably, two North American technicians, in conjunction with a group of middle-class ELSP students, conducted this research. *RAM* created a special section in its pages devoted to the DC social documentation section, where Lowrie published the concluding essay on the origins of children registered in the São Paulo municipal park schools' project. The final result revealed that there was a pattern of intensive ethnic segregation.[20]

In 1937, the process of analysing São Paulo and its population was complemented by the work of DC chief engineer, Bruno Rudolfer.[21] He divided São Paulo into administrative zones comprised of districts. One of these districts gathered together the three current most densely populated 'proletarian' areas. The study defined and demarcated the limits of what a poor urban area was, especially where ethnic segregation by circumstance was reinforced by the cultural segregation implicit in district planning. In 1936, the Jockey Club, which had been a symbol of a working neighbourhood since the nineteenth century, moved to a new 'garden city' residential district, constructed by the City of São Paulo Improvements and Freehold Land Company. Following the new cultural policy, the vacant space was donated to the DC project of model parks for poor neighbourhoods.

Immigrants crowded the outskirts of São Paulo during the 1930s, and migrants built new outskirts. Nonetheless, the reports about São Paulo produced by DC researchers crafted an official, culturally driven rhetoric of segregation that attributed to different areas of the city characteristics that confirmed or emphasized specific locations as the places for different social classes. While municipal intellectuals in their research studies invented a 'new' past, based on concepts of ethnicity and identity, municipal engineers built this new past into a present marked by sharper sociofunctional borders.

From 1935 to 1938, intellectual and technical writing in the municipal journal reflected the professional network that supported Prado's administration in these years. *RAM* proved to be the privileged channel that allowed for interaction among a heterogeneous group of liberal professionals, writers, technicians, intellectuals and officials from different departments. *RAM* served as the intermediary between the municipality and the population's practical needs, and between the municipality and other levels of government power.

In 1936, in an article about paving, DOP chief engineer Plínio Antonio Branco spoke of the importance of technical autonomy and its scope (1936b: 67–80).[22] The article boasted that successful use of this technology had improved public services. Given that these experiments increased the value of private companies' lands, the municipality also developed studies to tax these properties and to have the public share from benefits generated by DOP urban improvements. This was realized in the additional tax on profits (*Taxa de Melhoria*). The measure was instituted in April 1936 and a new DOP division was created especially for developing it. In the October 1936 issue, DOP engineers analysed the real square-metre value of urban land and evaluated the private sector contribution to the additional tax. This same *RAM* reflected on the impact of the new Act by publishing influential leaders' letters approving the tax. Highlighting the law's provocative context, this issue also presented real estate advertisements announcing that a private company guaranteed its clients 'all public urban benefits/services' on its lands (*RAM* 28, 1936). Nonetheless, at this time, the company was not yet being charged for the profits coming from these public improvements.[23]

Municipal engineers advocated that all public services be executed by private companies under public supervision and should be subject to competition. Accordingly, the old formula of unconditional public concession should be replaced by 'cooperation', a new formula that harmonized the interests of industrialists and consumers (Branco 1936a: 143). In the search for the limits and shared responsibilities between public and private, *RAM* stressed a liberal municipal approach to business, which struggled within authoritarian federal parameters. The studies of DOP engineers express the paradox of trying to create a modern liberal administration in times of anti-liberal and nationalist policies. For example, it was thought that changes in the municipality should follow a system analogous to the liberal North American city manager system. Quoting from the *National Municipal Review*, Branco argued that municipal officers should perform just like American entrepreneurs (1934: 34). Yet these ideas clashed with the political climate of centralization and nationalization. In August 1936, *RAM* defended public service and local autonomy and argued that municipal affairs should be exempted from federal and state approval (Teixeira 1936).

Though immersed in contradictions, the themes and subjects that *RAM* developed were timely. For example, when *RAM* published articles dealing with municipal concessions, light and power services were already being criticized and bombarded by the media. In May 1937, backed by widespread public discontent, the journal proposed that the electrical company allow direct DOP supervision to improve traffic in downtown São Paulo (Teixeira 1937). Moreover, *RAM* exemplified the municipal 'team spirit' in this May 1937 edition, with a DC official formally answering media criticism about the construction of a municipal stadium (Miranda 1937). Internal problems and the building process reflected a mixture of interests involving the municipality and two powerful private firms, the City of São Paulo Improvements and Freehold Land Company and the *Escritório Ramos de Azevedo*. *RAM*'s posture was anchored in ELSP professor Emilio Willems's essay on public opinion and the role of media (1937), whereas an article on public service concessions to private firms not only subtly referred to the theme but also explicitly offered theoretical support for the DOP director's decision to demand that Light and Power submit itself to total municipal supervision (Teixeira 1937). Thus municipal officers brought directly to civil society the work they sought to advance within the administration.

The October 1937 issue of *RAM* dealt with the municipal estate registry organization, CI (Zagottis 1937). Before its publication, this DOP study was presented to the Municipal Engineers' Society (SEM). This civil professional association evaluated the DOP proposal in a seminar that included the participation of DC and DOP officers such as Rudolfer and Branco. During the seminar, participants sought to mesh liberal ideals within a corporate organizational pattern. The study emphasized the role of the manager–engineer and stated that the municipal organization should take into consideration both the nature of its service and the engineering profession when building its organizational chart. There should be an autonomous division, specializing in specific municipal method and spread throughout the different departments. The study evolved and in January 1938 the engineers working on the estate registry (CI) section presented the taxation and real estate evaluation of the city (Zagottis 1938: 229). Backed by tables and calculus, *RAM* re-evaluated all municipal estates according to their location in the city.[24] However, less than four months after this, the *Estado Novo* put an end to these efforts. Mayor Francisco Prestes Maia's administration ignored the studies and effectively imploded their ideas within the apparatus.

After Mayor Maia replaced Fábio Prado in São Paulo's administration, *RAM* resumed its important role as a cultural publication, but lost its links with other units within the administration. It turned into an exclusive DC journal, rather than an expression of different municipal departments' work. In June 1938, the first *RAM* of Maia's administration contained the last article that Lowrie published in Brazil. He left his academic position at the ELSP and his municipal position at the DC. On 11 July 1938, the *O Estado de São Paulo* published a small note referring to a farewell lunch in the select Automóvel Club for Professor Samuel H. Lowrie, who was returning to the USA.

Conclusion

The 1934 constitution gave a job description of the new intellectual professional. Intellectual workers (*trabalhador intelectual*) were all those professionals dedicated to cultural practices (*atividades culturais*) and devoted to the 'development of sciences, arts, languages and culture in general' (Milliet 1936: 605). These professionals wrote a history for São Paulo as public servants in a quest for identity and citizenship. The municipal apparatus implicitly referred to issues of identity not only in its organization but also in its published written record. In the *RAM*, DC population studies researchers devoted themselves to understanding the ethnic and racial composition of São Paulo's urban population by surveying the living conditions of a working-class population that most of them were a part of, and whose spaces the social researchers delimited and identified for good. In this sense, Lowrie's inquiries into family budgets and the municipal engineers' research on new paving methods were part of the same routine. It was remarkable that most of these professionals were just ordinary officers or young scholars raising serious questions about the impact of urban growth. Issues of identity intersected with symbols of paulista political culture and melted away political contradictions in the common task of remembering 1932. The Prado administration's urban renewal programme was fully devoted to this task.

These symbols of identity effectively fused different political currents within the administration, one marked by a technical 'scientific' approach (the DOP) and the other marked by a technical 'intellectual' approach (the DC). The work of DOP and DC officials reflected both the technical basis of their urban politics and the political basis of their urban interventions. Each of these social activities, the reorganization of the municipal administration, the writings produced for *RAM* and the construction of visible symbols of paulista identity, was part of a transition through which the city of São Paulo was passing. In each field of endeavour, people were conceiving of or striving for a modern, professional, middle-class status for themselves and others in society. In their efforts, both public and private, they moved across or fell back from this threshold in circumstances that changed from day to day. The process was non-linear and non-rhythmic but, over time, it led to the self-conception of São Paulo as the middle-class, professional centre of modernizing Brazil.

Involved in many issues at the same time, these professionals contributed to a new capitalist society shaped by the rise of industry, urbanism and sociopolitical conflicts. As a result, São Paulo underwent progressive urban reform. Politically oriented, this administrative process determined where different social groups would fit into municipal reform strategy by ultimately determining the nature of these groups. Under the arrangements of the time, office holder positions intertwined with powerful political, technical and bureaucratic levels. Accordingly, professionally trained municipal experts became an important political group, incorporated into the municipal polity. In this context, many little-known professionals, such as Lowrie, Miranda and Branco, and some renowned professionals, such as Maia, Pierson and Andrade, developed their commitment to a broad spectrum of political reforms, from the development of social sciences to popular education, and from the extension of democracy to the improvement of working conditions.

In 1949, the municipality asked Nelson Rockefeller, the head of the International Basic Economic Corporation (IBEC), for professional advice on São Paulo's urban growth. IBEC sent a group of consultants, headed by urban planner Robert Moses, to report upon the city's more immediate problems. Moses noticed the political importance of the new professionals. He stated, among other factors, that unusual political conditions had turned the municipal government of São Paulo into a unique and unorthodox public organization, 'the creature of the state' (1950: 10). Nonetheless, he acknowledged that the work of public professionals could overcome this political condition given that good solutions resulted from 'the ability and sincerity of [those] officials' (ibid.). It was those officials, entrusted with the programme, who could muster public support.[25] Overall, municipal government assumed the status of manager and organizer by incorporating in its chart new social techniques and professions.

The 1930s and 1940s forged a new intellectual group in São Paulo in the form of waged professional employees committed to applying their expertise in the social arena. As public servants and professors, these middle-class salaried professionals assumed influential positions. Emerging from the 1932 political turmoil, the municipal body of professionals and employees helped to delineate a peculiar though concise work practice through policies and decisions taken as part of their daily responsibilities. Immersed at a time when blurred public and private sector responsibilities were starting to take new shapes, the technically oriented municipal employee was a person who brought together the skills of a property dealer, the academic rigour of an intellectual and the stubborn dedication of a bureaucrat.

Notes

1. DOP, the acronym used here, stands for all other names the department received before 1936: municipal works service (*Serviço de Obras Municipais*, 1898–1900); municipal works directorate (*Diretoria de Obras Municipais*, 1900–1913); works and highways directorate (*Diretoria de Obras e Viação*, 1913–35); works and municipal services directorate (*Diretoria de Obras e Serviços Municipais*, 1935) and public works department (*Departamento de Obras Públicas*, 1936–45).

2. Paulo Duarte, Fábio Prado's right-hand man, narrated this episode twice; first in his eulogy at Prado's funeral (1964: 40–41) and second in his memoirs (1976a: 226).

3. In 1936, São Paulo's mayor made eight *contos* monthly, the highest official municipal wage.

4. These departments were employee registry, treasury, public works (DOP), public services, juridical, culture (DC) and hygiene.

5. Saboya (1878–1952) started working as an auxiliary in the newly organized DOP in 1899 and became its director in 1928. During the 1932 revolution, he commanded a regiment formed by DOP employees (Cardim 1953: 346).

6. After the 1932 revolution, the federal government suspended the diplomas issued by Mackenzie (high school and college) and eliminated the course of architecture of the School of Fine Arts.

7. The author identified the engineers by name, the ethnicity of their surnames, place and date of birth, education (date of graduation), role in the 1932 revolution, residence and the different jobs they held, in the public and/or private spheres.

8. In 1935, the city of São Paulo had just one public high school (*Ginásio do Estado*, established in 1894, and 38 private institutes of which 24 were Catholic schools (Bittencourt 1990: 39). Of all the private schools existing in Brazil in 1939, one-third were in São Paulo state. Of all public schools, half were in São Paulo (Schwartzman 1991: 190).

9. The DOP engineers Cássio Vidigal and Henrique Neves Lefèvre defended municipal interests as congressmen in the São Paulo Constituent Assembly of 1935.

10. The word 'free' in Free School of Sociology and Politics (ELSP) stood for the institution's independence from government resources (Silva 1994: 87). The school had the character of a foundation and sought to educate people to perform technical and administrative occupations and to master bureaucratic theory and work methodology, the discipline of social engineering (Lowrie 1935). As for the DC, Milliet (1964: 36) described it as an extension of the newly created University of São Paulo (USP).

11. Paul Vanorden Shaw (born in 1898) received his PhD at Columbia University in 1930. Although Shaw praised the DC as a whole, he was a furious critic of 'socialist' ideas. Joseph Lee (1862–1937) contributed to the National Education Association of the United States, the NRA, the department of hygiene (Russell Sage Foundation) and the department of public recreation (American Civic Association). Howard Braucher (1881–1949) studied public recreation and its use in wartime.

12. According to Limongi (1989), both FFCL/USP and ELSP served as brokers. These schools filled up municipal and state occupation charts with professionals, the ELSP training students to work in private industries and

the USP forming a specialized workforce mainly for academia and public administrative careers.

13. The New York contacts were, for example, Columbia University, the New York Municipal Recreation Department and the Rockefeller Foundation.

14. Recollections of Willems include that of Brazilian president Fernando Henrique Cardoso, who attended USP during the 1950s (Santos 1988) and anthropologist Thomas Gregor (1997), who met Willems at Vanderbilt University during the 1970s.

15. Limongi (1989) wrote about the ELSP and the discipline of sociology in São Paulo on the basis of Lowrie's manuscript of 1935. Cyro Berlinck (1958) acknowledged Lowrie's role in the creation of the school, while Rubens Borba de Moraes depicted Lowrie as 'an exemplar of a researcher, [whose] studies on demography were remarkable, the very first official to work on census criticism' ('Anos de Formação' 1998).

16. The 1934 constitution stated that only native-born and naturalized Brazilians could practise a liberal profession. It recognized foreign qualifications only for native Brazilians, except for those who legally exercised liberal professions on the day of the constitution's enactment or represented legal cases of international reciprocity (Milliet 1936: 588). Lowrie fitted into the second category. However, foreign municipal officers had to be naturalized and have a voting card to enjoy the benefits of a permanent municipal employee position (Duarte 1976b: 208).

17. In Milliet's diaries, Lowrie is cited only once as the 'foreign sociologist who noticed and found strange the slowness of the Brazilian urbanization process, even in industrial São Paulo state' (Milliet 1949: 318).

18. The DC park programme followed American playground and German kindergarten precedents. The parks, located in working-class, crowded neighbourhoods, were intended to serve five thousand children, although, as Lowrie's research showed in 1936, they catered for only 10 per cent of this number.

19. See Dantas (1995: 15–50) about other DC studies on working-class families by Davis and Lowrie.

20. The percentage of blacks remained small and formed the subject of Lowrie's last article for *RAM* (1938).

21. Rudolfer was DC division of social documentation chief engineer, ELSP professor of statistics (1933–42) and Pierson's assistant (1939).

22. Born in 1896, Branco studied in Brussels before attending POLI (1915–20). He was subsequently state officer (1921–22), DOP engineer in the 1930s and municipal services chief from 1943 to 1951 (Hilton 1971, Cardim 1951).

23. See Mehrtens (2000), 248–98 on how this company used sites and municipal stadium construction as a vehicle for negotiating tax exemption with the municipality.

24. There was a huge difference between official and market values. Whereas a building in downtown São Paulo had an average municipal value rate of 20 *contos*, its estimated market value was 58 *contos* (Zagottis 1938: 253).

25. Support came from the average paulista citizen who was eager for the city's advancement and jealously guarded its reputation. However, proud of their city, they were against any radical, drastic urban changes. As Moses put it, they represented 'a middle-of-the-road citizen, at heart no revolutionary in his philosophy of municipal administration' (1950: 12).

CHAPTER NINE

The 'iron triangle' of municipal government: trade unions, bureaucracy and political parties in a French town (Toulouse, 1910–1970)

Jean-Yves Nevers

This chapter considers the impact of municipal trade unions on the transformation of local government in French cities during the twentieth century. Although the subject has not featured prominently in French historical and sociological literature (Hoffmann-Martinot 1991), from the 1900s the trade union movement played a vital role, procedurally and practically, in changing the condition of the workforce. In 1952, this change was finally acknowledged in the promulgation of a national status close to the one given to state civil servants in 1946 (Thoenig 1982, Burdeau 1989). The right to strike was legalized and municipal trade unions, considered until then simply as private associations, were formally recognized. Yet in reality the national measures represented the culmination of a continuous process. In certain towns, not only had trade unions and associations been recognized from the early twentieth century as legitimate workplace representatives, but they also had become the privileged partners of the town council and mayor in discussions and negotiations on a range of issues relating to jobs and staffing, such as wages, career structures, working conditions and job creation.

This situation is the one experienced in Toulouse, a town in the south-west of France. As early as the 1920s, the Toulouse trade union movement had acquired a strong bargaining position in the local bureaucracy thanks, in part, to the institutionalization of *paritarisme*, a co-management system with an equal representation of town councillors and staff representatives. Although its role was theoretically advisory, *paritarisme* in fact functioned as a system of decision making, which offered the necessary resources to the union for consolidating its influence among the workforce. The formal integration of union representation within the municipal organization, and the very strong links of interdependence forged between union leaders, managers of the services and leaders of the ruling political party, constituted the 'iron triangle' that maintained the structure of Toulouse's municipal power-base during the years between 1925 and 1970.

The national and local context

In most Western countries, the first decades of the twentieth century represented a pivotal period in the modernization of municipal government. New methods of management and various forms of civil service systems were progressively adopted in local government bureaucracies. These reforms could vary according to national contexts, but in general their declared aim was to increase the efficiency of municipal services by improving the professional competence of employees and by sheltering them from political pressures. For example, in its quest to combat the corruption of political machines and establish 'good government', the American municipal reform movement sought to impose measures that effectively depoliticized local government and professionalized the bureaucracy (Banfield and Wilson 1963, Ross et al. 2001). Under its influence, a large number of towns and cities across the United States adopted various strategies aimed at promoting the smoother operation of municipal functions. These ranged from the 'non-partisan ballot', which banned political parties from competing in municipal elections, to the institution of the city manager and the 'merit system', which aimed to improve standards of recruitment.

In France, changes during the first half of the century developed along broadly similar lines, although they took different political forms. Between 1890 and 1930, most urban districts adopted a set of rules and procedures concerning recruitment, career development, conditions of service and salary grades (Nevers 1975, 1991, Dumons and Pollet 1992, Dumons et al. 1998, Cohen 1998). These pioneering initiatives were local in origin, but gradually permeated outwards by means of horizontal exchanges between cities. The municipal management of foreign cities, notably in Britain and Germany, was studied and often followed. For example, the British example of Whitley Councils provided inspiration for the *commissions paritaires* (joint commissions), set up in several French cities including Bordeaux and Toulouse (Bourdon 1974).[1] A series of laws, the most important implemented in 1919 and 1930, gradually extended these local initiatives to all urban municipalities. As stated previously, legislation of 28 April 1952 finally gave France's 250 000 municipal employees a national status similar to that granted six years earlier to state civil servants (ibid.).

The promulgation of the national status is generally considered as having ended the period of relative autonomy for the municipalities. One of the effects of the 1952 law and of subsequent legislation was to 'nationalize' many of the functions of staff management. For the municipal workforce, wage negotiations became integrated with those of the entire public service. The application and modification of status, and the establishment of norms fixed for local jobs, especially relating to functions, qualifications and payments, came under the competence of a national committee. This was composed of 12 staff representatives, matched by an equal number of mayors' representatives, while three central government representatives acted as arbitrators. Local authorities kept a degree of autonomy only in matters of employment and dismissal, promotion and discipline, and various service conditions arrangements, including working hours and the awards of bonus and supplementary payments.

In the context of the status of French local government employees during the course of the twentieth century, what was distinctive about Toulouse? Originally the administrative and commercial capital of a rural region, from the 1920s Toulouse became increasingly industrialized. Demographic expansion was stimulated by work opportunities created in the aeronautical industry, the service sector and universities. Between 1900 and 1975 the city's population increased from 150 000 inhabitants to 370 000 and, as in other large French cities, municipal government grew at a brisker pace than population levels. Toulouse had one employee for every 115 inhabitants in 1900, but in 1975 the ratio was one in 44. Over the same period, the total number of municipal jobs rose from 1200 to more than 8000. Reflecting the diversity of work opportunities and qualifications, the municipal administration covered a heterogeneous range of services. In 1900, the 'uniformed services', including the local police force, firefighters and city toll-collectors, comprised around half of the workforce. The technical and environmental services comprised one-third, and were responsible for maintaining and cleaning the city's thoroughfares, the upkeep of public parks and gardens, water provision and the collection of household refuse. The remainder of the staff worked in various administrative, social and cultural services, such as museums, the school of fine arts, the school of music and the opera.

The number of employees decreased after the Second World War, as a result of the transfer of municipal policing functions to the state and, during 1941 and 1942, the removal of city toll-collecting responsibilities, which affected some 750 staff. However, this was counter-balanced by the growing number of employees in technical services from the 1960s, and by subsequent expansion of the sports, leisure and cultural services. Thereafter the organization chart of the administration remained stable. Serving as the mayor's right hand, the *secrétaire général* had authority over the whole municipal service, although in practice authority was often delegated to the managerial staff of technical services, particularly the chief engineer and city architect. Moreover, for some high-ranking posts, recruitment was the joint responsibility of the mayor and central government. This applied to the managers of services such as the school of music, the school of fine arts, museums and the police force.

As for the political profile of Toulouse, from 1888 to 1906 mayors from the centre-left *Parti républicain radical-socialiste* hereafter 'republican' controlled the city, although throughout this time the town council included a socialist minority. During the early twentieth century city politics went through a period of considerable flux, during which socialist mayors (1906–8 and 1912–19) alternated in power with republican mayors (1908–12 and 1919–25). However, from 1925 the socialist party established an entrenched electoral position, which allowed it to govern on its own from 1925 through to 1940. From 1944 to 1971 it headed a broad alliance with parties of the centre and the right, including radicals, Christian democrats and Gaullists.

The unionization of municipal administration and services

As with other categories of workers in the early twentieth century, French municipal employees joined collective organizations to defend their sectional interests and coordinate common aims. Because their social position was ambiguous, given their commitment to maintain public services, this process had distinctive characteristics. The public nature of their work had been progressively recognized by law, which meant that they secured certain advantages in terms of job stability. On the other hand, they were also subject to the same constraints affecting state civil servants, in particular the prohibition of strike activity and trade union membership. Such legal strictures did not prevent the rapid development of a range of associational organizations, although these tended to develop along different lines from trade unions: for instance, mutual, insurance and friendly societies, as well as bodies representing specific interest groups, especially professional associations.

Yet during the first decade of the twentieth century, more militant manifestations of protest were experienced at different levels within the state administration. Despite legal constraints and government opposition, state civil servants went on strike and created trade union organizations (Burdeau 1989).[2] Although municipal employees did not take part in these strikes, they were sufficiently encouraged to organize themselves. For instance, in 1903, staff representatives from several towns combined to create the *Fédération nationale des travailleurs municipaux* (national federation of municipal workers). The intense social struggles that followed the First World War led the government to recognize the *de facto* existence of union organization among state civil servants, without formally recognizing its legal existence, and municipal trade unions were in a similar situation of almost semi-legality.

In Toulouse before 1900 there was no trade union representing the whole municipal workforce, although very partial forms of expression existed among individual interest groups. For instance, some employees were members of a professional 'union'. Within the municipal coalition, several councillors who represented various socialist and trade union groups supported worker demands and grievances. In 1896, the socialist minority suggested a series of measures to the town council, designed to improve wages and conditions of service.[3] During the early years of the twentieth century, the relatively low level of organization and collective mobilization of municipal employees was linked to the multiplicity of jobs and qualifications. In 1914, the first defined salary scales distinguished almost 150 different jobs, functions and hierarchical levels. Additionally, the attachment to professional union membership for certain skilled staff, along with the social distance that separated white-collar employees from the mass of the workforce, retarded the emergence of collective solidarity within the municipal administration. But the most determining factor was undoubtedly the weight of patronage and political pressure exerted by elected representatives on employees. It proved difficult for many workers to break the bonds of personal dependence that tied them to town councillors, especially in matters of recruitment and promotion.

Between 1900 and 1914, as in most French urban communities, the collective organization of the Toulouse municipal staff developed spectacularly. During this period two rival unions were created. The first was the *Syndicat des employés et ouvriers municipaux de Toulouse* (union of Toulouse municipal employees and workers), which had close connections with the republican party. The claims it made suggest that it mainly represented qualified office clerks, and the union's secretary, who signed the project of status approved by the radicals in 1910, occupied the position of departmental head. The second union, the *Syndicat des travailleurs municipaux de Toulouse* (union of Toulouse municipal workers), was close to the socialist party. It followed the objectives enshrined in the broad programme of national unions, associated with the classic global objectives of the labour movement at the time, notably the eight-hour day and statutory minimum wage. However, it also pursued more specific, localized demands, including limiting the arbitrary power of mayors and introducing formal salary scales, pension schemes and provision for retirement.

Alongside these two local union organizations were several professional associations, such as those representing the fire brigade and municipal police. These came under the dual authority of the state representative and the mayor. Although separate from the trade unions, the professional organizations did not escape sharp politicization. For instance, the municipal police had both a 'republican association' and a 'socialist association', and conflict between the two was frequently profound. So sharp were the political differences that the police chief eventually requested that control of the municipal constabulary be taken over by the state. Such competition and conflict demonstrated the pervasive influence of political vote catching within the municipal administration. The cleavages were sharpened by the rapid succession of republican and socialist municipalities and the refinements made to personnel strategy under the different administrations.

After the First World War the two competing unions merged into a single union, the *Syndicat du personnel des services publics de la ville de Toulouse* (public service staff union of the city of Toulouse), affiliated to a national federation representing all categories of public sector employees within local communities, including health and hospital services. This federation belonged to the main national union, the *Confédération Générale du Travail* (CGT). At the same time, the occupational associations of the municipal police, firefighters and city toll-collectors became trade unions. Consolidating their base, there was a robust and rapid growth of membership throughout the inter-war period. In 1920, the new confederate union counted 590 members out of approximately 1600 employees, representing a membership rate of 37 per cent (Demelas et al. 1971). This number had increased threefold by 1937, to around 1800 members, so that by the eve of the Second World War union organization in administrative and technical services was around 75 per cent (Delpoux 1990). Collective organization was even more significant in services that had their own sectional union, such as the municipal police, which represented 360 out of 410 police officers, or 88 per cent of total staff.

The CGT was fragmented as a result of Cold War tensions, and in 1948 the reformist and anti-communist union *Force ouvrière* (FO) was created. In the Toulouse municipal administration, the FO inherited the power-base of the former union. In 1952, it gathered 78 per cent of the votes at the professional elections to nominate staff representatives to the *commission paritaire*. During the 1960s, the FO consolidated its influence, and achieved its best result in 1971 when it took 82 per cent of the votes. The result is especially striking because it was associated with a general increase in participation in professional elections, from 60 per cent in 1950 to 74 per cent in 1971. Moreover, it was within the context of growing numbers of municipal staff, from approximately 2500 to 6000. The influence of the FO varied according to the employees' level of qualification and their degree of integration within the municipal bureaucracy. It was weaker in services which had a strong autonomy, such as the school of music and the school of fine arts. It also had less influence among unskilled workers, frequently women, employed in services such as schools and canteens. Conversely, FO membership was strong among the skilled staff of the technical and administrative services, notably the male-dominated stratum of middle managers and technicians, such as deputy chief clerks, inspectors, clerks of works and draughtsmen. These categories constituted the heart of civic organization, the 'municipal family' according to the expression of one union leader, which shared most intensely the values and corporate culture of the municipal administration.

Of course, the phenomenon of increased unionization between the 1920s and 1960s was not confined to the municipal services of Toulouse. It represented a general trend that touched the industrial and tertiary sectors, and probably, in relation to administration, all of the French urban municipalities. However, it should be noted that in the municipal services, as in certain large bureaucracies of the state, such as the post office and the national education service, the rate of union membership increased very quickly, outstripping levels achieved in the private sector. A high level of unionization thus became a structural feature of the public sector. Such collectivity was not linked to conflict between employees and their 'elected' employers but, on the contrary, indicated the strong integration of trade unionism in the day-to-day working of the administration. This can be largely attributed to two factors. Firstly, the rapid spread of unionization after the First World War revealed the progress of a corporate culture within the municipal services that could transcend the diversity of occupations, fragmentation of services and hierarchical stratification. The so-called 'municipal family' had emerged under the protective wing of the union, which in turn became an important element of unification. Secondly, the influence obtained by the union apparatus was dependent upon its institutionalization as a partner of elected representatives in the co-management system set up from 1914 to 1940.

The institutionalization of municipal trade unionism

Three stages can be distinguished in the process of trade union institutionalization and the creation of the co-management system. The first stage was completed on the eve of war in July 1914, when the socialist-dominated municipal council formally recognized freedom of association and gave the trade unions' collective status as the legitimate voice of the workforce. Indeed, the rules explicitly permitted 'the free association of employees and workers based on the union law of 1884', and not on the 1901 law on associations.[4] They further stipulated, 'The union representatives shall be able to intervene directly with the municipal administration to articulate the collective claims of their members.'[5] Among other provisions, the regulation allowed for these claims to be jointly investigated. It also stressed that revisions to the regulation could be made 'only in collaboration' with the union of municipal workers.[6] These measures represented an important step forward compared with the regulation voted four years previously by the radical municipality, in which there was no provision for the right of association or union activity.[7] In 1914, they represented the declared aim of socialist councillors, which featured prominently in their election programme, that trade union membership be encouraged and declared that it was desirable to have a strong and unified union as a partner in negotiations. Because the new staff status had not been endorsed by national regulation, elected representatives were aware of its legal precariousness. Its application and efficiency depended on favourable local circumstances, and in consequence the presence of a powerful trade union movement constituted the best guarantee for preserving the regulation in the event of political changeover.

A second and equally important stage was accomplished in 1922 when, at the union's request, the republican and conservative municipal coalition created a *commission paritaire* or joint commission. This was renewable every year and had a wide remit 'to study, in the best spirit of collaboration, the claims of the workforce, improvements to make in the functioning of services, salary scales and categorizations [and] the possible reduction of staff numbers …'.[8] From the time of its creation, the joint commission engaged in considerable activity, although its first years were characterized by recurring power struggles between the union, elected members and the hierarchy of services. For example, elected members were opposed to the fact that the joint commission could discuss important budgetary decisions. In the course of a survey on staff numbers, the head clerks refused to answer questions posed by the commission's union representatives, on the basis that this would call into question their hierarchical authority. It was through these kinds of conflicts, beyond formal regulation, that procedures and usages gradually came to define the joint commission's areas of competency.

The third decisive stage came in 1926 with the introduction of a new regulation by the socialist town council, elected the previous year. This formalized the existence and role of the joint commission and explicitly granted the monopoly of staff representation to the CGT. Indeed, the regulation specified that 'the administration, apart from the professional grouping of police, shall recognize only one trade union member as representative'.[9] The 1926 provision was aimed at forestalling the implantation of competing trade unions, notably the pro-communist union, born out of a split from the CGT in 1921. However, the regulation was relatively generous in its provisions. It gave guarantees to union representatives who 'will be able to exert freely their mandate in the corporative domain'. It authorized 'time-off without pay to the trade union's permanent representative' and assured their eventual reintegration into municipal employment. The nomination of staff representatives to the 'disciplinary committee', and other important joint committees, was also left to the union's discretion. The trade union was present, through its joint commission representatives, on the panel of recruitment examinations. Along with the mayor and municipal council, it became sole representative on numerous other joint investigative committees set up between 1925 and 1940, including, for instance, a committee that proposed measures to reduce overstaffing.

Compared with the regulation of 1914, that of 1926 marked a considerable strengthening of trade union prerogatives. From that time onwards, the union had the legitimacy and resources that allowed it to become a decisive player within the municipal power structure. However, in excluding union pluralism and in granting the monopoly of staff representation to a sole trade union with which they had very close ideological links, socialist municipal leaders had allowed partisan politics to enter decisively into the conduct of staff relations. At the same time, the measure had advantages for elected representatives in securing management efficiency. Wage disputes were likely to be less volatile under co-management, while staff cooperation was more readily forthcoming in developing public services as part of the ruling party's programme of 'municipal socialism'.

The *paritarisme* and joint management system endured from the 1930s until the mid-1970s, although there were changes to the trade union profile. After the Liberation, the institutional and statutory framework that had determined the role and function of staff representation was largely maintained through the entrenched position of the FO. Yet, concerning the right of association and the exercise of the union's mandate, in 1949 a new staff status was implemented, which had the effect of diluting, for the main part, the arrangements of 1926. It recognized union pluralism and insisted that the choice to belong or not to belong to a trade union should have no consequences for employees' careers. However, these more limited arrangements did not undermine the position of the FO. The town council, now under a socialist- and centre-led coalition, opted for an electoral system on a majority basis for the joint commission, rather than proportional representation. The effect was to give the monopoly of staff representation to the FO, thus perpetuating *de facto* the dominant position that the trade union CGT had attained before the war. The monopoly was confirmed a few years later when the town council renewed the 1949 regulation within the scope of applying the 1952 law, which had extended national status to municipal staff. Urged to give a verdict on the joint commission's mode of operation, the town council pronounced itself in favour of election on a majority basis.

The 'iron triangle': trade union, ruling party and bureaucracy

The institutionalization of a co-management system associated with union monopoly existed by right between 1920 and 1949, and thereafter continued by fact. Significantly, it lasted throughout the period when the socialist party ran the municipality of Toulouse, from 1925 to 1940, then from 1944 to 1971. This process created a formidable structure of municipal power, the 'iron triangle' based on the interdependence of the interests of the dominating trade union, the ruling party and the bureaucratic hierarchy.

Each of these three categories took advantage of the situation, although the majority union was the main beneficiary. This union constituted an imposing organization, which became an integral part of the municipal bureaucracy, almost a 'state-within-a-state'. As has been seen, it received substantial support from the workforce, about 75 per cent of the votes at the professional elections. At its peak, before union membership declined generally during the 1980s, it claimed that around 3000 members were paying contributions. The FO was one of the biggest municipal workers' unions, comparable with those of Marseilles, Lille and Bordeaux (Orio 1993). It had a large number of party workers and considerable material resources placed at its disposal by the town council. Its structure was closely modelled on the organization chart of the municipal bureaucracy. Each service had its own union section or sections, and each of these possessed an office and included one or several representatives on the administrative committee, which numbered 67 by 1951. The authoritative central office, elected by the committee and its secretaryship, was empowered to present the sections' expressed claims before the municipal employers. Structurally, the union resembled a highly centralized pyramidal organization, which afforded scant space for the initiatives of grassroots militants. This mode of organization was intended to guarantee the power-base of the ruling group, representing the union on one side, and the mayor and *secrétaire général* on the other. The union secretary thus attained a powerful position, with direct and permanent access to the town clerk, as the head of administrative authority, and the mayor, as the municipality's political leader.

Between the 1920s and 1970s there was significant stabilization of the union's leadership profile, especially from the 1940s. This was reflected by the leaders' occupational orientation, as many of them emerged from the stratum of middle or senior managers. Over time the professional connection became an essential characteristic of the integration of union organization with the municipal administration, to the extent that several managers of services came to hold positions of union responsibility. A kind of osmosis existed between the bureaucratic hierarchy and the union 'hierarchy', which undoubtedly was a determining factor in extending the trade union's sphere of influence.[10] According to personal testimonies, many managers of services who were also union representatives put direct pressure on their subordinates to become members, notably at times of appointment and the granting of tenure. Staff were well advised to join, in order to secure the protection of their seniors and ensure promotion prospects. Union influence became self-perpetuating, as members protected themselves within the system by putting identical pressures on their subordinates. The systematic or almost systematic *encartage* (insertion) was effectively a form of post-entry closed shop, and the payment of contributions represented a quasi-obligatory ticket of entry to the market of favours and individual perquisites. Yet, at the same time, union members could be diverted from their own aims in order to serve wider bureaucratic interests. Trade union membership became a device for managers to reinforce their authority on junior staff and more generally it reinforced the administration's autonomy from political power.

During the years 1925–70, the close links between the dominating trade union and the socialist party relied on their shared ideological objectives. There was thus a frequent overlapping of membership between the two groups. From 1925 to 1940, several elected representatives were members of the CGT and others, two deputy mayors in particular, were well-known 'historical leaders' of the workers' movement of Toulouse. The triple career of one *secrétaire général* demonstrates how extensive the phenomenon of multi-membership could be, and also illustrates how far the process of 'osmosis' permeated politics, union activism and the bureaucratic hierarchy. Recruited in 1913 as the mayor's special secretary, and therefore to a 'political' job, he later pursued a brilliant municipal career that took him to departmental headship in 1929, and then to the deputy mayor's office. In 1937, he finally reached the top of the municipal bureaucracy as *secrétaire général*. Yet his ascension within the hierarchy was by no means incompatible with trade union responsibilities, since he became secretary of the Toulouse local employees' union from 1930 to 1935, and one of the principal leaders of the regional federation of public services and health unions. At the same time he pursued a political career as a local elected representative. He was mayor of his native village, then *conseiller général* of a rural area in 1929. As such he occupied an important position on the council of the *département*, as a member of the board committee. Active within the ruling committee of the socialist party's local section, he went on to become secretary of the party's local federation.

After the Liberation, the onset of political pluralism within the town council put an end to the exclusive private dialogue between the dominant trade union and the socialist party, which had ruled the municipality since 1925. No longer able to govern alone, the socialists had to seek alliances and share responsibilities. They were also confronted by elected representatives from the communist party, who aspired to the leadership of the left and now had a majority influence within the CGT, the biggest trade union in France. At stake was maintaining the continuing close relationship between the FO and the socialist party, both literally and strategically.

For FO leaders, holding on to their acquired advantages and maximizing their capacities for action entailed giving privileged support to the mayor, undisputed leader of the socialist party, chief of the political coalition and the effective 'boss' of municipal services. By this means, the FO retained its monopoly of access at the heart of the municipal power structure. And it was here that the executive had a role in distributing staff perquisites: collective advantages, such as wage increases, and, above all, individual benefits such as bonuses, special allowances and other 'selective incentives'. These had the aim of securing the support and commitment of the mass of employees, and thwarting tendencies for them to become 'free-riders'. Thanks to the distribution of incentives that could be reserved for its members, the trade union was able to put pressure on staff for membership, support and loyalty. Its monopolistic position in the joint commission and its direct and permanent access to the centres of political and administrative power, the offices of mayor and town clerk, secured an important controlling influence. Yet another important incentive was the support given to staff by the ruling political coalition and the mayor during conflicts between the union movement and central power. These related especially to the wage negotiations that had been 'nationalized' after the war. Strike pay considerably minimized the costs of protest action and favoured the massive mobilization of the workforce. More generally, the ruling union also wished to retain the benefits of important resources, such as the disposal of jobs, premises and vehicles, which were bestowed by the town council.

For the mayor and the socialist party, it was a question of using the union as a means of controlling staff, electorally handing over influence and eventually creating a breeding ground for the recruitment of militants. Firstly, as the 'boss' of the municipal bureaucracy, the mayor and his party were concerned to show voters, whether they were taxpayers or users, that they could manage public services with efficiency; that is, without conflict or disturbance. In this context, it is clear that support from the union's leadership, which in turn had the support of 70 per cent of employees, was a decisive asset. Secondly, it was a matter of catching the votes of the mass of employees.[11] Along with their families, relations, friends and neighbours, their votes represented a stock of substantial support for a party that had a relatively narrow electoral base. Thus, by the end of the 1960s, the municipality's 6000 employees represented a potentially valuable segment of the socialist electorate, which totalled almost 30 000, or 25 per cent of all votes cast in local elections. This quest for the employees' electoral support, as voters and eventually as electoral agents, inevitably required the active support of the trade union. Moreover, the municipal workforce could also be used to exert wider electoral influence over the provision of public services. Thirdly, leaning on the double influence of municipal managers and union representatives, the ruling party could attract a resource vital for boosting its basic political activities – militants.

During the period from 1944 to 1960, the widespread influence of the trade union and its presence in the hierarchy of municipal services made it much more than a mere cog in the wheel of the ruling party. Indeed, the opposite was closer to the truth, since the electoral influence of the socialist party and its survival at the head of the municipal coalition was dependent on the support of the FO. It is evident that a *de facto* solidarity existed, representing the strategic interests of the leaders of the local union, the ruling party and the head officers of municipal bureaucracy. Each of these three groups had strong reasons to maintain privileged relations with the other two, and thus contributed to perpetuating the 'iron triangle'.

Union power and municipal management

What was the impact of this power structure on municipal management? Of course, a precise evaluation would be impossible in a brief and limited study such as this. It is difficult to disentangle factors that depended on very general conditions and those that arose from the specific effect of union power within the 'iron triangle'. Moreover, there could be different evaluations depending on different perspectives. Individual employees have to be taken into account, as well as the collective entity of the administrative bureaucracy, which can be viewed either as an employer or as an enterprise providing public services. Then there are the elected representatives, the voters and the taxpayers.

In Toulouse, as in other French cities, rapid transformation of municipal staff conditions took place during the inter-war years. From a state of precariousness, arising from political changes and the mayor's arbitrary power, the workforce attained a much more stable position, thanks to the institution of rules and the negotiated statutory guarantees at the local level between the employers and union representatives. Staff also benefited from the protection of real 'union power', which operated in tandem with the elected members at various levels of the co-management system. Obviously, there was a price to pay, individually, to benefit in full from this protection and its advantages. Staff were required to give a certain allegiance to the dominant trade union and, beyond that, to the party ruling the municipality and the hierarchy of services. But this dependence was very moderate compared with the brutal forms of political subordination that dominated towards the end of the nineteenth century in the municipal services, when substantial numbers of staff could be dismissed as a result of political change or when strict partisan loyalty was demanded.[12]

As a result of their collective organization, municipal employees became important participants in local policy. Town council debates provide striking evidence of the elected representatives' changing attitudes towards the workforce, and the recognition of dignity and respect that helped to motivate their capacity for collective action. Union members contributed to the unification of the 'municipal family', which extended beyond the diversity of occupational categories employed within the services. They consequently played an essential part in the formation of a 'community for collective action'. Of course, it is difficult to evaluate their efficiency at the level of acquired advantages. This must take into account the collective action costs assumed by members. Judging by the relative rarity of strike action, the co-management system seems to have maintained its costs at a very low level for the employees. Between 1925 and 1940, a period of high social tension, the workforce withdrew their labour for only two hours, in 1933, to protest against the policies of central government. Similarly, in the troubled period following the Liberation, strike action was directed against the government and not against local elected representatives, and the phenomenon generally remained rare until the beginning of the 1970s. Furthermore, the costs to employees were sharply reduced, as has been seen, by the provision of strike pay, on one side, and by the political support given to elected representatives on the other.

It is also difficult to assess the situation relating to the collective advantages acquired in terms of payment and conditions of service. In the volatile climate of the years between 1925 and 1940, the trade union's aim was to obtain the automatic indexation of wages to the cost of living, as a protection against inflation. The municipality had accepted this measure in 1927, but central government vetoed it, and the period of deflation between 1929 and 1934 rendered it null and void. It was in fact during this period of deflation that employees increased their power by fighting for a straightforward wage freeze. The 1925–40 period was marked by the flattening of the payments grid, because of the incidence of low wages. For the post-Liberation period, it is difficult to evaluate the specific benefits of the co-management system in the matter of wages since these were practically indexed to those of state civil servants and were negotiated at the national level. In general, during the 1950s and 1960s, local staff payments were relatively low compared with those of the private sector. The municipalities experienced difficulties recruiting skilled workers, and so more advantageous conditions of work and an increasingly complex bonus system compensated for low wages. Yet, for existing employees, the difficulties of recruiting skilled staff and the creation of a large number of jobs provided openings for internal promotion.

What was the impact of the co-management system on municipal administration and local public policies, especially relating to productivity and efficiency, and the standard of services provided to the public? Of course, it would be excessive to attribute the influence of 'union power' to the quasi-constant progression of staff costs in municipal expenditure, from approximately 35 per cent in 1900 to almost 50 per cent in 1970. Far more important factors were the general progression of the cost of skilled labour, national social measures and the extension of certain services arising from demographic growth. However, without falling into conservative theories which denounce 'greedy bureaucrats', factors that could probably be associated with the power of the ruling trade union were the extension of municipal interventionism, resistance to privatization and the costs linked to excessive numbers of staff.[13] The question of overstaffing in some municipal services was indeed the subject of continual debate within the town council, which several times tried to involve the union in implementing retrenchment measures, but without success. A complete evaluation should take into account the important advantages for the elected members and, beyond, for the population, in relation to the relative rarity of open conflict and strike action.

The direct impact of the co-management system on local policies seems not to have been very important. There were clear limits that were acknowledged and respected between the fields of competence of the trade union and the elected representatives over staff policy. Union leaders never really questioned the legitimacy of elected representatives as far as the definition of municipal aims was concerned. Instead, the impact of union power was exerted as an indirect constraint, which reduced the room for manoeuvre for both the council and the mayor. This was especially so at times of economic strain, when measures to cut back on staff expenditure had to be made. From this perspective, during the years between 1945 and 1965, union power constituted a conservative influence, which considerably checked the capacity of the municipal administration to adapt to urban growth. But it can also be seen that, from 1925 to 1940, the joint co-management system created favourable conditions for a general increase in management efficiency and the municipal government's efforts to mobilize the workforce around a collective project of 'municipal socialism', as was shown by the scale of civic achievements throughout this period.

Conclusion

During the first decades of the twentieth century, the unionization of the workforce and the institutionalization of a co-management system were active factors in the modernization of Toulouse's municipal government. It contributed decisively towards the decline of patronage and political pressure that had hitherto characterized the relationship between local elected representatives and the municipal workforce. An established partnership involving the local union, the ruling party and the head of bureaucracy became a structural element in the city's municipal government for almost 50 years.

Yet in what way does the Toulouse case-study represent the French experience? It can be suggested, albeit on the basis of rather scattered indications, that a power structure similar to that of Toulouse existed in other towns, notably those that were controlled for a long period by the same political party. However, there are various qualifications to this argument. In towns with a communist municipality, the strong party organization overrode the trade union, which was considered more as an instrument for controlling the workforce than an autonomous partner, equal to the elected representatives (Brunet 1980). Elsewhere, in towns governed by the right or centre–left and where the organization of the ruling party was weak, the place of the trade union was closer to that occupied in the bureaucracies of state control or even in some private enterprises. This was the case in Lyons, for example. Yet it was probably the towns governed by the socialist party, such as Lille, Bordeaux and Marseilles, which exerted a local power structure similar to that of Toulouse. By the 1980s, in most of France's large cities, the 'iron triangle' had been destabilized by a substantial decrease in union membership, by the rise of alternative forms of local leadership, by the implementation of new public management techniques and by various policies of retrenchment.

Notes

1. Whitley Councils were responsible for arbitrating in cases of conflict between the district council and its agents and of elaborating collective conventions (Bourdon 1974: 34). However, the idea of mixed commissions in which town councillors and staff representatives were associated is older. In Toulouse this type of commission was anticipated in the status voted in 1910 and 1914.
2. A union federation of state civil servants, the *Fédération nationale des fonctionnaires*, was created in 1905 and an organization in defence of union rights in 1906, the *Comité de défense du droit syndical*.
3. In response, the mayor passed, in 1897, the first statutes that applied to a large proportion of the municipal workforce. Provisions introduced recruitment through examinations and a system of partial promotion based on length of service.
4. These laws both established the right to association, although in different ways. The 1884 law allowed for the creation of trade unions in the private sector, while the 1901 law made the legal existence of any type of association possible. Excluded from the 1884 law, municipal and state employees used the 1901 law to create legal associations, but these groups did not benefit from the same rights or privileges as private sector unions established under the 1884 law.
5. Report of the town council debates, session 30 July 1914, Municipal Bulletin, Municipal Archives of Toulouse.
6. Regulation of the municipal personnel, session 30 July 1914, Municipal Bulletin, Municipal Archives of Toulouse.
7. The regulation voted in 1910 by the town council with a radical majority planned to set up a 'staff council', but it made no allusion to trade unions.
8. Report of the town council debates, session 22 August 1922, Municipal Bulletin, Municipal Archives of Toulouse.
9. Regulation of the town personnel, session 25 June 1926, edited in the Municipal Bulletin, Municipal Archives of Toulouse.

10. This experience has also been observed in other public administrations and certain national enterprises.
11. Studies have shown that the participation of local staff in municipal elections was more important than that by other social categories, and that their votes were, on average, more favourable to the incoming mayor. For the USA, see Banfield and Wilson (1963), for the 1950s and early 1960s.
12. For a comparison with other cities, see Cohen (1998).
13. The question of the bureaucracy's role in the increase of public expenditure has been much debated, especially relating to periods of crisis. Empirical research has shown that the impact of employees' union activity on percentages of local expenditure is very limited. See, in particular, Clark and Ferguson (1983).

CHAPTER TEN

A (North) British end-view: the comparative experience of municipal employees and services in Glasgow (1800–1950)

Irene Maver

The introductory chapter to this collected volume has already given detailed consideration to recent scholarship on municipal employees and services within the United Kingdom.[1] Judging from the lion's share of accessible published material, it is evident that historians have focused territorially on London and Glasgow. This is not surprising, as by the 1930s London County Council (LCC) and Glasgow Corporation had by far the largest concentration of local government employees in urban Britain.[2] Yet even before this time a range of commentators, inside and outside the UK, were aware of the value of Glasgow in illustrating points about the complexities of urban administration. For instance, Albert Shaw, an American journalist and urban reformer, gave the city extensive scrutiny in his 1895 investigation into British municipal government. He was clearly struck by the scope and sophistication of functions, as they related to a community approaching 750 000 people. In an indirect reference to London, Shaw enthused '[as] a distinct and complete municipal organism, Glasgow may claim not the second, but the first place among communities of Great Britain' (1895b: 69) Over a century later, in a comparative study of British urban government between 1840 and 1950, Glasgow Corporation's chief officials were used as telling examples of the power of bureaucratic influence, especially during the pre-1914 heyday of 'municipal socialism' (Doyle 2000: 295–8). By its quantitative and qualitative distinctiveness, the Scottish city has long presented a revealing case study, and this chapter will build upon previous historical analyses to consider continuity and change in municipal administration over a broad time span.

Yet Glasgow was distinctive in another way. Although the municipality had important points of comparison with English cities like Birmingham and Manchester, as well as London, its Scottish identity meant that there were crucial differences of approach to local governance. During the 1900s, in words that still have resonance, one trenchant analyst of Scottish affairs argued that these had not been sufficiently recognized by her contemporaries: 'English ignorance of what goes on beyond the Border is proverbial, and foreigners appear to have no conception that Scotland has still its own laws and its own method of administration. Even the great German handbooks of political science make no mention of Scotland' (Atkinson 1904: 2).

In Scotland the evolution of urban communities under the separate legal system meant that the administrative unit of the 'burgh' was a term by no means interchangeable with the 'borough' of England and Wales. For instance, Scottish towns and cities traditionally had more financial autonomy and, according to one comparative study of 1939, municipalities could more readily secure local legislation to inaugurate and extend trading undertakings, such as gas supplies and public transport (Harris 1939: 189, 205–6). This legal dimension had relevance for the evolution of Glasgow's civic bureaucracy. The need to protect corporate assets and landholdings helped to encourage administrative expansion during the eighteenth century, and the police laws from 1800 consolidated professionalism in the environmental sphere (Maver 1995: 244–5, 251–2). Moreover, Scotland's eighteenth-century reputation as a 'managed' society, much influenced by the political ascendancy of the legal profession, was extended into the institutional framework of local government (Paterson 1994: 31–4). The power of Glasgow's town clerks, as described in this chapter, was evidence of how long the legacy lingered.

Indeed, Shaw commented approvingly that, although Scots had 'eagerly embraced the *régime* of the steam-engine and the factory system', the municipalities, in their functional form, retained stabilizing elements of continuity with the past (Shaw 1889: 37). A seemingly paradoxical blend of conservatism and progress had helped to shape the mechanisms of urban governance. One 1990s historian, in an attempt to conceptualize Scottish civil society and its relationship to the British state, has referred more obliquely to the emergence of a 'middle way' during the nineteenth century, whereby the powers devolved to localities were sustained by means of 'a complex and highly penetrative legal system' (Morton 1998: 351). The structures, and therefore the bureaucracy, provided a solid base from which public policy could be implemented. Modernizing, interventionist strategies were further legitimized by emphasizing the deep-rooted tradition of civic virtue. In Glasgow the rhetoric of public service was strongly coloured by the Scottish brand of evangelical Presbyterianism, which sought to construct the 'city of God' through municipal activism (Brown 1996). The moral mission was subsequently appropriated by the Labour party, which consolidated its electoral base during the 1920s and 1930s by projecting a socially inclusive vision of civic cooperation. Municipal employees thus operated almost continually in an environment where the political ideal had to be metamorphosed into reality, and it is scarcely surprising that Glasgow's leading officials promoted the city not just positively, but zealously.

Of course, within the UK the visionary qualities of the 'civic gospel' and 'municipal socialism' were by no means confined to Glasgow, although the ideological impulse had gathered momentum relatively early in the Scottish city (Fraser 1990: 63–5). And, despite supreme confidence about their governing abilities, Glasgow's municipal leaders and officials were quite prepared to look beyond immediate Scottish influences in their commitment to improve the urban environment. The last section of this chapter considers the impact of external ideas on Glasgow, as they affected the administration of services and the growth of professionalism. A number of parallels and contrasts will also be made by relating developments in Glasgow to themes explored in other contributions to this volume. For instance, in his study of municipal engineers in nineteenth-century Turin, Filippo De Pieri has shown that state centralization in the wake of Italian unification during the 1860s did not necessarily erode autonomy at the local level; as in Scotland, administrative continuities with the past persisted. Conversely, Emmanuel Bellanger's study of town clerks (*secrétaires généraux*) in the Paris region reveals the evolution of a very different professional identity from their Scottish counterparts. The former rose through the ranks of the municipal bureaucracy from relatively humble beginnings; the latter were highly qualified members of the Scottish legal fraternity. In the course of the analysis that follows, more comparisons will be made, as a means of emphasizing the distinctiveness, or otherwise, of the Glasgow experience.

The evolution of the civic bureaucracy

Urban governance in Scotland has origins in the burghal system of authority, stretching as far back as the twelfth century. Until the Union of the Scottish and English parliaments in 1707, the Crown had power to elevate communities into royal burghs, granting exclusive trading privileges along with rights of jurisdiction, notably in relation to securing an ordered environment. According to one pioneering analyst of Scottish local government, the system reflected 'much uniformity of privilege, custom and constitution', which was underpinned by considerable uniformity of administration (Keith 1915/16: 230). A crucial forum for promoting interconnections between urban communities was the Convention of Royal Burghs, which from the 1570s met annually to discuss matters of common interest, especially the regulation of commercial activities and civic functions. The Convention survived until the reform of Scottish local government in 1975, and represented a form of collective organization that was unknown in England and Wales until the creation of the Association of Municipal Corporations in 1872 (Keith-Lucas and Richards 1978: 180).[3]

Continuity, a high degree of administrative cohesion and concern for regulation were thus characterizing features of the Scottish system, and had implications for the evolution of the civic bureaucracy. Glasgow's town clerks provide a useful illustration, as they can be positively identified as operating from the mid-fifteenth century, although the office had been established much earlier, to serve the needs of the burgh court (McGrath 1995: 23–4). Over time, because of increasing reliance on formal law procedures, the town clerks came to establish an entrenched position within the municipal administration, not only in juridical affairs, but also in the complex spheres of burghal landholding and property transactions.

Unlike France, where the influential *secrétaires greffiers* had lost their status in the post-Revolutionary period, Scottish town clerks retained a strong municipal base. According to one historian of the National Association of Local Government Officers (NALGO), the power of Scotland's 'seigneurial' clerks was still potent in the 1920s, which meant that the trade union's district organizer had to hone his negotiating skills vigorously (Spoor 1967: 91). The status of town clerks was, of course, relative to the size of the municipality and the scope of its activities, but the extension of local government functions to newly populous communities during the nineteenth century inevitably multiplied administrative opportunities. Legislation in 1833, 1850 and 1862 had allowed for the creation of separately elected burghal entities, with their own bureaucratic apparatus. By the 1900s, in addition to the traditional 66 royal burghs, over 119 police burghs had emerged, and size was not necessarily an indicator of quality within this extensive grouping (Atkinson 1904: 74). During the 1880s, the police burgh of Hillhead, immediately adjacent to Glasgow, employed the eminent local government lawyer, James Muirhead, as its clerk, a position that gave rise to accusations that he was the controlling influence in a community of some 8600 inhabitants (Sweeney 1990: 165–6). The image of the manipulative bureaucrat was long-standing in Scotland. Henry Cockburn, himself a lawyer, depicted Edinburgh town council in the 1800s as under the thraldom of John Gray, its principal town clerk. With heavy irony, Gray was summed up as 'a respectable and useful officer, with an exclusive devotion to the town-council, but with such municipal wisdom, and such an intimate acquaintance with their affairs, that he was oftener the master than the slave' (Cockburn 1910: 88–9).

However debateable the extent of civic decadence under Scotland's *ancien régime*, the important electoral reforms of 1833 undoubtedly afforded financial leeway for extending municipal interventionism and encouraging much-needed social and environmental improvements.[4] Yet administrative reform of Scottish local government was a prolonged and piecemeal process, and the continuing suspicion of officialdom was testimony to what some saw as the inherent conservatism of the system. Undoubtedly, the influence of the Scottish legal profession helped to bolster the authority of town clerks. The parliamentary architects of the reform legislation in 1833 were Edinburgh-based lawyers who, for all their willingness to concede the principle of electoral accountability, were still prepared to protect their close-knit fraternity. In 1837, the House of Lords further safeguarded the status of town clerks when it ruled that in the royal burghs they should hold their appointment for life. As one legal expert subsequently put it, 'whatever the terms of his employment, he certainly cannot be deprived of his office by the magistrates and council summarily, and without process of law' (Marwick 1879: 347–8).

The effect of the ruling on Glasgow was to ensure the continuation of the formidable James Reddie as principal town clerk; his civic career went on to span almost 50 years, from 1804 to 1852 (Maver 1995: 254–5). Dearly as the Liberal-dominated municipal leadership would have liked to remove the politically uncongenial Reddie, they were legally powerless to do so, unless he committed a gross act of malfeasance. Such strictures did not apply in England and Wales, although the steely character of town clerks such as Joseph Heron in Manchester and Samuel Johnston in Nottingham had strong echoes of the Scottish mode of operation (Doyle 2000: 297). Although Reddie was made to appear by his opponents as anti-progressive, a fossil from an autocratic era, the circumstances of his recruitment had reflected concern for a greater degree of professionalism within Glasgow's governance. Unusually for the 1800s, the new town clerk was required to devote his energies full-time to municipal responsibilities. Remuneration was high, to compensate for exclusion from private practice. Reddie's skill in advocacy was the primary rationale for his appointment, at a time when Glasgow still had the busiest civil court in Scotland. Crime, policing and the ordered environment were major preoccupations in the fast-growing city, and in urban Scotland generally public safety was a matter of key concern. Reflecting the European experience, the concept of policing had a wide remit in Scotland, where a wide range of services, such as cleansing, lighting and road maintenance, also came under police control.

For England and Wales the origins of the local government 'reform period' have been identified with the 1829 Metropolitan Police Act, which introduced professional policing for London (Doyle 2000: 290). However, as the career of Reddie indicates, the Scottish response was earlier, with Glasgow and Edinburgh employing full-time constabularies from 1800 and 1805, respectively (Carson and Idzikowska 1989: 271). There were also influences from further back. Patrick Colquhoun, lord provost (mayor) of Glasgow between 1782 and 1784, was a pioneering publicist of ideas on preventative policing (Gash 1986). While his emphasis on moral reform reflected traditional Scottish Presbyterian concerns about antisocial behaviour, Colquhoun also related the moral dimension to contemporary influences that were designated 'policy science' in France, Germany and Spain (Fraile 1998: 22–3). He relocated to London later in the 1780s, where his views were disseminated widely, and influenced Benthamite thinking. Given this context of ideas, Glasgow's 1800 Police Act projected a professional approach to environmental control. Writing in 1909, John Lindsay, then deputy town clerk of Glasgow, wrote glowingly about the solid administrative precedent set by the legislation. The 'good model,' he argued, '[was] framed many, many years ago by some one whose personal identity is absolutely lost, but whose good professional and official work still remains' (Lindsay 1909: 10).

Historian Graeme Morton has recently taken Lindsay's optimism several stages further by claiming that the police Acts represented the beginnings of Scotland's 'self-administration of civil society', which empowered localities to legislate directly for community needs (Morton 1998: 354–5). Moreover, these developments occurred before the liberal ethos of 'local self-government' had taken root in Victorian Britain, following the electoral and municipal reform legislation of the 1830s.[5] In pre-reform Scotland the bureaucratic infrastructure evolved to facilitate the long-standing guardianship responsibility of the burghs, under the extraordinary demands of social and industrial change. Within its detailed terms of reference, Glasgow's 1800 Police Act itemized the employees needed for the practical implementation of the new administration. These ranged from a corps of 'Scavengers' (street sweepers and refuse collectors) to assorted 'Clerks, Servants, Watchmen, and Other Officers', who worked to assist the magistrates in 'preserving the good Order of the said City'.[6] Patrolling the streets was a highly visible means of controlling the urban environment, and the much-vaunted professional qualities of the new constabulary gave added legitimacy to the civic preoccupation with vigilance. More subtly, the bureaucracy could also be used to monitor the population by means of statistical returns, bills of mortality and census enumeration. In 1814, James Cleland, a former town councillor, was appointed to the influential paid position of superintendent of public works, with a wide remit that included statistical analysis (Maver 1995: 245–6). His subsequent prolific output made him well known throughout the UK, left a legacy of detailed factual information about the industrializing city and established an enduring tradition of social investigation within the municipal domain.

While Lindsay was effusive about the substance of Glasgow's early police legislation, he was also complimentary about individual officials, notably John Burnet, who served as clerk to the city's Police Board during the 1840s (Lindsay 1909: 18). Burnet's legal expertise was such that he went on to head the administration of the city's celebrated municipal water supply from Loch Katrine. Lindsay diplomatically did not relate that Burnet's predecessor had been dismissed in 1842 for alleged professional incompetence, although politics rather than ability had provoked this response (Sweeney 1990: 119–20). As far as police board functions were concerned, 'professionalism' also was not universally applied. Thus, in light of Amy Greenberg's analysis of American and European firefighting practices, it is worth pointing out that Glasgow's fire department was inaugurated under direct police authority in 1807.[7] Yet, unlike the police force, it was a part-time service. The firefighters were paid volunteers, selected on the basis of residency near to the central police office and ownership of suitably sturdy horses, to transport the equipment. For decades controversy over expenditure bedevilled the progress of the department, with local fire insurance companies accused of undue parsimony in their contribution to the city's protection. It was not until 1870 that the department acquired its first steam engine. Three years later it purchased its own stud of horses, and in 1878 the fire brigade was made a permanent standing force (Bell and Paton 1896: 152–5).

Notwithstanding its significance as a tangible expression of Scottish self-administration, the 'empowerment' of the burghs, in the form of localized devolution sanctioned by the central state, developed as an administrative expedient, to safeguard the interests of the increasingly assertive middle classes. It has also been questioned how far the notion of permanent and experienced administrative structures actually found favour in cost-conscious urban communities (McCaffrey 1998: 27–8, 35–6). As has been seen, Glasgow's professionalism was open to interpretation, and there was no compulsion on communities to adopt police powers. Moreover, in 1846, centralizing tendencies were already evident in the Glasgow area, with the merger of the various police authorities that had been established for the city and adjacent industrial districts. Political reasons played a key part in this process; the separately elected boards had acquired a reputation for radicalism, which clashed with the more patrician attitudes of Glasgow's magistrates and councillors (Maver 1996a: 451–3).[8] Particular cause for concern was the politicization of the bureaucracy in such a sensitive sphere as policing. From the municipal perspective, arbitrary decisions about hiring and firing on the basis of partisan loyalties were seen as socially destabilizing. The centralization of 1846 was intended to maintain administrative continuity as well as pool resources, providing a foretaste of the 'efficiency' arguments that came to be forcefully articulated in municipal circles by the end of the century. At a relatively early period, administrative reform was seen as both preserving and advancing the public good of the community.

Glasgow's police restructuring of 1846, under direct civic control, had the effect of transforming the city territorially as well as administratively. The absorption of outlying communities more than doubled the previous area of jurisdiction, with obvious implications for the provision of services and the role of municipal employees. The extended city began to consolidate its status among towns that 'sought to use municipal powers for social improvement', with the high-profile acquisition of Loch Katrine in 1855 serving as a declaration of civic intent about interventionist strategy (Fraser 1993: 260, Maver 1996a: 454–7). The employment of experienced officials like Burnet was reflected in other municipal growth areas. A notable example was John Carrick, appointed in 1844, with particular responsibility for Glasgow's built environment. His original job-title was superintendent of streets, but over time his commitments multiplied, and he was eventually redesignated city architect in 1862. Described in one recent history as 'the first of the great Glasgow architect-organizers', Carrick enjoyed a career which was inextricably bound up with the progress of the town council's ambitious 'Haussmannian' city improvement scheme, implemented from 1866 in an effort to clear some of the most decrepit slums and restructure the urban heartland (Glendinning et al. 1996: 256, Edwards 1993). Carrick's rise to prominence in Glasgow parallels the consolidation of the *Ufficio d'arte* in Turin, under chief engineer Eduardo Pecco, not least in his dedication to full-time service and his longevity in office.[9] Responsible for the design of a number of public buildings, including police offices, public baths and the municipal meat market, Carrick was still energetically working for the town council up to his death in 1890.

The city architect's specialist knowledge was indispensable in the context of Glasgow's mid-Victorian public health priorities. As Carrick subsequently wrote, in 1859 he formed part of an investigative committee to learn at first hand from sanitary experience elsewhere in the UK. In its report to the town council, the 'more cleanly habits of the English working-classes' were attributed, in part, to superior administration and stricter enforcement of the regulations (Carrick 1884: xxiii). The committee's recommendation to appoint a medical officer of health (MOH), along with an inspectorate, was authorized by a local police Act of 1862, an arrangement subsequently enshrined on a permanent basis in Scotland-wide legislation of 1867 (Robertson 1998: 72–3). Glasgow's first full-time MOH, James Burn Russell, acknowledged that the new sanitary task-force initially had an uphill task in combating Glasgow's 'fever-flood', notably of typhus. However, a sense of civic purpose prevailed: 'House to house visitation was begun, overcrowding was put down, the scavenger sallied forth with his broom, the lime-washer with his brush, temporary hospitals were run up, and medicines were dispensed' (Russell 1905b: 22). By the 1870s a staff of 42, excluding clerks, was in place in the sanitary department. These included five women inspectors, described in one official publication as 'missionaries of cleanliness', whose job was to disseminate the virtue of a dirt-free household (Bell and Paton 1896: 197–8). During the course of the nineteenth century, Glasgow's municipal employees, as agents of the drive for urban regeneration, were becoming more than just functionaries; they embodied the ideal of good governance by means of reshaping the moral character of the population.

Municipal employees, efficiency and 'model' management

The diversity of Glasgow's municipal expertise was immediately associated with articulate officials like Burnet, Carrick and Russell, whose flair for promoting the city was reflected from the 1860s in an impressive flow of publications about the dynamism of the city's public services. These included Burnet's pioneering history of the city's water supply, Carrick's detailed account of Glasgow's nineteenth-century structural improvements and Russell's diverse and prolific output on public health.[10] The overwhelmingly business profile of elected representatives, and the presence of wealthy entrepreneurs among the most prominent civic activists, was also conducive to the construction of a persuasive public relations machine.

Glasgow's carefully nurtured image was partly an attempt to counter criticism of expensive new undertakings, such as the water and gas supplies and city improvements. Hints of vested interests, especially in property transactions, were also submerged by the projection of the progressive and professionally run city (Maver 1996a: 460–61). The expansion of the municipal bureaucracy consequently continued, despite populist calls for stricter economy, especially after 1868, when the urban franchise in Scotland was extended to all male householders. A significant sign of changing times was the appointment of James D. Marwick as town clerk in 1873. The implementation of Glasgow's municipal policy was steered for the next 30 years by this dominating figure, whose starting salary of £2500 reflected the regard that councillors had for his abilities, and made him by far the highest-paid local government official in the UK. As has been explained in a recent analysis of Glasgow's municipal managers, Marwick's exacting standards created a role model that was evident in the authoritative style of leadership that characterized assorted civic departments and also legitimized the notion that high remuneration would ensure loyalty, impartiality and incorruptibility (Maver 2000: 72–3).

There were, of course, historic roots for Marwick's unique position among British town clerks, which related to the peculiar circumstances of Reddie's appointment during the 1800s, as well as the traditional influence of the Scottish legal profession. Nevertheless, Marwick's arrival in Glasgow, from the town clerkship of Edinburgh, allowed for an overhaul of the municipal administrative structure. A much clearer delineation of responsibilities resulted from his thorough reorganization of the office. Marwick was particularly anxious to regulate the basis of new appointments, preferring that his clerks, like himself, should devote their energies solely to municipal service. Previous practice, whereby junior staff members were often employed on an agency basis from outside law firms, was discontinued thus setting an important precedent for the town council generally (Sweeney 1990: 527–8). Marwick's senior deputies were impressively qualified law graduates from the universities of Glasgow and Edinburgh; indeed, the latter institution was his own *alma mater*. In addition to the long-standing statutory functions associated with royal burghs, they shared the law, conveyancing and parliamentary work for Glasgow's assorted municipal departments and trusts. However, apart from the town clerk's pivotal role, there was little coordinating organization between the utilities and services operating by the 1870s, and which had emerged over time according to individual needs and circumstances. Reflecting the excessive departmentalization that generally prevailed in British local government (Waller 1983: 286), Glasgow town council was prone to establishing distinctive domains for municipal managers, allowing them considerable personal freedom of action.

By 1889, Albert Shaw was making observations about the Scottish municipal system, which he compared favourably with its English and

American counterparts. With particular emphasis on Glasgow, he was impressed by the direct line of delegated responsibility from council committees to permanent officials, whom he praised for their expertise and efficiency (Shaw 1889: 35–6). It should be stressed that his continuing championship of Glasgow, 'a type of modern city with a highly developed and vigorous municipal life', was due in part to the abundant information with which he had been supplied by officials, notably Carrick and Russell (Shaw 1895b: 70). From his experience of Glasgow, Shaw firmly identified the bureaucracy as a stabilizing influence in the politicization of municipal affairs and made no secret of his disdain for mass democracy's unpredictable and 'irresponsible' impact on businesslike government (Shaw 1895b: 106, Fraser 1993: 261). Such emphasis on the impartiality of leading officials helped to burnish the image of single-minded dedication to public service, and James Dalrymple, the high-profile manager of Glasgow's tramways department from 1904, made a virtue out of his refusal to vote in municipal elections (Maver 1996b: 224). Yet, as Marwick's case strikingly illustrates, politics strongly coloured the choice of many appointments. For all his reticence on the matter after taking office, in his pre-town clerk persona he had served briefly as a Liberal councillor in Edinburgh, and ideological compatibility was an important reason for his recruitment to Glasgow.

The 1890s represented a period of profound administrative change in Glasgow, due to the first major extension of civic boundaries since 1846. Marwick had made it his personal mission to achieve the 'Greater Glasgow', and the positive projection of the city by the council's public relations machine represented part of a calculated strategy to convince central government of the need to expand the municipality. After a prolonged and expensive campaign, 2327 hectares of suburban territory were eventually incorporated in 1891, and thereafter councillors and officials set about rationalizing and restructuring the enlarged civic organization. Significantly, their task was directed by more than localized priorities. The debate about administrative reform was being conducted throughout the UK, both in the sense of redefining units of governance, such as the county councils in 1889, and in the wider sphere of devolving powers, to help relieve parliament's burden of domestic responsibilities. Moreover, a *fin de siècle* approach to innovation, to distinguish the new century from the old, gave a progressive edge to reformers' arguments. The Fabian-influenced Mabel Atkinson was consciously looking forward when she suggested 'co-operation and corporate action' as the dual imperatives for efficiency in local government (Atkinson 1904: 3). Back in 1893, Robert Crawford, an elected civic representative in Glasgow and devotee of the 'municipal socialist' ideas of Joseph Chamberlain, wrote ardently about the need for uniting and centralizing the bureaucratic apparatus. As he put it, the aim was to erode obstructive departmental barriers and effect 'due economy of both money and labour' (Crawford 1893).

The need for greater control and cohesion was all too evident from the sheer size of the civic workforce, numbering 10 000 by the mid-1890s. At the time these figures exceeded even the staffing of the LCC, although local government growth in the metropolis soon eclipsed the Scottish city (Clifton 1989: 9–10). In Glasgow new utilities, notably the tramways and electricity departments, had added to the civic establishment, while traditional commitments were increasing in step with the expanding population. Shaw reported with relish that over 1000 men were employed in the cleansing department as scavengers, whose contribution to efficiency during the horse-drawn era was to accumulate manure from city thoroughfares, for onwards processing as saleable fertilizer. Another substantial section of employees was the corps of police officers, numbering 1400 in 1895, whose 'strong sense of fidelity' was encouraged by superior working conditions, including the introduction of retirement pensions in 1891 (Shaw 1895b: 96–7, 110). As Shaw indicated, a more scientific approach towards human resources management was undoubtedly preoccupying civic representatives during this reforming decade. In 1893, for example, the experience of English local authorities was investigated, to compare arrangements for the grading of salaries and provision of pensions for non-police personnel. The LCC, with its classified four-tier grading structure and provident scheme for retirement, represented the kind of ordered approach that most appealed to Glasgow's 'efficiency' enthusiasts. As was stressed in the subsequent report to town councillors, employee strength in numbers constituted a 'powerful weapon' in the event of industrial disputes, and incentive schemes were thus highly desirable to counter disaffection.[11]

Despite the rhetoric about efficiency and progress during the 1890s, municipal conditions of service, even for the white-collar workforce, were not as 'model' as councillors liked to claim. Superannuation represented a particularly sluggish example of employer inaction, paralleling the prolonged experience of Montreal's workforce in securing a retirement plan.[12] In Glasgow the 1893 proposals were talked about, a draft scheme was delineated, but elected representatives could not agree on its precise form. Over the years the subject was periodically revived, notably in 1908, when a scheme was conclusively rejected (*Glasgow Herald*, 20 August 1908). The Liberal government's commitment to introducing state-sanctioned old-age pensions, along German lines, was seen as obviating the need for change.[13] It was not until 1923, 30 years after the original proposals, and following sustained pressure throughout Britain from NALGO, that Glasgow Corporation inaugurated a scheme for employees aged 20 and over. Even the less contentious issue of grading had languished until 1899, when the previous discussions were resuscitated by John Lindsay, then employed as administrative head of the police department. The scheme that finally emerged in 1902 was similar to the LCC clerical structure, except with five classifications rather than four.

Grading structures were an attempt to overcome departmental differentials and allowed employees greater scope for job mobility within the civic bureaucracy. Yet the benefits of more uniform administration, as envisaged by Crawford in 1893, were ambiguous. In 1895, there had been a major centralizing reorganization when the police and other civic trusts came to be vested in one controlling authority, the Corporation of the City of Glasgow. The fragmented structure that had evolved as a result of the legal limitations of burghal authority could now, theoretically, be overcome. However, in reality considerable departmental autonomy remained. In her analysis of the Corporation's clerical staff during the 1900s, R. Guerriero Wilson (1998), 226–7 suggests that departments continued to operate like 'individual small businesses', where working conditions varied enormously according to managerial practices and personalities. Nor did greater uniformity necessarily coalesce over the prewar period. A recurring criticism of the tramways department under Dalrymple's management from 1904 to 1926 was that he ran the Corporation's biggest service as if it was his own business enterprise (Maver 1996b: 224). On the other hand, from an industrial relations perspective, there were advantages in retaining the departmental focus. Concentrating employees in distinctive units diminished the prospect of establishing a cross-departmental identity, and diluted the strength of the collective bargaining machinery. The early history of municipal trade unionism in Glasgow was associated with specific departmental grievances that triggered a recruitment drive, although over the 1900s worker organization began to transcend lines of demarcation.

There were favourable conditions for trade union expansion among the workforce during the 1890s. The determination of councillors to municipalize the private tramways company, partly to protect civic interests in the developing sphere of electric traction, brought them together with local union representatives, who saw a range of staff benefits under public ownership (Fraser 1993: 264–7, Maver 1996b: 216–17). Concern to appear as the 'model' employer added to the enlightened image, especially after John Burns, trade union leader and outspoken exponent of 'municipal socialism' on the LCC, lavishly praised Glasgow's civic management and working conditions (Burns 1892: 677–8). In response, London Progressivism was seen as dynamic by many of Glasgow's municipal activists, its visionary appeal strongly echoing the long-standing evangelical moral mission in the Scottish city (Pennybacker 1995). Absorbing much from the London experience, Labour representatives began to be elected as councillors in Glasgow, and were particularly successful in 1896, when nine were returned. A loosely organized group, and by no means all socialists, they were instrumental in achieving the principle of the minimum wage for municipal employees in 1898 (Fraser 1993: 269). One year later the Gas Workers' and General Labourers' Union of Great Britain and Ireland, an organization with London roots, attempted to secure negotiating rights for staff within the Corporation. However, its leaders were identified by councillors as too militant and politically motivated for harmonious industrial relations, revealing that, even in Glasgow, there were limits to the advance of municipal socialism (Maver 1996b: 219–20).

Despite this rejection, Labour councillors successfully pursued the principle of trade union recognition, and in 1904 another national organization, the Municipal Employees' Association (MEA), began to recruit at departmental level. The MEA had originated among LCC manual workers, once again emphasizing the trade union links with the metropolitan labour movement (ibid.: 227). As its title suggests, the MEA recruited solely in the local government sector, and this exclusivity was greatly preferred by Glasgow's civic leaders. In comparison, white-collar trade unionism was slower in coming. NALGO, which had been founded in London in 1905, drew its original membership from English local authorities. While service conditions issues like superannuation had been a major reason for its creation, NALGO was initially more a blend of professional association and friendly society than trade union. Scottish municipal employees began to be recruited from 1911, although the membership activities of Glasgow Corporation staff around this time are not specifically mentioned in NALGO's official history (Spoor 1967: 42–3). Yet, perhaps significantly, in 1913 the Corporation instituted entrance examinations for clerical and administrative workers, a move that represented the kind of merit-based selection process for which NALGO was campaigning. A formal Glasgow branch was eventually inaugurated in 1919 (Bell 1989: 29) and, unlike the trade union experience of Toulouse, described elsewhere in this volume, separate organization for white-collar and manual workers persisted until the 1990s.[14] It is highly revealing that chief officials were the driving force in the creation of the NALGO branch, above all the ubiquitous John Lindsay, who since 1912 had been following in Marwick's footsteps as the city's town clerk.

National and international influences on municipal Glasgow

The twentieth-century increase in local government trade unionism indicated a greater degree of collaboration across individual municipalities, in recognition that shared experiences could be mutually beneficial. The unions were ahead of the employers, who for decades guarded conditions in their individual localities. The question of fixing national standards through a Whitley-style joint negotiating machinery, covering England and Wales and (separately) Scotland, had foundered in 1921. It was not until 1937 that a Joint Industrial Council was inaugurated north of the border, an arrangement that until the 1960s remained unsatisfactory for the unions, because Scottish employers tended to be less generous than their southern counterparts (Spoor 1967: 79–89, 379–83). However, the employers' groups involved – the Scottish County Councils' Association, the Counties of Cities Association and the Convention of Royal Burghs – had a history of pooling expertise in a number of areas. The need to protect local authority interests, especially over the thorny questions of finance and central–local government relations, often compelled a collective response. From the last quarter of the nineteenth century, following the creation of the Association of Municipal Corporations in 1872, there was also cross-border cooperation. As Hamish Fraser has shown, organized pressure from the larger urban municipalities, anxious to protect their gas enterprises, ensured strict government controls over the development of the fledgling electricity supply industry throughout the UK (Fraser 1990: 70). From the early 1880s, Scottish cities, notably Glasgow and Aberdeen, had been prominent participants in the campaign, and their town clerks acted as legal agents on the municipalities' behalf.

Glasgow town council had long been receptive to urban innovation elsewhere, as was demonstrated by the experience of John Carrick, as part of the 1859 delegation investigating comparative public health administration. Nor was such interest confined to the British Isles. From the 1860s, the accessibility of Europe via the expanding shipping and railway network meant that civic representatives and officials could more readily visit continental cities. As has been well documented, Paris under the Second Empire became an early focus of their attention (Edwards 1993: 88–9, Maver 1996a: 460, 1998: 334–5). Municipal leaders readily identified with the bold 'Haussmannian' planning project, and referred to it repeatedly in efforts to persuade citizens of the virtues of their own city improvement scheme. A fact-finding delegation to Paris in June 1866 included the city's first MOH, Professor William Gairdner, as well as the much-travelled Carrick. Their presence indicated more than commitment to civic professionalism; it also represented concern to reinforce the aesthetic qualities of urban design by means of sanitary control, a blend of priorities that was thought to have worked well in Paris. The subsequent lengthy report of the visit was glowing in its testimonial to the French capital, the summer sunshine clearly having mellowed Scottish attitudes. What most struck delegation members was the openness and salubrity they experienced, compared with the claustrophobic and corrosive atmosphere of industrial Glasgow.[15]

As many of Glasgow's municipal leaders shared a deeply ingrained Liberal–evangelical ethos, moral order was considered to be another important benefit of Parisian-style restructuring. They consequently identified with what they saw as 'the diminished turbulence and restlessness' of Paris, 'the uprooting of Socialism and Communism, the cultivation everywhere of the arts of peace'.[16] This upbeat appraisal of social harmony in Paris was soon overturned in 1871 by the trauma of the Commune; however, it is revealing that the Napoleonic mode of governance found favour in Glasgow, to the extent that the 1866 delegation expressed admiration for 'the great strength given to the executive under the Continental systems of administration'.[17] Legal constraints on regulatory enforcement were recognized as tempering similar developments at home, but the Glaswegians did their best to transform the inner city with broad thoroughfares, prestigious buildings and open spaces. Carrick was a keen exponent of the monumentalism of 1860s Parisian architecture, which he promoted as a deliberate contrast to the less grandiose, indigenous style. Amidst all the post-1866 structural upheaval, Carrick and his close colleague, Russell, acted as eloquent points of communication between councillors and the public. Their openness to outside ideas helped to consolidate Glasgow's modernizing image, and set standards for other cities to follow. Joseph Chamberlain, Birmingham's radical mayor, absorbed such influences a decade later, when the dual rationale of 'health and morality' underpinned ambitious improvement plans for the English city (Morris 2000: 413).

Paris was by no means the sole focus of civic attention in Glasgow from the 1860s. The consolidation of local government powers had made it imperative to learn from a range of cities, especially in the fast-developing sphere of public health administration. During 1866, the Glasgow delegation made a point of visiting Brussels and Amsterdam, to investigate the mechanisms for sewage disposal adopted by the two cities. They were only prevented from visiting German cities because of the war with Austria. Closer to home, London's Metropolitan Board of Works (MBW), which since 1856 had provided a highly professionalized focus for the city's infrastructural development, included Glasgow among several municipalities seeking advice on drainage and sewerage schemes. The MBW's eminent, full-time engineer, Joseph Bazalgette, duly acted as consultant to the Scottish city, although in the short term his proposals proved too costly for the town council, already under criticism from electors because of the expense of city improvement plans (Clifton 1992: 126–7, Bell and Paton 1896: 140). Yet London was not necessarily a role model, according to MOH Russell, in an address to the British Medical Association in 1876. He commented on the unease felt by a Glasgow delegation on a recent visit to the capital, to study working-class housing erected by assorted philanthropic agencies. The London vogue for new tenement apartments, sometimes seven storeys high, all too readily echoed the discredited style of Glaswegian multi-occupancy living, which city improvements were aiming to eradicate (Russell 1905a: 135–8). Russell's criticisms, voiced in a national forum, suggest that the interchange of professional ideas about social welfare was extending beyond the sphere of direct municipal involvement.

From the 1870s the conjunction of sanitary and aesthetic improvements in civic priorities was reflected in a more proactive strategy towards public well-being, especially the provision of cultural amenities. While this was a phenomenon throughout Britain, Glasgow's municipal leaders were concerned to demonstrate that they were being imaginative and outward looking about their responsibilities. In 1877, James Paton was appointed curator of the city art galleries. Two years later, because of the large number of valuable Flemish and Dutch paintings in the collection, he was sent to Belgium and The Netherlands to learn about methods of conservation and display. The example of Brussels, in particular, came to exert a strong influence on Glasgow's cultural policy. As Paton reported, the Belgian national museums and galleries had the kind of integrated approach that fostered both community identity and national unity.[18]

Similarly, in 1878, Duncan Maclellan, superintendent of public parks, was despatched on a lengthy tour of European cities. His primary objective was to visit the Paris *Exposition Universelle*, showing the importance of the international exhibitionary impulse in drawing together experts from a range of disciplines: in this case, the developing sphere of leisure and recreation. It is worth emphasizing that Glaswegians had been attending the Paris *Expositions* since 1867, when municipal representatives first officially displayed the Scottish city's newly accredited coat-of-arms. The 1900 *Exposition*, an extravaganza where nations vied with each other to reach new heights of competitive display, so impressed Glasgow Corporation visitors that several exhibits were acquired second-hand for use the following year at the city's own

International Exhibition (Kinchin and Kinchin 1988: 56, Rodgers 1998: 8–32). Back in 1878, Maclellan's learning experience of urban Europe was aided considerably by the 'genial' summer climate. This favourable impression of continental lifestyles appeared in his report to councillors, where he placed great stress on the apparent benefits of fresh air, open spaces and sunshine in encouraging 'rational' behaviour (Maclellan 1878: 7).

Maclellan's successor as parks superintendent, James Whitton, continued the tradition of European travel as a means of educating civic officials (Maver 1998: 340–42). His detailed observations of a visit in 1897 were particularly revealing about attitudes towards the modernizing mission of continental municipalities:

> The widening and improving of streets, the clearing away of common-place buildings to give greater space around those of architectural dignity or historic interest, the prominence given to new buildings for government or municipal purposes (itself a noteworthy feature), the general excellence of the electric lighting of the streets, and the great use made of electrical traction on tramways – these, along with many other minor matters, made it apparent that our continental neighbours, especially the Germans, are very much alive to the fact that modern requirements and a beautiful city mean a greater inflow of that commodity which is universally desired, and many more comforts and privileges which the possession of money secures.[19]

As described by Bénédicte Zimmermann, the economic and social functions of 'local self-administration' in *Kaiserreich* Germany were having an impact on informed Glasgow opinion.[20] The German Empire had replaced the old French Empire in the hearts and minds of civic practitioners, especially as it seemed to project the kind of efficiency and order to which they aspired. Moreover, 'Greater Glasgow' expansionism during the 1890s was encouraging the search for models that could help municipal leaders come to terms with larger-scale commitments. Germany thus had considerable relevance, with Berlin the prime example of a city that was growing fast, yet had developed an appropriate mechanism for dealing with the attendant pressures (Shaw 1895a: 333–5).

The power of the professionals was a feature of the German system, and had appeal for those in Glasgow who admired a strong executive role in administration. Indeed, there were obvious parallels between the Glasgow town clerk and the German *bürgermeister* in terms of their paid, professional status, their legal training and the control they could exercise over the administrative function. It was in this stabilizing context during the 1900s that admirers of the German system saw sense in edging the town clerk's position nearer to that of a Scottish *bürgermeister*, for the purposes of coordinating civic strategy. Germany was not the only country where professional expertise was being encouraged in the public sector; in the United States the recent idea of the city manager was having widespread appeal, not least to act as a check on the corruption rife in municipal politics. Bernard Aspinwall has exhaustively explored Glasgow's transatlantic civic connections at the time, commenting on the extent of councillors' knowledge about the USA, which was probably the most advanced of any British representative body (Aspinwall 1984: 139).

In 1905, after Marwick's retirement, a blend of German and American influences contributed to a radical attempt to redefine the Glasgow town clerkship. However, the proposal was thwarted by the Scottish legal profession, which doggedly refused to countenance any change in status. Above all, the prospect of recruiting a person unqualified in Scots law was deemed to be wholly unacceptable, which meant that the original plan to appoint an English-trained solicitor had to be withdrawn (Maver 2000: 73–4). Yet, for all the professional opposition, there were still strong advocates of a city manager up to the Second World War, and Glasgow was apparently the only British municipality where the debate remained robust (Harris 1939: 90).[21] By this time there was no longer a radical rationale behind the argument; anti-socialist councillors were anxious to undermine the political ascendancy of the Labour party, arising from postwar electoral democratization, and saw the city manager as a convenient neutralizing device.

In the years immediately before the First World War, Glasgow's civic officials were frequent travellers to Europe and North America. In 1905, James Dalrymple was famously 'borrowed' by the Progressive mayor of Chicago to advise on the city's transport system (Aspinwall 1984: 179–80). Dalrymple subsequently acted as a consultant for tramways development in Bombay and São Paulo, the latter city shown by Cristina Mehrtens to have been particularly open to outside ideas.[22] In addition to providing technical expertise during the 1900s, Glasgow's municipal personnel also served in an ambassadorial capacity. The *Entente Cordiale*, encouraged between Britain and France from 1904, sparked renewed interest in cross-Channel cooperation, and considerable press publicity was given to an official visit to French cities in 1907. Pierre-Yves Saunier has examined the background to this interchange, with specific reference to the initiative of Edouard Herriot, mayor of Lyons, in welcoming representatives from British municipalities (Saunier 1999: 28). In 1906, a delegation from Lyons had toured Glasgow, Edinburgh and Manchester, and the following year Herriot took the opportunity to offer reciprocal hospitality to all three municipalities. There were practical exhibitions organized for the visitors to Lyons, with emphasis on public health, but the lofty themes of 'the world's peace and the uninterrupted march of civilization' featured forcefully in the rhetoric of the Glasgow delegation.[23]

However, up to August 1914, the city's German connections continued to be strong, especially after Daniel Macaulay Stevenson became lord provost in 1911. A radical Liberal and dedicated internationalist, his brother-in-law, Robert Heidmann, was *bürgermeister* of Hamburg. Along with town clerk Lindsay, Stevenson headed a delegation to Düsseldorf in 1912, at the invitation of the German government. As the subsequent Corporation report made quite explicit, no English city was similarly represented.[24] The occasion was a municipal congress, accompanied by a large-scale civic exhibition, where the themes of town planning, public utilities and social welfare formed the central displays. Inevitably, the First World War and its dislocating aftermath helped to undermine some of the international networks previously established, and introspective attitudes meant that enthusiasts like Stevenson were accused of pro-German sympathies. However, it is significant that in 1913 the International Union of Local Authorities (IULA) had been founded in Belgium, and from the mid-1920s made strenuous efforts to re-establish municipal relationships across national boundaries.[25]

Glasgow Corporation, meantime, became caught up in the financial crisis arising from the Depression, which hit the city's heavy industrial base particularly hard. That the Labour party became the controlling power within the Corporation from 1933 did not initially inspire business confidence, unlike the more collaborative experience of Montreal's municipal government.[26] Yet Labour politicians remained acutely aware of the impact of public relations, above all journalist Patrick Dollan, the driving force behind their civic organization, who became lord provost in 1938. A high-profile visit to New York the following year, to coincide with the World's Fair, not only aimed to restore Glasgow's international reputation, but, according to Dollan, provided the starting point for professional interchange between municipalities in Scotland and the USA. This related especially to the training of employees, and he declared his commitment to introducing American ideas of 'progressive development' to younger Corporation officials (*Glasgow Herald*, 11 August 1939). Although they were expressed by a socialist of impeccable 'Red Clydeside' credentials, there was a turn-of-the-century 'efficiency' edge to such aspirations. War, at all events, soon cut across Glasgow's international municipal mission, which never had the same potency in the post-1945 climate of central government-inspired reconstruction.

Conclusion

This broad overview of Glasgow's municipal employees and services from the pioneering Police Act of 1800 has necessarily been selective, and the themes highlighted to some extent reflect the current state of research into the Scottish city. As Michèle Dagenais points out in her analysis of 1930s Montreal, the trend towards state centralization has tended to overwhelm historians' interest in the administrative role and function of local government during the inter-war period. The experience of Glasgow is no different. Yet the unprecedented scale of operations during the 1930s, as extensive new responsibilities such as schooling were taken over by the Corporation, suggests further areas of investigation, in order to give deeper insight into the organization of the largest municipal workforce in the UK outside London. Moreover, while postwar nationalization of utilities like gas and electricity supplies, as well as several aspects of health and social services, caused the Corporation to lose some of its key workers, almost 49 000 staff were still employed by the early 1950s. How far the 'welfare state' cut across Glasgow's civic responsibilities is a question yet to be fully addressed, especially in light of the 1975 changes to Scottish local government. The creation of Strathclyde Regional Council, the largest elected local authority in Europe between 1975 and 1996, which served over two million people, can be seen in some respects as an extension of 'Greater Glasgow' administrative expansionism, even though the region was intended to diminish the domination of the city in the west of Scotland.

Beyond Scotland, other areas of research have been indicated by the contributions to this book, including analyses of particular categories of staff, the influence of municipal trade unions, employer–employee relations and the impact of new administrative practices. The growth of professionalism has been a recurring theme, not only in the context of education and training, but in the dissemination and exchange of ideas locally, nationally and internationally. Glasgow's overseas connections were evidently wide-ranging from the 1860s; establishing how typical this experience was within other large municipalities would make an intriguing point of comparison. In the twenty-first century, the term 'local self-government' is being revived in an effort to stem the alienation of the public from overcentralized government and encourage citizenship and greater community participation. As has been shown throughout this volume, the history of what this meant in practice, from as far back as the 1800s, is worthy of further illumination at the comparative level.

Notes

1. See Chapter 1.
2. In 1933, the LCC reached its maximum number of employees, 85 676 (Clifton 1989: 10). On the eve of the Second World War, Glasgow Corporation was by far the biggest employer of the 'provincial' British cities, with a workforce of 44 069 (Harris 1939: 86).
3. In 1975, the Convention of Royal Burghs became the Convention of Scottish Local Authorities (COSLA), which at the time of writing (2001) projects itself as 'the representative voice of Scotland's unitary local authorities'.
4. The Burgh Reform Act of 1833 bestowed electoral rights in royal and parliamentary burghs on £10 property owners. This 'democratization' in Scotland was relative. The overall valuation of property was lower than in England and Wales, which meant that the right to vote was more exclusive.
5. George Montagu Harris placed the concept of local self-government in the context of John Stuart Mill's classic definition: 'all businesses purely local – all which concerns only a single locality – should devolve upon the local authorities' (Harris 1939: 5–6).
6. GCA [Glasgow City Archives] DTC 14.3.1 (1831 [1800]), Glasgow Police Act, 1800.
7. See Chapter 3.
8. Separate police boards existed for the city of Glasgow and the communities of Anderston, Calton and Gorbals. All were significant industrial growth areas, notably in textile manufacture. The election of police commissioners, to serve the boards, was on the basis of ratepayers' rights of representation, a situation that did not prevail in civic government until 1833. However, in Glasgow the police boards were always under the jurisdiction of the town council's magistrates.
9. See Chapter 2. A professional architect, Carrick was replaced in 1890 by Alexander B. Macdonald, a Glasgow University-trained civil engineer.
10. See, for example, Carrick (1884). As well as producing numerous official reports for Glasgow Corporation, Russell wrote for professional colleagues in the medical and sanitary spheres. He was also well known for his polemical writing about the state of Glasgow's public health. A list of his published papers, mostly journal articles, appears in Chalmers (1905), xxix–xxii.
11. GCA DTC 14.1.26 (1892/95), *Glasgow Corporation: Special Committee on Council Work, 1892–1895*, 127.
12. See Chapter 7.
13. German influences on British social policy, including pensions, form the theme of Hennock (1987).
14. See Chapter 9. UNISON was created in 1993 from a merger of three public sector unions, including NALGO. The MEA merged with a number of unions in 1924, including the Gas Workers' and General Labourers' Union, and from 1989 the union has been known as the GMB (originally from General, Municipal and Boilermakers).
15. GCA DTC 14.2.2 (1866), *Notes on Personal Observations and Inquiries in June, 1866, on the City Improvements of Paris, etc: with Appendix*, 17–18.
16. Ibid., 8–10.
17. Ibid., 10.

18. GCA DTC 14.2.26 (1879), *Report on a Visit to Museums and Galleries in Holland and Belgium, 1879, by James Paton*, 14.
19. GCA MP 32.823 (1899), *Report by Mr James Whitton, Superintendent of Parks, on his visit to continental parks, gardens, etc., 1897*, 4.
20. See Chapter 5.
21. Scottish local government reorganization in 1975 created the post of chief executive, which replaced that of town clerk. Scots law qualifications were not a prerequisite for the job.
22. See Chapter 8.
23. GCA MP 34.152 (1909), *Speeches Delivered in Connection with the Visit of Representatives of British Municipalities to Lyons and other Cities in France*, 14.
24. GCA C2.1.13 (1913), *Report of Representatives to the Düsseldorf Municipal Congress and Exhibition*, 1.
25. For the background to the origins of municipal internationalism, see Payre and Saunier (2000) and Saunier (2001), as well as the contributors to Saunier (2002).
26. See Chapter 7.

Bibliography

Abbot, Andrew (1988), *The System of Professions: An Essay on the Division of Expert Labor*, Chicago: University of Chicago Press.

Actes de la Recherche en Sciences Sociales (2000), Special Issue, 'Sur la science de l'Etat', June (133).

Adickes, Franz and Beutler, A.D. (1903), *Die sozialen Aufgaben der deutschen Städte*, Leipzig: Duncker and Humblot.

Adorno, Salvatore (1996), 'Professionisti, famiglie e amministrazione in una periferia: Siracusa 1860–1930', in Malatesta, Maria (ed.), *Storia d'Italia, Annali 10: I professionisti*, Turin: Einaudi, 623–65.

Adorno, Salvatore (1998), 'Storie di impiegati comunali in una città meridionale dell'Ottocento', in Soresina, Marco (ed.), *Colletti bianchi. Ricerche su impiegati, funzionari e tecnici in Italia fra '800 e '900*, Milan: Franco Angeli, 72–109.

Adorno, Salvatore and Sorba, Carlotta (eds) (1991), *Municipalita e borghesie padane tra Ottocento e Novecento: alcuni casi di studio*, Milan: Franco Angeli.

Agulhon, Maurice, Girard, Louis, Robert, Jean-Louis and Serman, William (eds) (1986), *Les maires en France du Consulat à nos jours*, Paris: Publications de la Sorbonne.

Aimo, Piero and Bigaran, Maria Pia (eds) (1986), *Istituzioni e borghesie locali nell'Italia liberale*, Milan: Franco Angeli.

Alaimo, Aurelio (1990a), 'Bologna', in ISAP, *Le riforme crispine*, vol. 3, *Amministrazione locale*, Milan: Giuffrè, 3–80.

Alaimo, Aurelio (1990b), *L'organizzazione della città: amministrazione comunale e politica urbana a Bologna dopo l'unità (1859–1889)*, Bologna: Il Mulino.

'Amtliche und gewerkschaftliche Arbeitslosenzählung in Stuttgart' (1902), *Correspondenzblatt der Generalkommission der Gewerkschaften Deutschlands*, 17 November, 46.

Anderson, Annelise Graebner (1979), 'The development of municipal fire departments in the United States', *Journal of Libertarian Studies*, 3(3), 331–59.

Andrade, C. (1996), 'Barry Parker em São Paulo', paper presented at the IV SHCU, November.

'Anos de Formação' (1998), 'Exhibition Catalogue', Escola de Sociologia e Política, May, 25–7.

Armstrong, Christopher and Nelles, H.V. (1983), *Monopoly's Moment: The Organization and Regulation of Canadian Utilities, 1830–1930*, Philadelphia: Temple University Press.

Aron, Cindy Sondik (1987), *Ladies and Gentlemen of the Civil Service: Middle-Class Workers in Victorian America*, New York: Oxford University Press.

Artibise, Alan F.J. (1975), *Winnipeg: A Social History of Urban Growth, 1874–1914*, Montreal: McGill-Queen's University Press.

Aspinwall, Bernard (1984), *Portable Utopia: Glasgow and the United States, 1820–1920*, Aberdeen: Aberdeen University Press.

Atkinson, Mabel (1904), *Local Government in Scotland*, Edinburgh and London: William Blackwood & Sons.

Bade, Klaus (ed.) (1984), *Auswanderer – Wanderarbeiter – Gastarbeiter. Bevölkerung, Arbeitsmarkt und Wanderung in Deutschland seit der Mitte des 19. Jahrhunderts*, Ostfildern: Scripta Mercaturae.

Baldissara, Luca (1994), *Per una città più bella e più grande: il governo municipale di Bologna negli anni della ricostruzione (1945–1956)*, Bologna: Il Mulino.

Baldissara, Luca (1998), *Tecnica e politica nell'amministrazione: saggio sulle culture amministrative e di governo municipale fra anni trenta e cinquanta*, Bologna: Il Mulino.

Balzani, Roberto (1991), *Un comune imprenditore: pubblici servizi, infrastrutture urbane e società à forlì, 1865–1945*, Milan: Franco Angeli.

Banfield, Edward G. and Wilson, James Q. (1963), *City Politics*, New York: Vintage.

Banti, Alberto Maria (1996), *Storia della borghesia italiana. L'età liberale*, Rome: Donzelli.

Barros, L. (1992), *Prefeitura. O poder em São Paulo*, São Paulo: PMSP/Cortez.

Bastos, A. (1969), *História da política revolucionária do Brasil I. 1930–1932*, Rio de Janeiro: Conquista.

Becker, Peter and Clark, William (2001), *Little Tools of Knowledge: Historical Essays on Bureaucratic and Academic Practices*, Ann Arbor: Michigan University Press.

Beckstein, Hermann (1991), *Städtische Interessen-Politik Organisation und Politik der Städtetage in Bayern, Preussen und im Deutschen Reich, 1896–1923*, Düsseldorf: Droste.

Bell, Sir James and Paton, James (1896), *Glasgow: Its Municipal Organization and Administration*, Glasgow: James Maclehose & Sons.

Bell, Karen R. (1989), 'A History of NALGO in Scotland', unpublished MPhil thesis, University of Strathclyde.

Bellamy, Christine (1988), *Administering Central–Local Relations, 1871–1919: The Local Government Board in its Fiscal and Cultural Context*, Manchester: Manchester University Press.

Bellanger, Emmanuel (2001), 'L'Ecole nationale d'administration municipale: des "sans-grade" devenus secrétaires généraux', *Politix* (53), March, 145–71.

Bellanger, Emmanuel, Pennetier, Claude, Siwek Pouydesseau, Jeanne, Velay, Michel and Yohana, Emmanuelle (2000), *Ville-employeur et personnel communal: élus et syndicalistes face à la question de l'emploi depuis 1919*, Paris: Programme de Recherche 'Ville et Emploi', Ministère de l'Equipement des Transports et du Logement.

Bender, Thomas (1999), 'Intellectuals, cities, and citizenship in the United States: the 1890s and 1990s', *Citizenship Studies*, 3 (2), 203–20.

Berlinck, C. (1958), *A Escola de Sociologia e Política de São Paulo, 1933–1958*, São Paulo: ESP.

Berman, Jay Stuart (1987), *Police Administration and Progressive Reform: Theodore Roosevelt as Police Commissioner of New York*, New York: Greenwood Press.

Berselli, Aldo, Della Peruta, Franco and Varni, Angelo (1988), *La Municipalizzazione nell'area padana: storia ed esperienze a confronto*, Milan: Franco Angeli.

Bigaran, Mariapia (1990), 'Il personale burocratico', in ISAP (ed.), *Le riforme crispine*, vol. 3, *Amministrazione locale*, Milan: Giuffrè, 859–92.

Bittencourt, C. (1990), *Pátria, Civilização e Trabalho*, São Paulo: Loyola.

Blackbourn, David and Eley, Geoff (1984), *The Peculiarities of German History*, Oxford: Oxford University Press.

Blackstone, Geoffrey Vaughan (1957), *A History of the British Fire Service*, London: Routledge.

Bledstein, Burton J. (1976), *The Culture of Professionalism: The Middle Class and the Development of Higher Education in America*, New York: Norton.

Blotevogel, Hans H. (ed.) (1990), *Kommunale Leistungsverwaltung und Stadtentwicklung vom Vormärz bis zur Weimarer Republik*, Cologne: Böhlau.

Blumin, Stuart M. (1989), *The Emergence of the Middle Class: Social Experience in the American City, 1760–1900*, New York: Cambridge University Press.

Bocquet, Denis and De Pieri, Filippo (2002), 'Public works and municipal government in two Italian capital cities: comparing technical bureaucracies in Turin and Rome, 1868–88', *Modern Italy*, 7(2), 143–52.

Boltanski, Luc and Thévenot, Laurent (1991), *De la justification. Les économies de la grandeur*, Paris: Gallimard.

Bourdieu, Pierre (1984), 'Espace social et genèse des classes', *Actes de la recherche en sciences sociales* (52/53), June, 3–12.

Bourdon, J. (1974), *Le personnel communal*, Paris: Editions Berger-Levrault.

Bourjol, Maurice (1975), *La réforme municipale*, Paris: Editions Berger-Levrault.

Bracco, Giuseppe (2000a), 'La finanza comunale', in Levra, Umberto (ed.), *Storia di Torino*, vol. 6, *La città nel Risorgimento (1798–1864)*, Turin: Einaudi, 97–131.

Bracco, Giuseppe (ed.) (2000b), *1859–1864. I progetti di una capitale in trasformazione. Dalla città dei servizi alla città dell'industria*, Turin: Archivio Storico della Città.

Branco, P. (1934), 'Contribuição para a reforma das organizações municipais', *RAM* (5), October, 33–42.

Branco, P. (1936a), 'Carta', *RAM* (24), June, 143.

Branco, P. (1936b), 'O arenito asfáltico paulista', *RAM* (28), October, 67–80.

Brayley, Arthur Wellington (1889), *A Complete History of the Boston Fire Department from 1630–1888*, Boston: John Dale and Company.

Brown, Callum (1996), '"To be aglow with civic ardours": the "Godly Commonwealth" in Glasgow, 1843–1914', *Records of the Scottish Church History Society* (26), 169–195.

Browne, Gary Larson (1980), *Baltimore in the Nation*, Chapel Hill: University of North Carolina Press.

Brunet, Jean-Paul (1980), *Saint-Denis, la ville rouge, 1890–1939*, Paris: Hachette.

Brunet, Jean-Paul (1981), *Un demi-siècle de gestion municipale à Saint-Denis la Rouge (1890–1939)*, Paris: Cujas.

Burdeau, F. (1989), *Histoire de l'administration française du 18 au 20ème siècle*, Paris: Montchrétien.

Burlen, Katherine (ed.) (1987), *La banlieue oasis: Henri Sellier et les cités-jardins, 1900–1940*, Paris: Presses Universitaires de Vincennes.

Burns, John (1892), 'Let London live!', *The Nineteenth Century* (31), April, 673–85.

Byrne, Tony (1994), *Local Government in Britain*, London: Penguin Books.

Calabi, Donatella (1997), 'L'architetto', in Malatesta, Maria (ed.), *I professionisti, Storia d'Italia. Annale 10*, Turin: Einaudi, 339–75.

Caracciolo, Alberto (1956), *Roma capitale. Dal Risorgimento alla crisi dello stato liberale*, Rome: Editori Riuniti (fifth edition, 1999).

Caracciolo, Alberto (1985), 'Le tre capitali d'Italia: Torino, Firenze, Roma', in De Seta, Cesare (ed.), *Le città capitali*, Rome and Bari: Laterza, 195–200.

Cardim Filho, C. (1951), *Problemas urbanos da capital*, São Paulo: PMSP.

Cardim Filho, C. (1953), 'Engenheiro Arthur Saboya', *Revista De Engenharia*, 11 (130), 346.

Cardoso, I. (1982), *A universidade da comunhão paulista*, São Paulo: Cortez.

Cardoza, Anthony L. (1997), *Aristocrats in Bourgeois Italy: The Piedmontese Nobility, 1861–1930*, Cambridge: Cambridge University Press.

Carpinelli, Saverio (1997), 'Il lavoro negli enti locali in età liberale', in Melis, Guido and Varni, Angelo (eds) (1997), *Le fatiche di Monsù Travet. Per una storia del lavoro pubblico in Italia*, Turin: Rosenberg and Sellier, 61–79.

Carrick, John (1884), 'Introductory chapter on the progress of Glasgow', in Robertson, David (ed.), *Glasgow Past and Present: Illustrated in Dean of Guild Reports and in the Reminiscences and Communications of Senex, Aliquis, J.B., etc.* (volume I), Glasgow: David Robertson & Co., xv–lx.

Carson, Kit and Idzikowska, Hilary (1989), 'The social production of Scottish policing, 1795–1900', in Hay, Douglas and Snyder, Francis (eds), *Policing and Prosecution in Britain, 1750 to 1850*, Oxford: Oxford University Press.

Cassedy, J. Albert (1891), *Firemen's Record*, Baltimore: Wm. Day and Company.

Castronovo, Valerio (1987), *Torino*, Rome and Bari: Laterza.

Chalmers, A.K. (ed.) (1905), *Public Health Administration in Glasgow: A Memorial Volume of the Writings of J.B. Russell*, Glasgow: James Maclehose & Sons.

Chandler, Alfred D., Jr. (1977), *The Visible Hand: The Managerial Revolution in American Business*, Cambridge: Harvard University Press.

Châtelet, Anne-Marie (1991), 'La conception haussmannienne du rôle des ingénieurs et architectes municipaux', in Des Cars, Jean and Pinon, Pierre (eds), *Paris-Haussmann*, Paris: Picard/Éditions du Pavillon de l'Arsenal, 257–66.

Ciucci, Giorgio (1989), *Gli architetti e il fascismo. Architettura e città 1922–1944*, Turin: Einaudi.

Clark, T.N. and Ferguson, L.C. (1983), *City Money, Political Processes,*

Fiscal Strain and Retrenchment, New York: Columbia University Press.

Claude, Viviane (1999), 'Le travail de la différence: expériences comparatives dans le champ municipal à Strasbourg (1900–1930)', *Genèses* (37), December, 114–34.

Clifton, Gloria (1989), 'Members and officers of the LCC, 1889–1965', in Saint, Andrew (ed.), *Politics and the People of London: the London County Council, 1889–1965*, London: Hambledon Press, 1–26.

Clifton, Gloria (1992), *Professionalism, Patronage and Public Service in Victorian London: the Staff of the Metropolitan Board of Works, 1856–1889*, London: Athlone Press.

Cockburn, Henry (1910 [1856]), *Memorials of his Time, 1779–1830*, Edinburgh: T.N. Foulis.

Cohen, William B. (1998), *Urban Government and the Rise of the French City: Five Municipalities in the Nineteenth Century*, New York: St Martin's Press.

Colleoni, Maria C. (1989), 'L'associazionismo professionale degli ingegneri italiani: dai collegi di fine Ottocento ai sindacati fascisti', *Il Politecnico di Milano nella storia italiana 1914–1963*, Milan and Bari: Cariplo-Laterza, 153–69.

Collin, Jean-Pierre (1994), 'Les stratégies fiscales municipales et la gestion de l'agglomération urbaine: le cas de la Ville de Montréal entre 1910 et 1965', *Revue d'histoire urbaine/Urban History Review*, 23 (1) November, 19–31.

Collin, Jean-Pierre (1997), 'City management and the emerging welfare state: evolution of city budgets and civic responsibilities in Montreal, 1931–1951', *Journal of Policy History*, 9 (3), 339–57.

Collin, Jean-Pierre and Dagenais, Michèle (1997), 'Évolution des enjeux politiques locaux et des pratiques municipales dans l'île de Montréal, 1840–1950' in Menjot, Denis and Pinol, Jean-Luc (eds), *Enjeux et expressions de la vie politique municipale (XIIe–XXe siècles)*, Paris: L'Harmattan, 191–221.

Copp, T. (1979), 'Montreal's municipal government and the crisis of the 1930s', in Artibise, Alan F.J. and Stelter, Gilbert A. (eds), *The Usable Urban Past. Planning and Politics in the Modern Canadian City*, Toronto: Macmillan.

Coppini, Romano Paolo (1994), 'Il Piemonte sabaudo e l'unificazione (1849–1861)', in Sabbatucci, Giovanni and Vidotto, Vittorio (eds), *Storia d'Italia*, vol. I: *Le premesse dell'Unità*, Rome and Bari: Laterza, 337–429.

Corrêa, M. (1987), *História da Antropologia no Brasil (1930–1960)*, São Paulo: UNICAMP.

Corrigan, Philip and Sayer, Derek (1985), *The Great Arch: English State Formation as Cultural Revolution*, Oxford: Basil Blackwell.

Crawford, Robert (1893), 'The principles of municipal reform: I, reform within the council', feature article in the Glasgow *Evening News*, 23 March.

Croon, Helmut, Hofmann, Wolfgang and Unruh, Georg-Christoph von (1971), *Kommunale Selbstverwaltung im Zeitalter der Industrialisierung*, Stuttgart: Kohlhammer.

Crossick, Geoffrey and Haupt, Heinz-Gerhard (1995), *The Petite Bourgeoisie in Europe, 1780–1914: Enterprise, Family and Independence*, London and New York: Routledge.

Curtis, Bruce (2001), *The Politics of Population: State Formation and the Census of Canada, 1840–1875*, Toronto: University of Toronto Press.

Dagenais, Michèle (1989), 'Itinéraires professionnels masculins et féminins en milieu bancaire: le cas de la Banque d'Hochelaga', *Labour/Le Travail* (24), 45–68.

Dagenais, Michèle (1992), *Democracy in Montreal from 1830 up to the Present*, Montréal: Ville de Montréal, Service du greffe.

Dagenais, Michèle (2000a), *Des pouvoirs et des hommes: l'administration municipale de Montréal, 1900–1950*, Montreal: McGill-Queen's University Press.

Dagenais, Michèle (2000b), 'Urban governance in Montreal and Toronto in a period of transition', in Morris, Robert J. and Trainor, Richard H. (eds), *Urban Governance: Britain and Beyond since 1750*, Aldershot: Ashgate, 86–100.

D'Ambry, Robert W. (1953), *Pioneers in Protection: The Story of a Century of Fire Insurance Service*, York, PA: Farmers Fire Insurance Company.

Dana, David D. (1858), *The Fireman*, Boston: James French and Company.

Dantas, M. (1995), *Contribuições da Sub-divisão de Documentação Social*, São Paulo: Secretaria de Cultura/DPH.

Davis, Donald (1985), 'The "metropolitan thesis" and the writing of Canadian urban history', *Urban History Review/Revue d'Histoire Urbaine*, 14 (2), 95–113.

Davis, H. (1935), 'Brazil's political and economic problems', *Foreign Policy Reports*, 11 (1), March, 1–12.

Delpoux, Yannick (1990), 'Étude sur la scission de la CGT et la naissance de la CGT Force Ouvrière en Haute-Garonne, janvier 1936–décembre 1948', unpublished thesis, Toulouse: University of Toulouse le Mirail.

Demelas, D., Pouliquen, M. and Ruquet, M. (1971), 'Le mouvement syndical à Toulouse 1878–1936', unpublished thesis, University of Toulouse le Mirail.

De Nicolò, Marco (ed.) (1996), *L'amministrazione comunale di Roma. Legislazione, fonti archivistiche e documentarie, storiografia*, Bologna: Il Mulino.

De Pieri, Filippo (1999), 'La capitale frammentata. Istituzioni e progetti urbani nella Torino del primo Ottocento', unpublished PhD thesis, Politecnico di Torino.

De Pieri, Filippo (2003), 'L'expertise manquée. Le Conseil des Édiles et le développement urbain de Turin, 1822–1848', in Bourillon, Florence and Coudroy de Lille, Laurent (eds), *Expertise et décision urbaines*, Créteil: Presses Universitaires de Creteil.

Dilcher, Gerhard (1976) 'Das Gesellschaftsbild der Rechtswissenschaft und die soziale Frage', in Vondung, Klaus (ed.), *Das Wilhelminische Bildungsbürgertum. Zur Sozialgeschichte seiner Ideen*, Göttingen: Vandenhoeck and Ruprecht, 53–66.

Dion, S. (1986), *La politisation des mairies*, Paris: Economica.

Dogliani, Patrizia (1992), *Un laboratorio di socialismo municipale: La Francia 1870–1920*, Milan: Franco Angeli.

Douwes, F.G.M. (1968), 'De grote brand in 1858', *Ons Amsterdam* (20), 267–71.

Doyle, Barry M. (2000), 'The changing functions of urban government: councillors, officials and pressure groups', in Daunton, Martin (ed.), *The Cambridge Urban History of Britain: Volume III, 1840–1950*, Cambridge: Cambridge University Press, 287–313.

Duarte, Paulo (1938), *Contra o vandalismo e o extermínio. No journal e na tribuna*, Colecao Departamento de Cultura v.19, São Paulo: Prefeitura Municipal de São Paulo.

Duarte, Paulo (1964), 'Eulogia', in *Fábio Pradio*, São Paulo: Anhambi.

Duarte, Paulo (1976a), *Memórias, Os mortos de Seabrook*, São Paulo: Hucitec.

Duarte, Paulo (1976b), *Memórias, Selva escura*, São Paulo: Hucitec.

Dubois, Vincent (1996), *Institutions et politiques culturelles locales: éléments pour une recherche socio-historique*, Paris: Comité d'Histoire du Ministère de la Culture.

Dubois, Vincent (ed.) (1998), *Politiques locales et enjeux culturels: les clochers d'une querelle, XIXe–XXe siècles*, Paris: Comité d'Histoire du Ministère de la Culture/La Documentation Française.

Dubois, Vincent (1999), *La politique culturelle: genèse d'une catégorie d'intervention publique*, Paris: Belin.

Dubois, Vincent and Dulong, Delphine (eds) (1999), *La question *technocratique: de l'invention d'une figure aux transformations de l'action*, Strasbourg: Presses Universitaires de Strasbourg.

Dumons, Bruno and Pollet, Gilles (1992), 'Fonctionnaires municipaux et employés de la ville de Lyon (1870–1914): légitimité d'un modèle administratif décentralisé', *Revue historique* (1), 105–25.

Dumons, Bruno and Pollet, Gilles (2001), 'Espaces politiques et gouvernements municipaux dans la France de la IIIe République: Eclairage sur la sociogenèse de l'Etat contemporain', *Politix*, 14 (53), 15–32.

Dumons, Bruno, Pollet, Gilles and Saunier, Pierre-Yves (1998), *Les élites municipales sous la Troisième République: Des villes du Sud-Est de la France*, Paris: Editions du CNRS.

Earnest, Ernest (1979), *The Volunteer Fire Company, Past and Present*, New York: Stein and Day.

Ebner, Michael H. and Tobin, Eugene M. (eds) (1977), *The Age of Urban Reform: New Perspectives on the Progressive Era*, New York: Kennikat Press.

Edwards, Brian (1993), 'Glasgow improvements, 1866–1901', in Reed, Peter (ed.), *Glasgow: the Forming of the City*, Edinburgh: Edinburgh University Press, 84–103.

Emerson, Ralph Waldo (1982), *Selected Essays*, ed. Ziff, Larzer, New York: Penguin Classics.

Engeli, Christian and Haus, Wolfgang (1975), *Quellen zum modernen Gemeindeverfassungsrecht in Deutschland*, Stuttgart and Berlin: Kohlhammer.

Engeli, Christian and Matzerath, Horst (eds) (1989), *Modern Urban History Research in Europe, USA and Japan*, Oxford: Berg Publishers.

Ernesti, Giulio (1988), 'La formazione dell'urbanistica in Italia: intersezioni di discipline, conflitti. Fra utopia e realtà', in Ernesti, Giulio (ed.), *La costruzione dell'utopia. Architetti e urbanisti nell'Italia fascista*, Rome: Edizioni Lavoro, 163–73.

Espagne, Michel (1999), *Les transferts culturels franco-allemands*, Paris: Presses Universitaires de France.

Falco, Luigi (1988), 'La formazione della disciplina e la nascita della "corporazione" degli urbanisti', in Ernesti, Giulio (ed.), *La costruzione dell'utopia. Architetti e urbanisti nell'Italia fascista*, Rome: Edizioni Lavoro, 197–206.

Farcy, Jean-Claude (1991), 'Banlieues 1891: les enseignements d'un recensement exemplaire', in Faure, Alain (ed.), *Les Premiers Banlieusards: aux origines des banlieues de Paris (1860–1940)*, Paris: Edition Créaphis, 15–69.

Faust, Anselm (1986), *Arbeitsmarktpolitik im Deutschen Kaiserreich.*

Arbeitsvermittlung, Arbeitsbeschaffung und Arbeitslosenunter-stützung 1890–1918, Stuttgart: Steiner.

Fecteau, Jean-Marie (1995), 'Un cas de force majeure: le développement des mesures d'assistance publique à Montréal au tournant du siècle', *Lien social et politiques – RIAC* (33), spring, 105–11.

Ferraresi, Alessandra (2000), 'Per una storia dell'ingegneria sabauda: scienza, tecnica, amministrazione al servizio dello Stato', in Blanco, Luigi (ed.), *Amministrazione, formazione e professione: gli ingegneri in Italia tra Sette e Ottocento*, Bologna: Il Mulino, 91–299.

Finegold, Kenneth (1995), *Experts and Politicians: Reform Challenges to Machine Politics in New York, Cleveland and Chicago*, Princeton: Princeton University Press.

Fisch, Stephan (1988), *Stadtplanung im 19. Jahrhundert: Der Beispiel München bis zur Ära Theodor Fischer*, Munich: Oldenbourg.

Fischer, Andrea (1995), *Kommunale Leistungsverwaltung im 19. jahrhundert. Frankfurt am Main unter Mumm von Schwarzenstein, 1868 bis 1880*, Berlin: Duncker and Humblot.

Forrest, Clarence H. (1898), *Official History of the Fire Department of the City of Baltimore*, Baltimore: Williams and Wilkins Co. Press.

Fougères, Dany (1995), 'Le public et le privé dans la gestion de l'eau potable à Montréal depuis le XIXe siècle', in Pothier, Louise (ed.), *L'eau, l'hygiène publique et les infrastructures*, Montréal: Groupe PGV, 51–73.

Fourcaut, Annie (1980), *Bobigny: Banlieue Rouge, 1890–1939*, Paris: Hachette.

Fourcaut, Annie (ed.) (1992), *Banlieue Rouge, 1920–1960. Années Thorez, années Gabin: archétype du populaire, banc d'essai des modernités*, Paris: Editions Autrement.

Fraile, Pedro (1998), 'Putting order into the cities: the evolution of "policy science" in eighteenth-century Spain', *Urban History*, 25 (1), 22–35.

Franchi, Michela (1999), 'Edilizia popolare a Parma durante il ventennio fascista', *Storia urbana* (86), 75–101.

Fraser, W. Hamish (1990), 'From civic gospel to municipal socialism', in Fraser, Derek (ed.), *Cities, Class and Communication: Essays in Honour of Asa Briggs*, Hemel Hempstead: Harvester Wheatsheaf, 58–80.

Fraser, W. Hamish (1993), 'Municipal socialism and social policy', in Morris, Robert J. and Rodger, Richard (eds), *The Victorian City: A Reader in British Urban History, 1820–1914*, London: Longman, 258–80.

Fraser, W. Hamish and Maver, Irene (eds) (1996), *Glasgow, Volume II: 1830 to 1912*, Manchester: Manchester University Press.

Frisch, Michael H. (1972), *Town into City: Springfield, Massachusetts, and the Meaning of Community, 1840–1880*, Cambridge: Harvard University Press.

Frost, L.E. and Jones, E.L. (1989), 'The fire gap and the greater durability of nineteenth-century cities', *Planning Perspectives*, 4 (4), 333–47.

Führer, Karl Christian (1990), *Arbeitslosigkeit und die Entstehung der Arbeitslosenversicherung in Deutschland 1902–1927*, Berlin: Colloquium Verlag.

Furner, Mary O. and Lacey, Michael J. (eds) (1993), *The State and Social Investigation in Britain and the United States*, Cambridge: Cambridge University Press.

Furner, Mary O. and Supple, Barry (eds) (1990), *The State and Economic Knowledge: the American and British Experiences*, Cambridge: Cambridge University Press.

Gabetti, Roberto and Griseri, Andreina (1973), *Architettura dell'eclettismo. Un saggio su G.B. Schellino*, Turin: Einaudi.

Gabetti, Roberto and Marconi, Paolo (1971), 'L'insegnamento dell'architettura nel sistema didattico franco-italiano (1798–1922)', *Controspazio*, III (3, 6, 9), 10–11.

Gagnon, Robert (1991), *Histoire de l'École Polytechnique de Montréal 1873–1990. La montée des ingénieurs francophones*, Montréal: Boréal.

Gagnon-Lacasse, Francine (1965), 'Évolution des institutions politiques de la Ville de Montréal (1921–1965)', unpublished MA thesis, Université de Montréal.

Galbani, Annamaria (1992), 'L'ufficio tecnico municipale da Domenico Cesa Bianchi a Giovanni Masera', in Rozzi, Renato, Boriani, Maurizio and Rossari, Augusto (eds), *La Milano del piano Beruto (1884–1889). Società, urbanistica e architettura nella seconda metà dell'Ottocento*, vol. I, Milan: Guerini e associati, 173–89.

Gardey, Delphine (1999), 'Mécaniser l'écriture et photographier la parole: utopies, monde du bureau et histoires de genre et de techniques', *Annales – Histoire et sciences sociales*, I (3), 587–614.

Gash, Norman (1986), 'A Glaswegian criminologist: Patrick Colqhuoun, 1745–1820', *Pillars of Government and Other Essays on State and Society, c.1770–c.1880*, London: Edward Arnold.

Gaspari, Oscar (1994), *Il segretariato per la montagna (1919–1965): Ruini, Serpieri e Sturzo per la bonifica d'alta quota*, Rome: Presidenza del Consiglio dei Ministri.

Gaspari, Oscar (1998), *L'italia dei municipi: Il movimento comunale in età liberale, 1879–1906*, Rome: Donzelli.

Gaspari, Oscar (1999), 'Ugo Giusti (1873–1953)', *Economia Pubblica* (1), 79–116.

Gaumer, Benoît (1995), 'Les services de santé publique des villes américaines: une longue tradition d'engagement municipal', *Lien social et politique – RIAC* (33), spring, 97–105.

Genèses (1999), special issue, 'Sciences du politique' (37), December.

Georges, Jocelyne (1989), *Histoire des maires (1789–1939)*, Paris: Plon.

Giannetto, Marina (1999), 'I tecnici delle comunicazioni fra età liberale e fascismo', in Varni, Angelo and Melis, Guido (eds), *Burocrazie non burocratiche. Il lavoro dei tecnici nelle amministrazioni tra Otto e Novecento*, Turin: Rosenberg and Sellier.

Giannini, M. Severo (1967), 'I Comuni', in Giannini, M. Severo (ed.), *I Comuni*, Vicenza: Neri Pozza, 11–47.

Gigierano, Geoffrey (1982), '"A Creature of Law": Cincinnati's paid fire department', *The Cincinnati Historical Society Bulletin*, 40 (2), 78–99.

Gilbert, Keith Reginald (1966), *Fire Engines and other Firefighting Appliances*, London: HMSO.

Gillot, Auguste (1986), *Un forgeron dans la cité des rois*, Paris: Editions Halles de Paris.

Glendinning, Miles, Macinnes, Ranald and Mackechnie, Aonghus (1996), *A History of Scottish Architecture: from the Renaissance to the Present Day*, Edinburgh: Edinburgh University Press.

Goudsblom, Johan (1992), *Fire and Civilization*, London: Penguin.

Gow, James I. (1986), *Histoire de l'administration publique québécoise 1867–1970*, Montréal: Presses de l'Université de Montréal.

Greenberg, Amy S. (1998a), *Cause for Alarm: The Volunteer Fire Department in the Nineteenth-Century City*, Princeton: Princeton University Press.

Greenberg, Amy S. (1998b), 'Fights/Fires: violent firemen in the nineteenth-century American city', in Spierenburg, Pieter (ed.), *Men and Violence: Gender, Honor, and Rituals in Modern Europe and America*, Columbus: University of Ohio Press, 159–89.

Greer, Alan and Radforth, Ian (eds) (1992), *Colonial Leviathan: State Formation in Mid-Nineteenth-Century Canada*, Toronto: University of Toronto Press.

Gregor, T. (1997), 'Emilio Willems Eulogy', Vanderbilt University, November.

Groh, Dieter (1973), *Negative Integration und revolutionärer Attentismus. Die deutsche Sozialdemokratie am Vorabend des Ersten Weltkrieges*, Berlin: Ullstein-Propyläen.

Grottrup, Hendrik (1973), *Die Kommunale Leistungsverwaltung:*

Grundlagen der Gemeindlichen Daseinsvorsorge, Stuttgart: Kohlhammer.

Guagnini, Anna (1993), 'Academic qualifications and professional functions in the development of the Italian engineering schools, 1859–1914', in Fox, Robert and Guagnini, Anna (eds), *Education, technology and industrial performance in Europe, 1850–1939*, Cambridge and Paris: Cambridge University Press and Éditions de la Maison des sciences de l'homme, 171–95.

Haber, Samuel (1964), *Efficiency and Uplift: Scientific Management in the Progressive Era, 1890–1920*, Chicago: University of Chicago Press.

Hall, Thomas (1997), *Planning Europe's Capital Cities: Aspects of Nineteenth Century Urban Development*, London: Spon.

Hardy, Anne (1993), *The Epidemic Streets: Infectious Disease and the Rise of Preventive Medicine, 1856–1900*, Oxford: Clarendon Press.

Harris, George Montagu (1939), *Municipal Self-Government in Great Britain: A Study of the Practice of Local Government in Ten British Cities*, London: P.S. King & Son.

Hazen, Margaret Hindle and Hazen, Robert M. (1992), *Keepers of the Flame: The Role of Fire in American Culture, 1775–1925*, Princeton: Princeton University Press.

Heffter, Heinrich (1950), *Die deutsche Selbstverwaltung im 19. Jahrhundert. Geschichte der Ideen und Institutionen*, Stuttgart: Koehler Verlag.

Heinhorn, Robin (1991), *Property Rules: Political Economy in Chicago*, Chicago: University of Chicago Press.

Hennock, E.P. (1987), *British Social Reform and German Precedents: the Case of Social Insurance, 1880–1914*, Oxford: Clarendon Press.

Hietala, Marjatta (1987), *Services and Urbanization at the Turn of the Century: the Diffusion of Innovations*, Helsinki: Societas Historicas Finlandiae.

Hill, Levi (1935), 'The municipal service', in Laski, Harold J., Jennings, W. Ivor and Robbins, William A. (eds), *A Century of Municipal Progress, 1835–1935*, London: Allen and Unwin, 109–52

Hilton, Ronald (ed.) (1971 [1948]), 'Preface to Part VI', *Who's Who in Latin America. A Biographical Dictionary of Notable Living men and Women of Latin America 2*, Stanford: Stanford University Press.

Hirsch, Paul (1908), *25 Jahre sozialdemokratischer Arbeit in der Gemeinde. Die Tätigkeit der Sozialdemokratie in der Berliner Stadverordnetenversammlung*, Berlin: Vorwärts.

Hirsch, Paul (1911), *Das Kommunal-Programm der Sozialdemokratie Preussens*, Berlin: Vorwärts.

Hodgetts, J.E. et al. (1975), *Histoire d'une institution. La Commission de la fonction publique du Canada, 1908–1967*, Québec: Presses de l'Université Laval.

Hoffmann-Martinot, Vincent (1991), 'Les employés municipaux et les politiques du personnel, une comparaison de huit pays, in *Annuaire des collectivités locales*, Paris: LITEC.

Hofmann, Wolfgang (1974), *Zwischen Rathaus und Reichskanzlei: Die Oberbürgermeister in der Kommunal- und Staatspolitik des Deutschen Reiches von 1890 bis 1933*, Stuttgart: Kohlhammer.

Hofmann, Wolfgang (1983), 'Aufgaben und Struktur der kommunalen Selbstverwaltung in der Zeit der Hochindustrialisierung', in Jeserich, Kurt, Pohl, Hans and Unruh, Georg von (eds), *Deutsche Verwaltungsgeschichte, vol. 3: Das deutsche Reich bis zur Ende der Monarchie*, Stuttgart: Deutsche Verlags-Anstalt, 578–644.

Holloway, Charles T. (ed.) (1860), *The Chief Engineer's Register and Insurance Advertiser, containing a Full Account of the Organization of the Baltimore City Fire Department, also The Laws of the State of Maryland and the Ordinances of the City of Baltimore etc ...*, Baltimore: Steam Press.

ISAP (Istituto per la scienza dell'amministrazione pubblica) (1990), *Le riforme crispine*, vol. 3, *Amministrazione locale*, Milan: Giuffrè.

Isin, Engin F. (1992), *Cities without Citizens: the Modernity of the City as a Corporation*, Montreal: Black Rose Books.

Jastrow, Ignaz (1898), *Die Einrichtung von Arbeitsnachweisen und Arbeitsnachweis-Verbänden*, Berlin: Hermann.

Joana, Jean (1998), 'L'action publique municipale sous la IIIe république (1884–1939)', *Politix*, 12 (42), 151–78.

Joana, Jean (2001), 'La commune contre le municipalisme: débat public et politiques municipales à Avignon sous la IIIe république (1884–1903)', *Genèses* (43), June, 89–111.

Kahn, Jonathan (1997), *Budgeting Democracy: State Building and Citizenship in America, 1890–1920*, Ithaca: Cornell University Press.

Keith, Theodora (1915/16), 'The Convention of the Burghs', *Proceedings of the Royal Philosophical Society of Glasgow* (47), 229–51.

Keith-Lucas, Brian and Richards, Peter G. (1978), *A History of Local Government in the Twentieth Century*, London: George Allen & Unwin.

Kinchin, Perilla and Kinchin, Juliet (1988), *Glasgow's Great Exhibitions: 1888, 1901, 1911, 1938, 1988*, Wendlebury: White Cockade.

King, William T. (1896), *History of the American Steam Fire-Engine*, Boston: William King.

Kocka, Jürgen (1980), *White Collar Workers in America, 1890–1940: A Social–Political History in International Perspective*, translated by Maura Kealey, London and Beverly Hills: Sage Publications.

Kocka, Jürgen (1989), *Histoire d'un groupe social: les employés en Allemagne, 1850–1980*, Paris: Editions de l'Ecole des Hautes Etudes en Sciences Sociales.

Köllmann, Wolfgang (1974), *Bevölkerung in der industriellen Revolution*, Göttingen: Vandenhoeck and Ruprecht.

Krabbe, Wolfgang (1979), 'Munizipalsozialismus und Interventionsstaat. Die Ausbreitung der städtischen Leistungsverwaltung im Kaiserreich', *Geschichte in Wissenschaft und Unterricht* (5), 265–83.

Krabbe, Wolfgang (1985), *Kommunalpolitik und Industrialisierung: Die Entfaltung der Städtischen Leistungsverwaltung im 19. und frühen 20. Jahrhundert. Fallstudien zu Dortmund und Münster*, Stuttgart: Kohlhammer.

Krabbe, Wolfgang (1989), *Die deutsche Stadt im 19. und 20. Jahrhundert*, Göttingen: Vandenhoeck and Ruprecht.

Kühl, Uwe (ed.) (2001), *Munizipalsozialismus in Europa*, Munich: Oldenbourg.

Ladd, Brian (1990), *Urban Planning and Civic Order in Germany, 1860–1914*, Cambridge, Massachusetts: Harvard University Press.

Laffin, Martin (ed.) (1998), *Beyond Bureaucracy? The Professions in the Contemporary Public Sector*, Aldershot: Ashgate.

Langewiesche, Dieter (1988), *Liberalismus in Deutschland*, Frankfurt/Main: Suhrkamp.

Larivière, Claude (1977), *Crise économique et contrôle social (1929–1937): le cas de Montréal*, Montréal: Éditions coopératives Albert St-Martin.

Latta, Alexander Bonner and Latta, E. (1860), *Origin and Introduction of the Steam Fire Engine Together with the Results of the Use of Them in Cincinnati, St Louis and Louisville, For One Year, also, Showing the Effect on Insurance Companies, etc*, Cincinnati: Moore, Wilstach, Keys and Company.

Laurie, Bruce (1973), 'Fire companies and gangs in Southwark: the 1840s', in Davis, Allen F. and Mark H. Haller (eds), *The Peoples of Philadelphia: A History of Ethnic Groups and Lower Class Life, 1790–1940*, Philadelphia: University of Pennsylvania Press, 71–88.

Lecomte, Catherine (1987), 'Le personnel communal de l'empirisme au statut', in *Fonction Publique et Décentralisation*, Lille: Presses Universitaires de Lille, 206–24.

Lecomte, Catherine (1989), 'La professionnalisation des fonctions publiques territoriales', *Jahrbuch für europäische verwaltungs geschichte*, 1, 151–75.

Léonard, Jean-François (1973), 'L'évolution du rôle du service d'urbanisme de la ville de Montréal dans l'orientation de la politique d'aménagement de la ville de Montréal (1941–1971)', unpublished MA thesis, Université du Québec à Montréal.

Lequin, Yves (1992), 'Le métier', in Nora, Pierre (ed.), *Les lieux de mémoire, tome III*, Paris: Gallimard, 376–419.

Leverenz, David (1989), *Manhood and the American Renaissance*, Ithaca: Cornell University Press.

Levi, Giovanni and Olmo, Carlo (eds) (1984), *Terra, uomini e istituzioni in una città che si industrializza: indagine su San Donato, 1850–1900*, Turin: Città di Torino, Circoscrizione San Donato-Campidoglio.

Lewek, Peter (1992), *Arbeitslosigkeit und Arbeitslosenversicherung in der Weimarer Republik 1918–1927*, Stuttgart: Steiner.

Lewis, William C. (1872), *A Manual for Volunteer or Paid Fire Organizations*, New York: William C. Lewis.

Limongi, Neto, F.P. (1989), 'A Escola Livre de Sociologia e Política', *História das Ciências Sociais no Brasil I*, São Paulo: Revista dos Tribunais.

Lindsay, John (1909), *Review of Municipal Government in Glasgow*, Glasgow and Edinburgh: William Hodge & Co.

Linteau, Paul-André (1992), *Histoire de Montréal depuis la Confédération*, Montréal: Boréal.

Lord, Kathleen (1984), 'Nineteenth-century corporate welfare: municipal aid and industrial development in Saint-Jean, Quebec, 1848–1914', *Urban History Review/Revue d'Histoire Urbaine*, 13 (2), 105–16.

Lorrain, Dominique (1991), 'De l'administration républicaine au gouvernement urbain', *Sociologie du Travail*, October–December, 461–83.

Lowe, Graham (1987), *Women in the Administrative Revolution: the Feminization of Clerical Work*, Toronto: University of Toronto Press.

Lowrie, S. (1935), 'Informações sobre a ELSP in Memorial apresentado aos senhores deputados', *RAM* (15), August, 99–117.

Lowrie, S. (1938a), 'O elemento negro na população de São Paulo', *RAM* (48), April, 5–56.

Lowrie, S. (1938b), 'Origem da população da cidade e diferenciação das classes sociais', *RAM* (43), January, 196–212.

Lucarini, Federico (1999), 'Per *un funzionario modello e moderno*. La formazione dei segretari comunali in Italia attraverso alcuni perdiodici dell'età giolittiana', in Varni, Angelo and Melis, Guido (eds), *Burocrazia a scuola. Per una storia della formazione del personale pubblico nell'Otto-Novecento*, Turin: Rosenberg and Sellier, 221–48.

Lussier, Hubert (1987), *Les Sapeurs-Pompiers au XIXe siècle: associations volontaires en milieu populaire*, Paris: A.R.F.-Éditions/L'Harmattan.

Lynch, Thomas (1880), *The Volunteer Fire Department of St Louis*, St Louis: R. Ennis.

Mabileau, Albert (1993), *À la recherche du local*, Paris: L'Harmattan.

Maclellan, Duncan (1878), *Notes of a Tour through Parts of Holland, Belgium, Germany and France*, Glasgow: Glasgow Corporation.

MacClelland, Charles E. (1991), *The German Experience of Professionalization*, Cambridge: Cambridge University Press.

Maggi, Stefano (1999), 'Ingegneri e amministrazione statale dopo l'Unità', in Giuntini, Andrea and Minesso, Michela (eds), *Gli ingegneri in Italia tra '800 e '900*, Milan: Franco Angeli, 63–80.

Magnusson, Warren (1983), 'The development of Canadian urban government', in Magnusson, W. and Sancton, A. (eds), *City Politics in Canada*, Toronto: University of Toronto Press, 3–57.

Maier, Hans (1980), *Die ältere deutsche Staats- und Verwaltungslehre*, Munich: Beck.

Malatesta, Maria (ed.) (1995), *Society and professions in Italy*, Cambridge: Cambridge University Press.

Malvardi, Aimé (1928), *De l'opportunité de retirer aux maires le droit de nomination des secrétaires de mairie*, Paris: Institut d'urbanisme de l'Université de Paris.

Mann, Heinrich (1964 [1918]), *Der Untertan*, Munich: Deutscher Taschenbuch Verlag.

Marchis, Vittorio (1984), 'Dalle scuole di ingegneria al Politecnico. Un secolo di istituzioni tecniche in Piemonte', *La formazione dell'ingegnere nella Torino di Alberto Castigliano. Le Scuole di Ingegneria nella seconda metà dell'Ottocento*, Genoa: Sagep, 19–44.

Martineau, R. (1906), *Les Secrétaires de Mairie*, Paris: Bonvalot-Jouve.

Marwick, James D. (1879), *Observations on the Law and Practice in Regard to Municipal Elections and the Conduct of Business of Town Councils and Commissioners of Police in Scotland*, Edinburgh: William Blackwood & Sons.

Maver, Irene (1995), 'The guardianship of the community: civic authority prior to 1833', in Devine, Thomas M. and Jackson, Gordon (eds), *Glasgow, Volume I: Beginnings to 1830*, Manchester: Manchester University Press, 239–77.

Maver, Irene (1996a), 'Glasgow's civic government', in Fraser, W. Hamish and Maver, Irene (eds), *Glasgow, Volume II: 1830 to 1912*, Manchester: Manchester University Press, 441–85.

Maver, Irene (1996b), 'Glasgow's municipal workers and industrial strife', in Kenefick, William and McIvor, Arthur (eds), *Roots of Red Clydeside, 1910–1914? Labour Unrest and Industrial Relations in West Scotland*, Edinburgh: John Donald, 214–39.

Maver, Irene (1998), 'Glasgow's public parks and the community, 1850–1914: a case study in Scottish civic interventionism', *Urban History*, 25 (3), 323–47.

Maver, Irene, (2000) 'The role and influence of Glasgow's municipal managers, 1890s–1930s', in Morris, Robert J. and Trainor, Richard H. (eds), *Urban Governance: Britain and Beyond since 1750*, Aldershot: Ashgate, 69–85.

Mazzanti Pepe, Fernanda (1998), *L'amministrazione del Comune di Genova tra '800 e '900*, Milan: Giuffré.

McCaffrey, John F. (1998), *Scotland in the Nineteenth Century*, Basingstoke and London: Macmillan Press.

McDonald, Robert A.J. (1996), *Making Vancouver 1863–1913*, Vancouver: University of British Columbia Press.

McGrath, James (1995), 'The medieval and early modern burgh', in Devine, Thomas M. and Jackson, Gordon (eds), *Glasgow, Volume I: Beginnings to 1830*, Manchester: Manchester University Press, 17–62.

McLeod, Roy M. (1988), *Government and Expertise: Specialists, Administrators and Professionals, 1860–1919*, Cambridge: Cambridge University Press.

Mehrtens, Cristina (2000), 'Urban Space and Politics: Constructing Social Identity and the Middle Class in São Paulo, Brazil, 1930s–1940s', unpublished PhD thesis, University of Miami.

Melis, Guido (1988), *Due modelli di amministrazione tra liberalismo e fascismo. Burocrazie tradizionali e nuovi apparati*, Rome: Pubblicazione degli archivi di stato.

Melis, Guido (1995), 'L'amministrazione', in Romanelli, Raffaele (ed.), *Storia Dello stato italiano dall' Unità ad oggi*, Rome: Douzelli.

Melis, Guido (1996), *Storia dell'amministrazione italiana, 1861–1993*, Bologna: Il Mulino.

Melis, Guido and Varni, Angelo (eds) (1997), *Le fatiche di Monsù Travet. Per una storia del lavoro pubblico in Italia*, Turin: Rosenberg and Sellier.

Melis, Guido and Varni, Angelo (eds) (1999), *Burocrazie non burocratiche. Il lavoro dei tecnici nelle amministrazioni tra Otto e Novecento*, Turin: Rosenberg and Sellier.

Melis, Guido and Varni, Angelo (eds) (2000), *Burocrazia a scuola. Per una storia della formazione del personale pubblico nell'Otto-Novecento*, Turin: Rosenberg and Sellier.

Miceli, S. (1989), 'Por uma das Ciências Sociais', *História das Ciências Sociais no Brasil I*, São Paulo: Revista dos Tribunais.

Milliet, S. (1936), *Índice das constituições federal e do estado de São Paulo*, São Paulo: DC.

Milliet, S. (1949), *Diário Crítico 7*, São Paulo: Martins.

Milliet, S. (1964), *Diário Crítico*, São Paulo: Martins.

Minard, Philippe (2000), 'Faire l'histoire sociale des institutions: démarche et enjeux', *Bulletin de la Société d'Histoire Moderne et Contemporaine*, 3–4, 119–23.

Minesso, Michela (1995), 'The engineering profession, 1802–1923', in Malatesta, Maria (ed.), *Society and the Professions in Italy, 1860–1914*, Cambridge: Cambridge University Press, 175–219.

Minesso, Michela (1996), 'L'ingegnere dall'età napoleonica al fascismo', in Malatesta, Maria (ed.) *Storia d'Italia, Annali 10: I professionisti*, Turin: Einaudi, 259–302.

Miranda, N. (1937), 'O Estádio Municipal de São Paulo', *RAM* (35), May, 67–82.

Monkkonen, Eric H. (1981), *Police in Urban America, 1860–1920*, Cambridge: Cambridge University Press.

Monkkonen, Eric H. (1988), *America Becomes Urban: the Development of US Cities and Towns, 1780–1980*, Berkeley: University of California Press.

Morgan, A. (1934), *Os engenheiros de São Paulo em 1932: Pela lei e pela ordem*, São Paulo: s.n.

Morris, Robert J. (2000), 'Structure, culture and society in British towns', in Daunton, Martin (ed.), *The Cambridge Urban History of Britain: Volume III, 1840–1950*, Cambridge: Cambridge University Press, 395–426.

Morris, Robert J. (1989), 'The reproduction of labour and capital: British and Canadian cities during industrialization', *Urban History Review/Revue d'Histoire Urbaine*, 18 (1), 48–62.

Morris, Robert J. (1997), 'Municipal politics in English and Scottish cities in the nineteenth century', in Pinol, Jean-Luc and Menjot, Denis (eds), *Enjeux et expressions de la politique municipale (XIIe–XXe siècles)*, Paris: L'Harmattan, 125–48.

Morris, Robert J. (2000), 'Governance: two centuries of growth', in Morris, Robert J. and Trainor, Richard H. (eds), *Urban Governance: Britain and Beyond since 1750*, Aldershot: Ashgate, 1–14.

Morris, Robert J. and Trainor, Richard H. (eds) (2000), *Urban Governance: Britain and Beyond since 1750*, Aldershot: Ashgate.

Morton, Graeme (1998), 'Civil society, municipal government and the state: enshrinement, empowerment and legitimacy, Scotland, 1800–1929', *Urban History*, 25 (3), 348–67.

Moses, Robert (1950), *Programa de melhoramentos públicos para a cidade de São Paulo*, New York: IBEC.

Most, Otto (1912), *Die deutsche Stadt und ihre Verwaltung. Eine Einführung in die Kommunalpolitik der Gegenwart*, Berlin: Göschen'sche Verlagshandlung.

Mozzarelli, Cesare (ed.) (1992), *Il governo della città nell'Italia Giolittiana: Proposte di storia dell'amministrazione locale*, Trento: Reverdito.

Musella, Luigi (1995), 'Professionals in politics: clientelism and networks', in Malatesta, Maria (ed.), *Society and the Professions in Italy, 1860–1914*, Cambridge: Cambridge University Press, 313–36.

Musi, Aurelio (1998), 'Burocrazia comunale e mediazione politica nel Mezzogiorno tra Ottocento e Novecento', in Soresina, Marco (ed.), *Colletti bianchi. Ricerche su impiegati, funzionari e tecnici in Italia fra '800 e '900*, Milan: Franco Angeli, 58–71.

Naunin, Helmut (1984), *Städteordnungen des 19. Jahrhunderts: Beiträge zur Kommunalgeschichte Mittel- und Westeuropas*, Cologne: Böhlau.

Nejrotti, Mariella (1994), 'Gli anni all'umanitaria', in Maurizio, Ridolfi (ed.), *Alessandro Schiavi: indagine sociale, culture politiche e tradizione socialista nel primo '900*, Cesena: Il Ponte Vecchio, 112–42.

Nevers, Jean-Yves. (1975), 'Système politico-administratif communal et pouvoir local en milieu urbain, le cas de la municipalité radicale-socialiste de Toulouse (1888–1906)', unpublished thesis, University of Toulouse le Mirail.

Nevers, Jean-Yves (1983), 'Du clientélisme à la technocratie – cent ans de démocratie communale dans une grande ville: Toulouse', *Revue Française de Science Politique*, 33 (3), July–September, 426–54.

Nevers, Jean-Yves (1984), 'Stress, stress, stress … Une municipalité face à la crise urbaine, à la crise fiscale et à la crise économique entre 1910 et 1940', paper presented at the CSU conference, 'Crise et politiques locales', Paris.

Nevers, Jean-Yves (1991), 'Enjeux et formes de la rationalisation dans l'administration d'une grande ville de 1900 à 1940', paper presented at the 'Cinquième journée de sociologie du travail', Lyons, 13–14 November 1991.

Nicoloso, Paolo (1987), 'Competenze e conflittualità nelle prime proposte sulla figura del tecnico urbanista', *Urbanistica* (86), March, 38–41.

Nicoloso, Paolo (1999), *Gli architetti di Mussolini. Scuole e sindacato, architetti e massoni, professori e politici negli anni del regime*, Milan: Franco Angeli.

Nigrelli, F. Carmelo (1992), 'Catania: il piano d'ampliamento della città del 1888', *Storia urbana* (58), 118–56.

Olmo, Carlo (1989), 'Turin et ses miroirs fêlés', *Annales ESC*, XLIV (4), 759–91.

Orio E. (1993), 'Relations professionnelles et tensions financières à Bordeaux', unpublished DEA (diplôme d'études approfondies), Institut d'Études Politiques de Bordeaux.

Orsoni, M. (1938), *Le personnel communal et l'autorité municipale*, Paris: Maurice Lavergne.

Osello, M.A. (1983), 'Planejamento urbano de São Paulo, 1899–1961', unpublished MA thesis, FGV.

Park, Clyde W. (1954), *The Cincinnati Equitable Insurance Company*, Cincinnati: Cincinnati Equitable Insurance Company.

Paterson, Lindsay (1994), *The Autonomy of Modern Scotland*, Edinburgh: Edinburgh University Press.

Pavone, Claudio (1964), *Amministrazione centrale e amministrazione periferica da Rattazzi a Ricasoli (1859–1866)*, Milan: Giuffrè.

Payre, Renaud (2001), 'Un possible non institutionnalisé: sociologie historique de la "science communale" (1900–1950)', in Deloye, Yves and Voutat, Bernard (eds), *Faire de la science politique. Pour une analyse socio-historique du politique*, Paris: Belin.

Payre, Renaud (2002), 'A science that was not: the *Science Communale* in France (1913–1949)', *Contemporary European History*, 11 (4), 529–49.

Pederzani, Ivana (1990), 'Como', in ISAP (Istituto per la scienza dell'amministrazione pubblica), *Le riforme crispine*, vol. 3, *L'amministrazione locale*, Milan: Giuffrè, 81–191.

Pennybacker, Susan D. (1995), *A Vision for London, 1889–1914: Labour, Everyday Life and the LCC Experiment*, London and New York: Routledge.

Penzo, P. Paola (1994), 'L'urbanistica e l'amministrazione socialista a Bologna, 1914–1920', *Storia urbana* (66), 109–43.

Petracchi, Adriana (1962), *Le origini dell'ordinamento comunale e provinciale italiano. Storia della legislazione piemontese sugli enti locali dalla fine dell'antico regime al chiudersi dell'età cavouriana (1770–1861)*, Venice: Neri Pozza.

Pfammatter, Ulrich (2000), *The Making of the Modern Architect and Engineer: The Origins and Development of a Scientific and Industrially Oriented Education*, Basle, Berlin and Boston, Massachusetts: Birkhäuser.

Pick, Alfred John (1939), *The Administration of Paris and Montreal. A*

Comparative Study, Montreal: The Witness Press.

Pinol, Jean-Luc (1999), 'Villes "riches", villes "pauvres" dans la France de l'entre-deux-guerres', *Vingtième siècle* (64), October–December, 67–82.

Poitras, Claire (1999), 'Construire les infrastructures d'approvisionnement en eau en banlieue montréalaise au tournant du XXe siècle: le cas de Saint-Louis', *Revue d'histoire de l'Amérique française*, 4 (52), 507–32.

Pollet, Gilles (1995), 'La construction de l'Etat social à la française: entre local et national XIXe et XXe siècles', *Lien social et politique-RIAC* (33), spring, 115–31.

Pyne, Stephen J. (1982), *Fire in America*, Princeton: Princeton University Press.

Regis, Daniele (1994), *Torino e la via diagonale. Culture locali e culture internazionali nel secolo XIX*, Turin: Celid.

Repaci, Francesco Antonio (1927), 'I dazi di consumo della città di Torino nell'ultimo secolo', *La Riforma Sociale* (1–2).

Report on the Fire Departments of Cincinnati and St Louis, and the Use of Steam Fire Engines. By Order of the Fire Underwriters of St Louis (1858), St Louis: George Knapp and Company.

Report of the Special Committee of the Baltimore United Fire Department in Reference to the Funds of Said Department (1859), Baltimore: James Young.

Riall, Lucy (1994), *The Italian Risorgimento: State, Society and National Unification*, London: Routledge.

Riall, Lucy (1998), *Sicily and the Unification of Italy. Liberal Policy and Local Power, 1859–1866*, Oxford: Clarendon Press.

Riess, Steven A. (1992), 'The city', in Cayton, Mary Kupiec, Gorn, Elliott J. and Williams, Peter W. (eds), *The Encyclopedia of American Social History: 2*, New York: Charles Scribner and Sons, 1259–75.

Roberts, Alasdair (1994), 'Demonstrating neutrality: the Rockefeller Philanthropies and the evolution of public administration', *Public Administration Review*, 54 (3), May–June, 221–8.

Robertson, Edna (1998), *Glasgow's Doctor: James Burn Russell, 1837–1904*, East Linton: Tuckwell.

Rodger, Richard (1993), 'L'interventionnisme municipal en Ecosse: civisme local, préoccupations sociales et intérêts des possédants', *Genèses*, 10, January, 6–30.

Rodger, Richard (1994), *Research in Urban History: A Classified Survey of Doctoral and Masters' Theses*, Brookfield: Scolar Press.

Rodger, Richard (1996), *A Consolidated Bibliography of Urban History*, Brookfield: Scolar Press.

Rodgers, Daniel T. (1998), *Atlantic Crossings: Social Politics in a*

Progressive Age, Cambridge, MA and London: Belknap Press of Harvard University Press.

Romanelli, Raffaele (1988), *Il comando impossibile. Stato e società nell'Italia liberale*, Bologna: Il Mulino.

Romanelli, Raffaele (1989), *Sulle carte interminate. Un ceto di impiegati tra privato e pubblico: i segretari comunali in Italia, 1860–1915*, Bologna: Il Mulino.

Romanelli, Raffaele (1995), 'Centralismo e autonomie', in Romanelli, Raffaele (ed.), *Storia dello stato italiano dall'Unità ad oggi*, Rome: Donzelli, 126–86.

Romeo, Rosario (1963), *Dal Piemonte sabaudo all'Italia liberale*, Turin: Einaudi.

Roper, Stephen (1876), *Handbook of Modern Steam Fire Engines, including the Running, Care, and Management of Steam Fire-Engines and Fire Pumps*, Philadelphia: Claxton, Remsen and Haffelfinger.

Rosanvallon, Pierre (1990), *L'Etat en France de 1789 à nos jours*, Paris: Seuil.

Ross, Bernard H. and Levine, Myron A. (2001), *Urban Politics: Power in Metropolitan America*, Ithaca, NY: Peacock Publishers.

Rosso, Franco (1994), 'Controllo architettonico e urbanistico a Torino: il *Conseil des Ediles* e le sue origini, 1562–1814', *All'ombra dell'aquila imperiale. Trasformazioni e continuità istituzionali nei territori sabaudi in età napoleonica (1802–1814)*, vol. 2, Rome: Ministero per i beni culturali e ambientali, Ufficio centrale per i beni archivistici, 610–58.

Rotelli, Ettore (1973), 'Le trasformazioni dell'ordinamento comunale e provinciale durante il regime fascista', in Fontana, S. (ed.), *Il fascismo e le autonomie locali*, Bologna: Il Mulino, 73–155.

Rudin, Ronald (1984), 'Boostering the French Canadian town: municipal government in Quebec, 1850–1900', *Urban History Review/Revue d'Histoire Urbaine*, 13 (2), 1–10.

Rugge, Fabio (1986), 'La "città che sale": Il problema del governo municipale di inizio secolo', in Bigaran, M.P. (ed.), *Istituzioni e borghesie locali nell'Italia liberale*, Milan: Franco Angeli.

Rugge, Fabio (1989a), 'Le scienze comunali in Germania. Il Kommunalwissenschaftliche Forschungzentrum', *Amministrare*, XXVI (3), December, 439–54.

Rugge, Fabio (1989b), *Il governo delle città Prussiane tra '800 e '900*, Milan: Giuffrè.

Rugge, Fabio (ed.) (1992), *I regimi della città. Il governo municipale in Europa tra '800 e '900*, Milan: Franco Angeli.

Rumilly, Robert (1974), *Histoire de Montréal. Tome IV (1918–1939)*, Montréal: Fides.

Rumilly, Robert (1975), *Histoire de Montréal. Tome V (1939–1967)*, Montréal: Fides.

Russell, James Burn (1905a), 'An address delivered at the opening of the section on public medicine at the annual meeting of the British Medical Association, Sheffield, 1876', in Chalmers, A.K. (ed.), *Public Health Administration in Glasgow: A Memorial Volume of the Writings of J.B. Russell*, Glasgow: James Maclehose & Sons, 126–46.

Russell, James Burn (1905b), 'The first half of the century: a period of awakening', in Chalmers, A.K. (ed.), *Public Health Administration in Glasgow: A Memorial Volume of the Writings of J.B. Russell*, Glasgow: James Maclehose & Sons, 1–26.

Saint, Andrew (ed.) (1989), *Politics and the People of London: the London County Council, 1889–1965*, London: Hambledon Press.

Saint Louis Fireman's Fund (1916), *History of the St. Louis Fire Department*, Saint Louis: Saint Louis Fireman's Fund.

Salvati, Mariuccia (1992), *Il regime e gli impiegati. La nazionalizzazione piccolo-borghese nel ventennio fascista*, Bari: Laterza.

Salvati, Mariuccia (ed.) (1993), *Per una storia comparata del municipalismo e delle scienze sociali*, Bologna: Clueb.

Santos, M.C.L. (1988), *Maria Antonia, uma rua na contramão*, São Paulo: Nobel.

Saunier, Pierre-Yves (1996) 'La Ville et la ville. Les hommes et les organismes de l'aménagement urbain, portraits des services municipaux de six villes de la région Rhône-Alpes', *Recherches contemporaines* (3), 1995–6, 121–37.

Saunier, Pierre-Yves (1997) 'Au service du plan: hommes et structures de l'urbanisme municipal à Lyon au 20e siècle', *Forma Urbis. Les plans généraux de Lyon du XVIe au XXe siècle*, Lyon: Archives Municipales de Lyon, 135–44.

Saunier, Pierre-Yves (1998), 'La ville comme antidote? ou à la rencontre du troisième type (d'identité territoriale)', in Haupt, Heinz-Gerhard, Miller, Michael G. and Woolf, Stuart (eds), *Regional and national identities in Europe in the XIXth and XXth centuries/Les identités régionales et nationales en Europe aux XIXe et XXe siècles*, The Hague: Kluwer Law International, 125–64.

Saunier, Pierre-Yves (1999), 'Changing the city: urban international information and the Lyon municipality, 1900–1940', *Planning Perspectives*, 14(1), 19–48.

Saunier, Pierre-Yves (2001), 'Sketches from the urban international: voluntary societies, international organizations and US foundations at the city's bedside, 1900–1960, *International Journal for Urban and Regional Research*, 25 (2), 380–403.

Saunier, Pierre-Yves (ed.) (2002), 'Municipal connections: co-operation

Links and transfers among European cities', *Contemporary European History*, 11 (6).

Saunier, Pierre-Yves and Payre, Renaud (2000), 'L'internazionale municipalista: L'Union Internationale des Villes fra 1913 e 1940', *Amministrare*, XXX (1–2), 217–42.

Scarpa, Ludovica (1983), *Martin Wagner e Berlino: casa e città nella Repubblica di Weimar, 1918–1933*, Rome: Officina.

Scarpa, Ludovica (1992) 'Politique et bureaucratie. L'administration des notables à Berlin au XIXe siècle', *Genèses* (7), March, 129–49.

Scarpa, Ludovica (1995), *Gemeinwohl und lokale Macht: Honoratioren und Armenwesen in der Berliner Luisenstadt im 19. Jahrhundert*, Munich: Saur.

Schachter, Hindy Lauer (1989), *Frederick Taylor and the Public Administration Community: A Re-evaluation*, Albany: State University of New York Press.

Scherer, R. (1987), 'Decentralização e planejamento urbano no município', unpublished PhD thesis, USP.

Schiera, Pierangelo (1971), *I precedenti storici dell'impiego locale. Studio storico-giuridico 1859–1960*, Milan: Giuffrè.

Schiesl, Martin (1977), *The Politics of Efficiency: Municipal Administration and Reform in America, 1880–1920*, Berkeley: University of California Press.

Schikowski, John (1895), *Über Arbeitslosigkeit und Arbeitslosenstatistik*, Leipzig: Friedrich.

Schott, Dieter (1999), *Die Vernetzung der Stadt: Kommunale Energiepolitik, öffentlicher Nahverkehr und die 'produktion' der modernen Stadt: Darmstadt – Mannheim – Mainz 1880*, Darmstadt: Wissenschaftliche Buchgesellschaft.

Schwartzman, Simon (1991), *A Space for Science. The Development of the Scientific Community in Brazil*, Philadelphia: Pennsylvania State University Press.

Shaw, Albert (1889), 'Municipal socialism in Scotland', *The Juridical Review*, I, 33–53.

Shaw, Albert (1895a), *Municipal Government in Continental Europe*, New York: The Century Co.

Shaw, Albert (1895b), *Municipal Government in Great Britain*, New York: The Century Co.

Sheehan, James (1971), 'Liberalism and the city in nineteenth-century Germany', *Past and Present* (51), 116–37.

Silbergleit, Heinrich (1912), *Das statistische Amt der Stadt Berlin 1862–1912*, Berlin: Grunert.

Silsby Manufacturing Company (1881), *History of the Silsby Steam Fire Engine*, Buffalo: Gries and Company.

Silva, M. (1994), 'Da Maria Fumaça das fábricas a ELSP (1922–1940)', unpublished PhD thesis, PUC/SP.

Siwek-Pouydesseau, Jeanne (1989), *Le syndicalisme des fonctionnaires jusqu'à la guerre froide, 1848–1948*, Lille: Presses Universitaires de Lille.

Smith, Carl (1995), *Urban Disorder and the Shape of Belief*, Chicago: University of Chicago Press.

Sorba, Carlotta (1987), 'Amministrazione periferica e locale', *Storia Amministrazione Costituzione, Annale ISAP*, 5, 153–85.

Sorba, Carlotta (1993), *L'eredità delle mura: un caso di municipalismo democratico (Parma 1889–1914)*, Venice: Marsilio.

Sorba, Carlotta (1998), 'Tecnici municipali nell'Italia liberale: percorsi di reclutamento e identità professionali', in Soresina, Marco (ed.), *Colletti bianchi. Ricerche su impiegati, funzionari e tecnici in Italia fra '800 e '900*, Milan: Franco Angeli, 134–47.

Soresina, Marco (ed.) (1998), *Colletti bianchi. Ricerche su impiegati, funzionari e tecnici in Italia fra '800 e '900*, Milan: Franco Angeli.

Spoor, Alec (1967), *White-Collar Union: Sixty Years of NALGO*, London: Heinemann.

Steinmetz, George (1993), *Regulating the Social. The Welfare State and Local Politics in Imperial Germany*, Princeton: Princeton University Press.

Stieber, Nancy (1998), *Housing Design and Society in Amsterdam: Reconfiguring Urban Order and Identity, 1900–1920*, Chicago: University of Chicago Press.

Stivers, Camilla (2000), *Bureau Men, Settlement Women: Constructing Public Administration in the Progressive Era*, Lawrence: University of Kansas.

St Louis Fireman's Fund (1914), *History of the St Louis Fire Department*, St Louis: Central Publishing Company.

Sweeney [Maver], Irene (1990), 'The Municipal Administration of Glasgow, 1833–1912: Public Service and the Scottish Civic Identity', unpublished PhD thesis, University of Strathclyde.

Tacchi, Francesca (1994), 'L'ingegnere, il tecnico della "nuova" società fascista', in Turi, Gabriele (ed.), *Libere professioni e fascismo*, Milan: Franco Angeli, 177–227.

Teaford, Jon C. (1984), *The Unheralded Triumph: City Government in America, 1870–1900*, Baltimore: Johns Hopkins University Press.

Teixeira, J. (1936), 'O Conceito de serviço público', *RAM* (26), August, 145–60.

Teixeira, J. (1937), 'Concessões de services públicos', *RAM* (35), May, 101–16.

Tennstedt, Florian (1981), *Sozialgeschichte der Sozialpolitik in Deutschland*, Göttingen: Vandenhoeck and Ruprecht.

Terallori, R. (1981), 'A orientação municipal e o poder local no estado, na primeira república', unpublished PhD thesis, USP.

Thoenig, Jean-Claude (1982), 'La politique de l'Etat à l'égard des personnels des communes (1884–1939)', *Revue française d'administration publique*, 23 (3), July–September, 487–517.

Topalov, Christian (1994), *Naissance du chômeur 1880–1910*, Paris: Albin.

Topalov, Christian (ed.) (1999), *Laboratoires du nouveau siècle: la nébuleuse réformatrice en France et ses réseaux, 1880–1914*, Paris: Editions de l'Ecole des Hautes Etudes en Sciences Sociales.

Troilo, Simona (1997), 'Chieti tra Otto e Novecento', *Storia urbana* (79), 127–66.

Tyrrell, Ian (1991), 'American exceptionalism in an age of international history', *The American Historical Review*, 96 (4), 1031–55.

Verhandlungen des dritten Deutschen Städtetages am 12. September 1911 zu Posen zur Frage der Arbeitslosenversicherung (1911), Berlin: Loewenthal.

Visconti Cherasco, Maria Carla (1996), 'Ernesto Balbo Bertone di Sambuy soprintendente ai giardini', in Comoli Mandracci, Vera and Roccia, Rosanna (eds), *Torino città di loisir. Viali, parchi e giardini tra Otto e Novecento*, Turin: Archivio Storico della Città, 221–37.

Waller, P.J. (1983), *Town, City and Nation: England, 1850–1914*, Oxford: Oxford University Press.

Wallington, Neil (1989), *Images of Fire: 150 Years of Fire-fighting*, London: David and Charles.

Warner, Sam Bass Jr. (1968), *The Private City: Philadelphia in Three Periods of Growth*, Philadelphia: University of Pennsylvania Press.

Weaver, John (1979), *Shaping the Canadian City: Essays on Urban Politics and Policy, 1890–1920*, Toronto: Institute of Public Administration of Canada/Institut d'Administration Publique du Canada.

Weber, Max (1964), *Wirtschaft und Gesellschaft*, vol. 2, 11th edn, Berlin: Kiepenheuer und Witsch.

Weisbrod, Bernd (1981), 'Wohltätigkeit und "symbolische Gewalt" in der Frühindustrialisierung. Städtische Armut und Armenpolitik in Wuppertal', in Mommsen, Hans and Schulze, Winfried (eds), *Vom Elend der Handarbeit*, Stuttgart: Klett-Cotta, 334–57.

Weitensteiner, Hans Kilian (1976), *Karl Flesch. Kommunale Sozialpolitik in Frankfurt am Main*, Frankfurt/Main: Haag and Herschen.

Wheeler, Norman W. (1876) *Report of Norman W. Wheeler, Engineer, upon Steam Fire Engines, Fire Extinguishers, etc.*, New York: New York Underwriters Agency.

White, John H. Jr. (1973), 'Origins of the steam fire engine', *Technology and Culture*, 14 (2, part 1), 166–9.

Wiebe, Robert H. (1967), *The Search for Order 1877–1920*, New York: Hill and Wang.

Wilentz, Sean (1984), *Chants Democratic: New York City and the Rise of the American Working Class*, New York: Oxford University Press.

Willems, E. (1937), 'Opinião pública e imprensa', *RAM* (35), May, 83–100.

Wilson, R. Guerriero (1998), *Disillusionment or New Opportunities? The Changing Nature of Work in Offices, Glasgow, 1880–1914*, Aldershot and Brookfield: Ashgate.

Wunder, Bernd (ed.) (1995), *Les influences du 'modèle' napoléonien d'administration sur l'organisation administrative des autres pays*, Brussels: International Institute of Administrative Sciences.

Young, Charles T.F. (1866), *Fires, Fire Engines and Fire Brigades*.

Zagottis, A. (1937), 'Estudo da organização dos services do cadastro geral', *RAM* (40), October, 239–67.

Zagottis, A. (1938), 'Em torno da publicação do trabalho cadastro dos Ben Imóveis', *RAM* (43), January, 225–54.

Zanni Rosiello, Isabella (ed.) (1976), *Gli apparati statali dall'unità al fascismo*, Bologna: Il Mulino.

Zimmermann, Bénédicte (1994), 'Statisticiens des villes allemandes et action réformatrice (1871–1914). La construction d'une généralité statistique', *Genèses* (15), March, 4–27.

Zimmermann, Bénédicte (2001), *La constitution du chômage en Allemagne. Entre professions et territoires*, Paris: Editions de la Maison des Sciences de l'Homme.

Zucconi, Guido (1989), *La città contesa. Dagli ingegneri sanitari agli urbanisti (1885–1942)*, Milan: Jaca Book.

Index